How the Internet Works

Eighth Edition

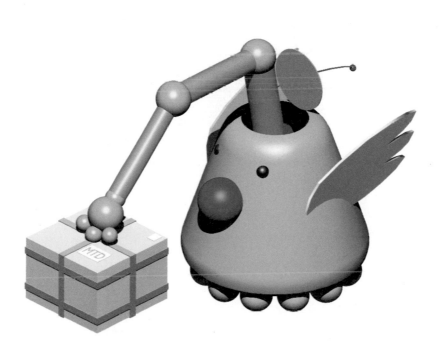

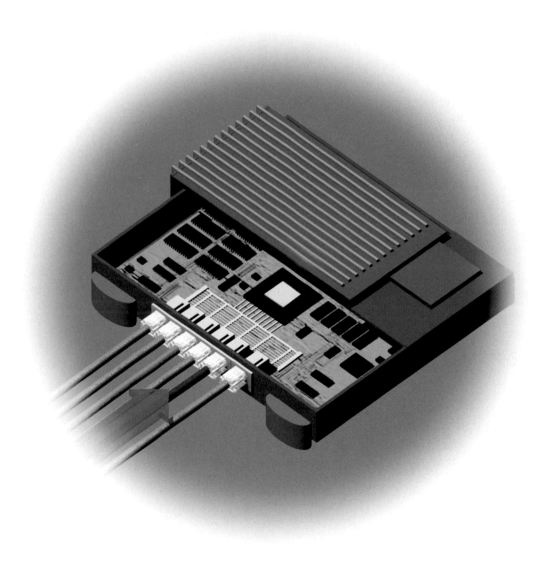

How the Internet Works

Eighth Edition

Preston Gralla

Illustrated by Michael Troller

800 East 96th Street
Indianapolis, IN 46240

How the Internet Works, Eighth Edition
Copyright © 2007 by Que Publishing

Associate Publisher	Greg Wiegand
Acquisitions Editor	Stephanie J. McComb
Development Editor	Kevin Howard
Managing Editor	Patrick Kanouse
Project Editor	Mandie Frank
Copy Editor	Linda Seifert
Indexer	Ken Johnson
Proofreader	Kathy Bidwell
Technical Editor	David Eytchison
Publishing Coordinator	Cindy Teeters
Interior Designer	Trina Wurst
Cover Designer	Anne Jones

International Standard Book Number: 0-7897-3626-8

Printed in the United States of America

First Printing: October 2006

09 08   4 3 2

Trademarks

Warning and Disclaimer

Bulk Sales

Que Publishing offers excellent discounts on this book when ordered in quantity for bulk purchases or special sales. For more information, please contact

U.S. Corporate and Government Sales

1-800-382-3419

corpsales@pearsontechgroup.com

For sales outside of the U.S., please contact

International Sales

international@pearsoned.com

Library of Congress Cataloging-in-Publication Data

Gralla, Preston.

How the Internet works / Preston Gralla, Michael Troller. -- 8th ed.

p. cm.

Includes index.

ISBN 0-7897-3626-8 (pbk. : alk. paper)

1. Internet--Popular works. I. Troller, Michael. II. Title.

TK5105.875.I57G72423 2007

004.67'8--dc22

2006027737

ABOUT THE AUTHOR

Preston Gralla is the award-winning author of 20 books, including *How Wireless Works*, *How to Expand and Upgrade PCs*, and *The Complete Idiot's Guide to Protecting Yourself Online*. He is an executive editor and columnist for CNet and ZDNet, is a technology columnist for the *Dallas Morning News*, and has written about technology for many magazines and newspapers, including *USA Today*, *PC Magazine*, the *Los Angeles Times*, *Boston Magazine*, *PC/Computing*, *Computerworld*, and *FamilyPC* among many others. Gralla has won several writing and editing awards, including one from the Computer Press Association for the best feature article in a computer magazine.

As a well-known expert on computers and the Internet, he has appeared frequently on numerous TV and radio shows and networks, including the *CBS Early Show*, CNN, National Public Radio's *All Things Considered*, MSNBC, CNBC, TechTV, and CNet Radio.

He was the founding managing editor of the well-known newspaper *PC Week* and a founding editor of *PC/Computing*. Under his editorship, *PC/Computing* was a finalist for General Excellence from the National Magazine Awards.

Gralla lives in Cambridge, Massachusetts, with his wife Lydia, children Gabriel and Mia, and a rabbit named Polichinelle. He also writes the free Gralla's Internet Insider email newsletter. To subscribe to it for free, send an email to preston@gralla.com with the words SUBSCRIBE NETINSIDER on the subject line.

Acknowledgments

THIS book, like the Internet, is a collaborative work. My name might be on the cover, but I am far from the only person involved in its creation.

Acquisitions editor Stephanie McComb was instrumental in getting the book off the ground, and as always, was a pleasure to work with.

The illustrator for the book, Michael Troller, deserves many thanks. His illustrations made this book a rich, visually pleasing experience.

Thanks also go to illustrators of past editions: Mina Reimer, Sarah Ishida, Shelly Norris, and Stephen Adams. And many thanks to the entire team at Que who produced the book, including Kevin Howard, Mandie Frank, Linda Seifert, Tammy Graham, and Ken Johnson.

Thanks also have to go to the many, many people I interviewed for this book. People from Quarterdeck Corporation, Chaco Communications, Progressive Networks, White Pine Software, Microsoft, Netscape, Headspace, SurfWatch Software, WebTV, Accrue, VDONet Corporation, America Online, Yahoo!, Hilgraeve, Fairmarket, eWallet, and Nuborn Technologies are only a few of the folks who gave their time to help me understand the nitty-gritty of how various Internet technologies work. Tim Smith offered me vital help as well.

I gleaned much information from the many FAQs and similar documents widely available on the Internet. I'd like to thank the anonymous authors of those documents, whoever they are.

Finally, big thanks have to go to my wife, Lydia. She put up with those occasional glassy-eyed looks that were replies to simple questions like, "Did you leave your keys in the refrigerator again?" She also endured my extreme absent-mindedness while I was figuring out ways to explain how firewalls, DSL, or zombies work when I should have been concentrating on more immediate matters.

We Want to Hear from You!

AS the reader of this book, *you* are our most important critic and commentator. We value your opinion and want to know what we're doing right, what we could do better, what areas you'd like to see us publish in, and any other words of wisdom you're willing to pass our way.

As an associate publisher for Que Publishing, I welcome your comments. You can email or write me directly to let me know what you did or didn't like about this book—as well as what we can do to make our books better.

Please note that I cannot help you with technical problems related to the topic of this book. We do have a User Services group, however, where I will forward specific technical questions related to the book.

When you write, please be sure to include this book's title and author as well as your name, email address, and phone number. I will carefully review your comments and share them with the author and editors who worked on the book.

Email: feedback@quepublishing.com

Mail: Greg Wiegand
           Associate Publisher
           Que Publishing
           800 East 96th Street
           Indianapolis, IN 46240 USA

Reader Services

Visit our website and register this book at www.quepublishing.com/register for convenient access to any updates, downloads, or errata that might be available for this book.

Introduction

IN the course of cruising the World Wide Web and clicking a link, have you ever wondered, "How does that work?" Or perhaps this question popped into your mind while you were transferring a file to your computer via FTP, or reading a newsgroup message, or when you first heard about technologies such as spam, cookies, and firewalls. Maybe you've wondered how a message sent from your computer travels through the vastness of cyberspace and ends up in the right email box halfway across the world. Have you ever wanted to know how search tools find the exact piece of information you want out of the millions of pieces of information on the whole Internet? How can you listen to music and view animations while surfing the Web?

This book is designed for everyone interested in the Internet. Its guiding principle is this: No matter how much of a cyberpro you are—or how much of a novice—there's a lot you don't understand about the Internet. Here's just one small example. I have a friend who has made his living with companies involved with the Internet for many years. He's a complete cyberpro who lives and breathes the Internet. One day, he almost whispered to me, "I don't like to admit this, but I don't know what a proxy server is. How does it work, anyway?"

He's not alone. The Internet changes so quickly and the technology advances so rapidly that it can seem almost impossible to keep up with all of it. If you're like just about everyone else involved in the Internet, your questions are similar to those of my friend. You'll find your answers here.

In Part 1, "Understanding the Internet's Underlying Architecture," I explain the underlying basics of the Internet: who runs it, how TCP/IP works, how to understand Internet addresses and domains, and similar topics. Here's where you'll find out about things such as routers and how the client/server architecture underpins virtually every aspect of the Internet.

Part 2, "Connecting to the Internet," depicts the various ways you can connect your computer to the Internet. There are myriad ways you can connect, such as via a cable modem, a digital subscriber line (DSL), an online service, a satellite, wirelessly, and many other ways. We'll cover all that, and more, in this section.

Part 3, "Communicating on the Internet," covers every aspect of Internet communications. It shows how email and newsgroups work, how IRC chat works, what email "spam" is and what you can do to prevent it, how instant messaging works, and how you can use the Internet and a technique called VoIP to make telephone calls anywhere in the world. And it also shows you how blogging works, which has become an increasingly important part of our culture.

Part 4, "How the World Wide Web Works," covers what has become by far the most popular part of the Internet—the World Wide Web. You'll learn virtually every aspect of how the Web works. It delves into how browsers work, how web server software works, and how Hypertext Markup Language (HTML) works. This section also covers the ways in which the Web is becoming integrated directly into your computer, how web pages are published and organized on a site, and every other aspect of the Web that is likely to be of interest to you. It also explains many of the newest web technologies, which will become even more important in the future, notable web services, and grid computing.

Part 5, "Using the World Wide Web," shows you the Web in actual real-world use. So you'll find out how Google is able to search the entire Internet and find exactly what you're looking for, and how map sites can give you driving locations anywhere you want to go. It also takes you behind the scenes of Wikipedia, a free, online encyclopedia put together entirely by thousands of volunteers.

Part 6, "Using Common Internet Tools," takes a close look at common Internet tools. Here's the place to learn about basic tools and services, such as telnet, and what happens when you use FTP to download a file to your computer. It's the section of the book that covers cutting-edge Internet technology. You'll find out how Java and ActiveX programming languages work, how JavaScript works, how agents can silently do your bidding for you, and how the Common Gateway Interface (CGI) works, which is a little-known but vital part of the Internet.

Part 7, "Enjoying Entertainment and Multimedia on the Internet," shows you how some of the most exciting parts of the Internet work—the various multimedia technologies. Whether you want to know how virtual reality or animations work, how streaming video works, how videoconferencing works, or how similar technologies work, you'll find it all here. And it also shows you how the iPod works, along with iTunes and podcasting.

Part 8, "Shopping and Doing Business on the Internet," covers intranets, how the Internet works with the outside world, and how you can shop online. You'll see how companies use Internet technologies to build their own private networks, called *intranets*. And you'll take a close look at the underlying technologies that let you shop on the Web, which accounts for billions of dollars a year in sales.

Finally, Part 9, "Protecting Yourself on the Internet," covers security concerns. The chapters in this part explain the controversial cookie technology that lets web servers put bits of information on your hard disk and use that information to track you, how the even-more controversial FBI system called Carnivore wiretapped people's use of the Internet to read their email, watch their web browsing, and more. They also look at the National Security Agency's Echelon program, which allows for web snooping and wiretapping on a global scale.

This part also shows how firewalls work, how viruses can attack your computer, and how cryptosystems allow confidential information to be sent across the Internet. It delves into how hackers can attack Internet service providers (ISPs) using so-called Denial of Service or "smurf attacks," and how they can attack your computer as well. This section also looks at how "spyware" can report on your surfing activities, and how your place of employment may monitor your Internet activities. And it covers the issue of pornography on the Internet and shows how parental-control software can prevent children from seeing objectionable material.

So, come along and see how the vast Internet works. Even if you're a cyberpro (and especially if you're not), you'll find out a lot you never knew.

P A R T

UNDERSTANDING THE INTERNET'S UNDERLYING ARCHITECTURE

FOR the first time ever, the world is at your fingertips. From your computer, you can find information about anything you can name or even imagine. You can communicate with people on the other side of the world. You can set up a teleconference, tap into the resources of powerful computers anywhere on the globe, search through the world's best libraries, and visit the world's most amazing museums. You can watch videos, listen to music and share music with others, and read special multimedia magazines. You can shop for almost anything you can name. You can do all this by tapping into the largest computer network in the world—the Internet.

The Internet isn't a single network; it is a vast, globe-spanning network of networks. No single person, group, or organization runs the Internet. Instead, it's the purest form of electronic democracy. The networks communicate with one another based on certain protocols, such as the Transmission Control Protocol (TCP) and the Internet Protocol (IP). More and more networks and computers are being hooked up to the Internet every day. Tens of thousands of these networks exist, ranging from university networks to corporate local area networks to large online services such as America Online and MSN. Every time you tap into the Internet, your own computer becomes an extension of that network.

The first section of this book is spent defining the Internet. It also examines the architectures, protocols, and general concepts that make it all possible.

Chapter 1, "What Is the Internet?" examines how the Internet runs. You'll look at who pays for the high-speed data backbones that carry much of the Internet's traffic and at the organizations that ensure that standards are set for networks to follow so the Internet can run smoothly. You'll also look at the various types of networks connected to the Internet.

Chapter 2, "How Computer Networks Send Data Across the Internet," explains how information travels across the Internet and describes how hardware, such as routers, repeaters, and bridges, sends information among networks. It also shows how smaller networks are grouped into larger regional networks—and how those large regional networks communicate among themselves.

Chapter 3, "How TCP/IP Works," covers the Internet's basic protocols for communications. You'll learn a little about basic Internet jargon, such as TCP/IP (short for Transmission Control Protocol and Internet Protocol). This chapter also explains how those protocols work and how special software such as Winsock enables personal computers to get onto a network originally designed for larger computers.

Chapter 4, "Understanding the Internet's Software Structure," looks at the Internet's client/server architecture. *Servers*—also called *hosts*—are powerful computers that perform functions such as delivering information or web pages, hosting databases, and handling email.

A *client* is your own computer and the software that sits on it, such as a web browser or piece of email software. Clients request information from servers, which do the heavy-duty processing and then send the information back to the client, which displays the information.

Chapter 5, "How Internet Addresses and Domains Work," takes the mystery out of the Internet's often confusing addressing scheme. You'll learn about Internet domains and addresses and will even be able to make sense of them. More than that, you'll learn how domain servers keep track of all the locations on the Internet and translate addresses such as www.zdnet.com into Internet IP addresses such as 134.54.56.120. You'll also learn how some computers are assigned new IP addresses by special servers every time they connect to the Internet.

Chapter 6, "How Routers Work," details how the most basic piece of hardware on the Internet—a router—works. *Routers* are combinations of hardware and software that perform the job of ensuring that all data is sent to the proper destination. Think of routers as traffic cops of the Internet. They use the IP addresses the name servers have translated to route the data. Routers look at the addresses and then send the data to the next-closest router to the destination and so on, until the data is finally delivered. They use *routing tables* to determine how to route the traffic, and they can also adjust the routes as the traffic on the Internet changes, thus ensuring that the data is routed in the most efficient way possible.

Whether you're a newbie or cyberpro, this section teaches you the basics of the Internet.

CHAPTER

1

What Is the Internet?

ONE of the most frequently asked questions about the Internet is "Who runs it?" The truth is that no centralized management of the Internet exists. Instead, it is a collection of thousands of individual networks and organizations, each of which is run and paid for on its own. Each network cooperates with other networks to direct Internet traffic so that information can pass among them. Together, these networks and organizations make up the wired world of the Internet. For networks and computers to cooperate in this way, however, a general agreement must take place about things such as Internet procedures and standards for protocols. These procedures and standards are laid out in requests for comment (RFCs) that are agreed on by Internet users and organizations.

A variety of groups guide the Internet's growth by helping to establish standards and by educating people on the proper way to use the Internet. Perhaps the most important is the Internet Society, a private, non-profit group. The Internet Society supports the work of the Internet Architecture Board (IAB), which handles much of the Internet's behind-the-scenes and architectural issues. The Internet Engineering Task Force (IETF) is responsible for overseeing how the Internet's TCP/IP protocols evolve. For information about the IETF, go to www.ietf.org. (See Chapter 3, "How TCP/IP Works," for details on TCP/IP protocols.)

The World Wide Web Consortium (W3C) develops standards for the evolution of the most well-known part of the Internet, the World Wide Web (find it at www.w3.org). The W3C is an industry consortium run by the Laboratory for Computer Science at the Massachusetts Institute of Technology (MIT).

Private companies oversee the registration of Internet domains, such as www.zdnet.com or www.quepublishing.com. These companies, called *registrars*, all must cooperate with one another to ensure that only one person or company can own a particular domain and that all the domains work properly. The registrars compete with one another as well in allowing people and businesses to register domains. Registering a domain costs money, and the registrars compete on cost and on giving extra services to those who buy domains.

Although all these types of organizations are important for holding together the Internet, at the heart of the Internet are individual local networks. These networks can be found in private companies, universities, government agencies, and online services. They are funded separately from each other and in a variety of manners, such as fees from users, corporate support, taxes, and grants. Many Internet service providers (ISPs), which provide Internet access for individuals, have networks as well. Individuals who want to access the Internet pay ISPs a monthly connection rate, so in that sense, everyone who uses the Internet helps pay for it.

The networks are connected in a variety of ways. For efficiency's sake, local networks join in consortiums known as *regional networks*. A variety of leased lines connect regional and local networks. The leased lines that connect networks can be as simple as a single telephone line or as complex as a fiber-optic cable with microwave links and satellite transmissions.

Private companies who make money by selling access to their lines build *backbones*, which are very high-capacity lines that carry enormous amounts of Internet traffic. Government agencies, such as NASA, and large private corporations pay for some of these backbones. The National Science Foundation also pays for some backbones.

How the Internet Comes Together

Organization of networks Because the Internet is a loose organization of networks, no single group runs it or pays for it all. Instead, many private organizations, universities, and government agencies pay for and run parts of it. They all work together in a democratic, loosely organized alliance. Private organizations range from small, homegrown networks to commercial online services, such as America Online and MSN, and private Internet service providers (ISPs) that sell access to the Internet.

Regional Network

Funding the Internet Through agencies such as the National Science Foundation, the federal government pays for some high-speed backbones that carry Internet traffic across the country and the world. The high-speed vBNS (very high-speed Backbone Network Services), for example, provides a high-speed infrastructure for the research and education community by linking together supercomputer centers. Often, a large corporation or organization such as NASA provides backbones to link sites across the country or the world. The government has also funded the Internet2, a super-fast network that can transfer data at an astounding 2.4 gigabits per second, for use by universities. The Internet2 is also developing a number of future Internet technologies that will allow for the creation of new Internet uses such as digital libraries, virtual laboratories, and distance-independent learning.

Regional networks
Regional networks provide and maintain Internet access within a geographic area. Regional nets can consist of smaller networks and organizations within the area that have banded together to provide better service.

Registrars Private companies called Internet *registrars* are responsible for registering Internet domains, such as www.zdnet.com, to people and businesses. A quasi-public company called the InterNIC used to have sole responsibility for doing this, but other registrars can now register domains as well.

Supercomputer Center

Online Services

Supercomputer Center

Internet service providers ISPs sell people monthly connections to the Internet. They run their own segments of the Internet and also might supply long-distance connections called *backbones*. Telephone companies are another source of long-distance connections for the Internet.

Internet Service Provider

vBNS Backbone

Internet Society

Internet Society The Internet Society is a private nonprofit organization that makes technological and architectural recommendations that pertain to the Internet, such as how TCP/IP and other Internet protocols should work. This body guides the direction of the Internet and its growth.

InterNIC The InterNIC and other registrars are responsible for maintaining the domains registered through registries. It tracks the connections between Internet addresses, such as 125.34.24.21, and domain names, such as www.zdnet.com.

InterNIC

Internet Registrars

Internet Registrars

Internet Registrars

An Internet Timeline

DARPA

1969 The U.S. Department of Defense funds ARPANET, a network that was the forerunner to the Internet. It let researchers link to remote computing centers and use those center's resources. Network nodes are set up at UCLA, Stanford Research Institute, the University of California Santa Barbara, and the University of Utah. The first actual use of the network came when someone named Charley Kline at UCLA tried to log into a computer at the Stanford Research Institute. A pattern was set that lasts until this day: The system crashed as he typed in the letter "G" in LOGIN.

1972 The first email program to manage, read, file, and respond to messages is written by Larry Roberts.

1974 The so-called "Fathers of the Internet" Vint Cerf and Bob Kahn publish a paper titled "A Protocol for Packet Network Interconnection," which defines the basic protocol for Internet communications, the Transmission Control Program (TCP).

TCP/IP

1982 The Transmission Control Protocol (TCP) and Internet Protocol (IP) protocol suite (TCP/IP) are formally established as the underlying protocols of the Internet. The Internet is defined as a network of networks.

1984 The Domain Name System (DNS) is introduced. The number of host computers on the Internet exceeds 1,000 for the first time.

1986 The NSFNET backbone is created, with a speed of 56Kbps. The Network News Transfer Protocol (NNTP) is designed to make it easier to create and use Usenet news groups over TCP/IP.

1988 A worm released by Robert Morris, Jr., a graduate student in Computer Science at Cornell, replicates so quickly that it clogs the Internet with traffic and closes down much of the Internet. Morris's father was at the time the Chief Scientist of the federal top-secret National Security Agency. CERT (Computer Emergency Response Team) is created in response to the worm.

1990   The World (world.std.com) becomes the first commercial provider of dial up access to the Internet.

1991   The World Wide Web is developed by Tim Berners-Lee at Swiss-based CERN (European Organization for Nuclear Research).

1993   The White House website goes live (www.whitehouse.gov). President Bill Clinton's email address is president@whitehouse.gov; Vice President Al Gore's is vice-president@whitehouse.gov.

1994   Yahoo is founded by Stanford graduate students David Filo and Jerry Yang. The first banner ads make their appearance on the Web. They run on www.hotwired.com and were for the beverage Zima and for AT&T.

1995   The online auction site eBay is founded, with the name Auctionweb, which is changed to eBay in 1997. The browser company Netscape goes public with an IPO.

1996   Google is begun as a research project by two Ph.D. students at Stanford, Larry Page and Sergey Brin.

1997   The terms *weblog* and *blog* are coined.

1999   The file-sharing software Napster is released, which allows people to share files, in particular music, with each other over the Internet.

2000   The high-speed Internet2 backbone deploys IPv6, the next generation of IP standards.

2001   Worms and viruses increasingly become a danger, with the Code Red worm and Sircam virus causing damage to businesses and individuals, and slowing down Internet access.

2002   Portions of the Internet become unusable after a distributed denial of service (DDoS) attack knocks out 8 of the Internet's 13 DNS root servers.

2003   The Recording Industry Association of America (RIAA) sues 261 people for alleged illegal distribution of copyrighted music files over the Internet.

2004   Online spending continues to climb and reaches a record high of 117 billion, a 26% increase over 2003.

2005   In January, the free online encyclopedia Wikipedia (www.wikipedia.com) reaches the mark of 900,000 articles.

2006   Phone communications over the Internet become increasingly popular with Voice over Internet Protocol (VoIP). New services such as Vonage tap into it, while cable companies offer their own VoIP plans, and services such as Skype use VoIP to offer free PC-to-landline calls.

Note
Thanks to the Hobbes's Internet Timeline for some of the information in this illustration. For the whole timeline, see http://www.zakon.org/robert/internet/timeline.

CHAPTER

2

How Computer Networks Send Data Across the Internet

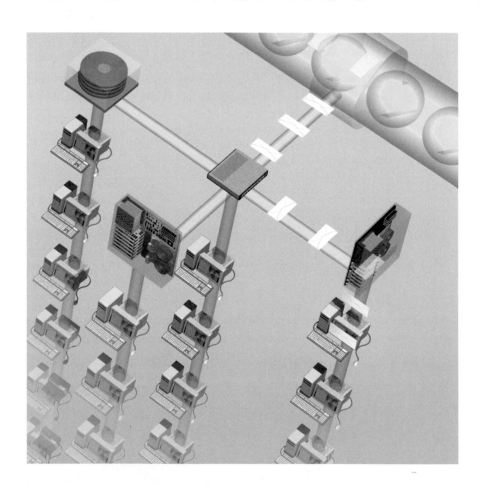

YOU might take for granted that when you send a piece of information across the Internet, it will always reach its intended destination. However, the process of sending that information is remarkably complex.

When you send information across the Internet, the *Transmission Control Protocol (TCP)*—the language computers use when communicating over the Internet—first breaks the information up into *packets*, smaller blocks of information that also contain a variety of data that helps the packets travel across the Internet. Your computer sends those packets to your local network, Internet service provider (ISP), or online service. From there, the packets travel through many levels of networks, computers, and communications lines before they reach their final destinations, which might be across town or around the world. A variety of hardware processes those packets and routes them to their proper destinations. This hardware is designed to transmit data between networks and makes up much of the glue that holds the Internet together. Five of the most important pieces of hardware are hubs, bridges, gateways, repeaters, and routers.

Hubs are important because they link groups of computers to one another and let computers communicate with each other. *Bridges* link local area networks (LANs) with one another. They enable data destined for another LAN to be sent there, while keeping local data inside its own network. *Gateways* are similar to bridges, but they also translate data from one type of network to another.

When data travels across the Internet, it often crosses great distances, which can be a problem because the signal sending the data can weaken over the distance. To solve the problem, *repeaters* amplify the data at intervals so the signal doesn't weaken.

Routers play a key role in managing Internet traffic. Their job is to ensure the packets always arrive at the proper destination. If data is being transferred among computers that are on the same LAN, routers often aren't necessary because the network itself can handle its internal traffic. Routers come into play when the data is sent between two different networks. Routers examine packets to determine their destinations. They take into account the volume of activity on the Internet, and they send the packet to another router that is closer to the packet's final destination. For more information on routers see Chapter 6, "How Routers Work."

All this hardware connects the many networks that make up the Internet. Corporate LANs are at the most local level of networks. Midlevel networks hook together these LANs using high-speed telephone lines, Ethernet, and microwave links. A *regional* network is a midlevel network in a geographic area. A *wide area network (WAN)* is another type of midlevel network. A WAN consists of an organization with many networked sites linked together.

When a packet travels from a computer on a LAN in a midlevel network to a computer somewhere else on the midlevel network, a router (or a series of routers) sends the packet to its proper destination. However, if the destination lies outside the midlevel network, the packet is sent to a network access point (NAP), where it is sent across the country or the world on a backbone. High-speed backbones such as the vBNS (very high-speed Backbone Network Services) can transmit data at an exceedingly high rate—155 megabits (millions of bits) per second (Mbps) or higher. Even faster backbones are being built that will transmit data at an astonishing 9.6 billion bits per second.

How Networks Talk with Each Other

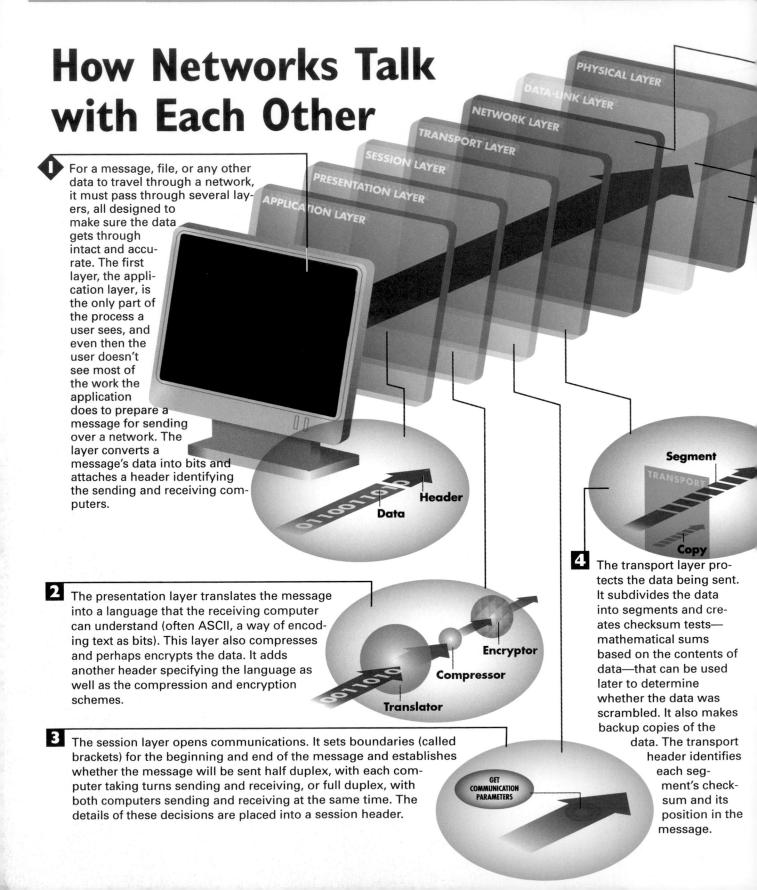

1 For a message, file, or any other data to travel through a network, it must pass through several layers, all designed to make sure the data gets through intact and accurate. The first layer, the application layer, is the only part of the process a user sees, and even then the user doesn't see most of the work the application does to prepare a message for sending over a network. The layer converts a message's data into bits and attaches a header identifying the sending and receiving computers.

2 The presentation layer translates the message into a language that the receiving computer can understand (often ASCII, a way of encoding text as bits). This layer also compresses and perhaps encrypts the data. It adds another header specifying the language as well as the compression and encryption schemes.

3 The session layer opens communications. It sets boundaries (called brackets) for the beginning and end of the message and establishes whether the message will be sent half duplex, with each computer taking turns sending and receiving, or full duplex, with both computers sending and receiving at the same time. The details of these decisions are placed into a session header.

4 The transport layer protects the data being sent. It subdivides the data into segments and creates checksum tests—mathematical sums based on the contents of data—that can be used later to determine whether the data was scrambled. It also makes backup copies of the data. The transport header identifies each segment's checksum and its position in the message.

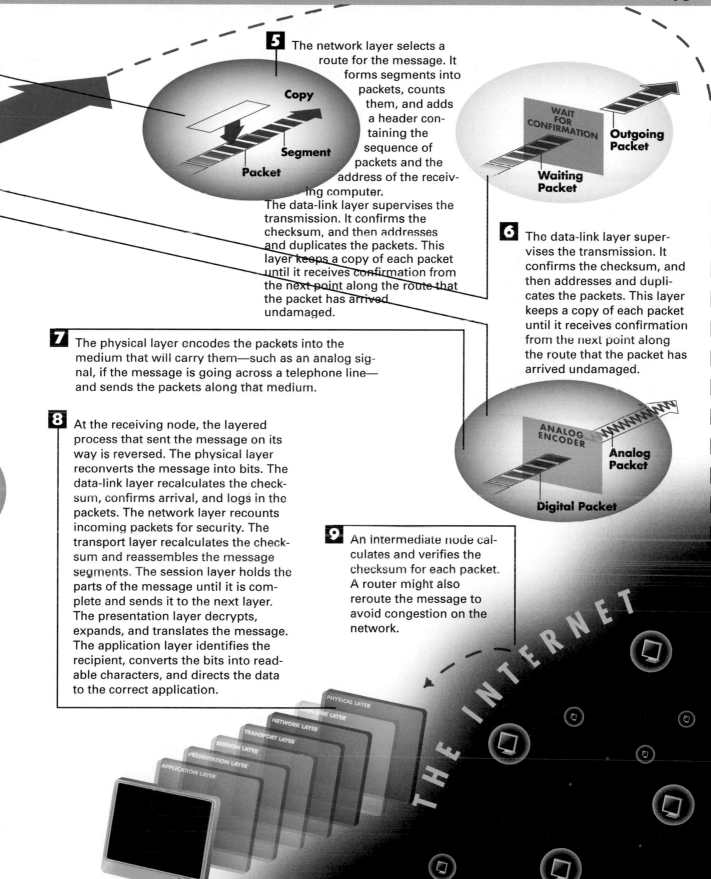

5 The network layer selects a route for the message. It forms segments into packets, counts them, and adds a header containing the sequence of packets and the address of the receiving computer.

Copy

Segment

Packet

The data-link layer supervises the transmission. It confirms the checksum, and then addresses and duplicates the packets. This layer keeps a copy of each packet until it receives confirmation from the next point along the route that the packet has arrived undamaged.

WAIT FOR CONFIRMATION

Outgoing Packet

Waiting Packet

6 The data-link layer supervises the transmission. It confirms the checksum, and then addresses and duplicates the packets. This layer keeps a copy of each packet until it receives confirmation from the next point along the route that the packet has arrived undamaged.

7 The physical layer encodes the packets into the medium that will carry them—such as an analog signal, if the message is going across a telephone line—and sends the packets along that medium.

8 At the receiving node, the layered process that sent the message on its way is reversed. The physical layer reconverts the message into bits. The data-link layer recalculates the checksum, confirms arrival, and logs in the packets. The network layer recounts incoming packets for security. The transport layer recalculates the checksum and reassembles the message segments. The session layer holds the parts of the message until it is complete and sends it to the next layer. The presentation layer decrypts, expands, and translates the message. The application layer identifies the recipient, converts the bits into readable characters, and directs the data to the correct application.

ANALOG ENCODER

Analog Packet

Digital Packet

9 An intermediate node calculates and verifies the checksum for each packet. A router might also reroute the message to avoid congestion on the network.

THE INTERNET

PHYSICAL LAYER

DATA-LINK LAYER

NETWORK LAYER

TRANSPORT LAYER

SESSION LAYER

PRESENTATION LAYER

APPLICATION LAYER

How Networks Link to the Internet

1 Whether at work or at home, you get onto the Internet via a variety of ways. You may connect to a LAN at your place of business via Ethernet networks and token-ring networks. Token-ring networks pass data in *tokens* from computer to computer in a ring or star configuration. In Ethernet networks, the data goes from a server to a computer on the network. At home, you can dial into a large computer connected to the Internet via an online service or a dial-in Internet service provider (ISP), or you can use another type of Internet service, such as a cable modem, Digital Subscriber Line (DSL) modem, or a satellite connection.

Dial Up

Server

vBNS Backbone

Satellite Link

TI Line

Router

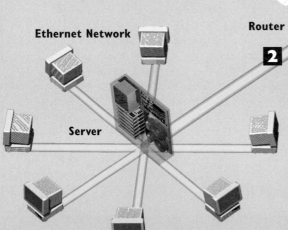

Ethernet Network

Server

Token-Ring Network

Server

2 After you're connected and you want to send or receive information, your requests and data are handled by routers on the Internet. *Routers* perform most of the work of directing traffic on the Internet. They examine the packets of data that travel across the Internet to see where the data is headed. Based on the data's destination, the packet is routed in the most efficient way—generally to another router, which in turn sends the packet to the next router, and so on. Routers also connect networks to each other.

3 The data can be transferred between networks in a number of ways. Dedicated telephone lines can transmit data at 56Kbps (kilobits per second). An increasing number of T1 leased telephone lines carry data between networks. A T1 link can carry data at 1.544Mbps. Higher-speed T3 links, which can carry data at 44.746Mbps, are being used as well. If you dial into an ISP from home, you might connect at a lower speed than at your office, where you might have higher-speed connections such as a T1 line. However, a variety of high-speed options are available for connecting to the Internet at home, such as cable modems or DSL connections.

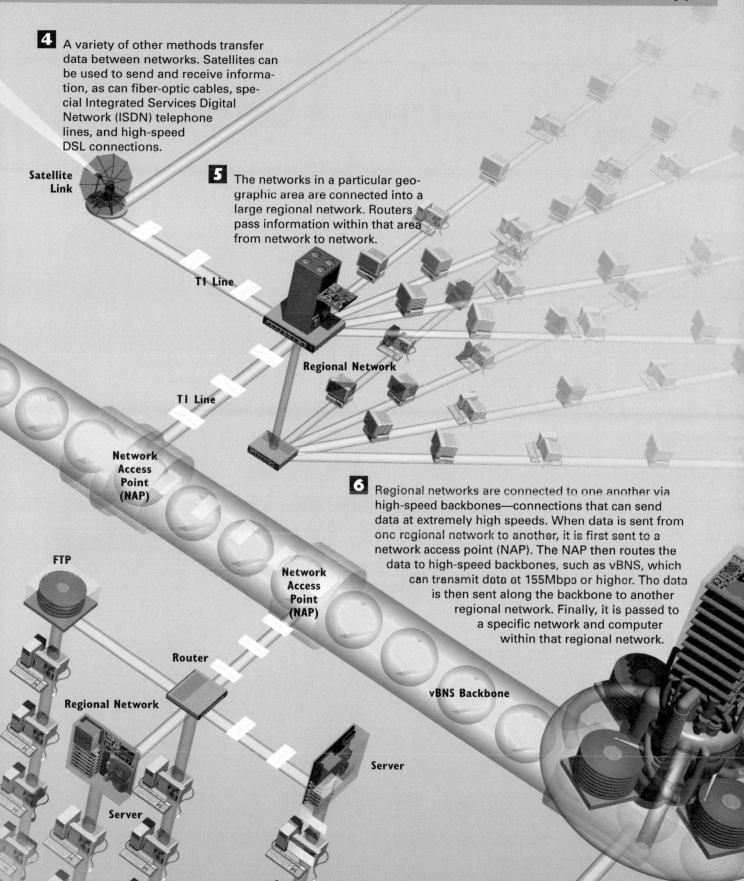

4 A variety of other methods transfer data between networks. Satellites can be used to send and receive information, as can fiber-optic cables, special Integrated Services Digital Network (ISDN) telephone lines, and high-speed DSL connections.

Satellite Link

5 The networks in a particular geographic area are connected into a large regional network. Routers pass information within that area from network to network.

TI Line

Regional Network

TI Line

Network Access Point (NAP)

FTP

Network Access Point (NAP)

6 Regional networks are connected to one another via high-speed backbones—connections that can send data at extremely high speeds. When data is sent from one regional network to another, it is first sent to a network access point (NAP). The NAP then routes the data to high-speed backbones, such as vBNS, which can transmit data at 155Mbps or higher. The data is then sent along the backbone to another regional network. Finally, it is passed to a specific network and computer within that regional network.

Router

Regional Network

vBNS Backbone

Server

Server

CHAPTER
3

How TCP/IP Works

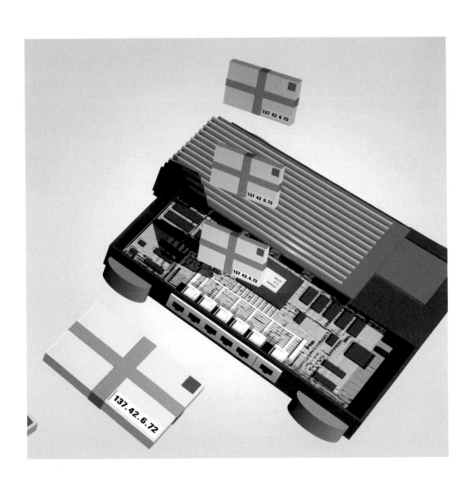

A seemingly simple set of ideas makes it possible for computers and networks all over the world to share information and messages on the Internet: Break up every piece of information and message into pieces called *packets*, deliver those packets to the proper destinations, and then reassemble the packets into their original form after they've been delivered so the receiving computer can view and use them. That's the job of the two most important communications protocols on the Internet—the Transmission Control Protocol (TCP) and the Internet Protocol (IP). They are frequently referred to as *TCP/IP*. TCP breaks down and reassembles the packets, whereas IP is responsible for ensuring the packets are sent to the right destination.

TCP/IP is used because the Internet is what is known as a packet-switched network. In a *packet-switched network*, there is no single, unbroken connection between sender and receiver. Instead, when information is sent, it is broken into small packets, sent over many different routes at the same time, and then reassembled at the receiving end. By contrast, the telephone system is a circuit-switched network. In a *circuit-switched network*, after a connection is made (as with a telephone call, for example), that part of the network is dedicated only to that single connection.

For personal computers to take full advantage of the Internet, they need to use special software that understands and interprets the Internet's TCP/IP protocols. This software is referred to as a *socket* or a *TCP/IP stack*, and it is built in to any computer that you buy, so you don't need to do anything special to access it. For PCs, the software is called Winsock. For Macintoshes, the software is called MacTCP. In both cases, this software serves as an intermediary between the Internet and the personal computer.

There are two primary ways that a computer can connect to the Internet and then use TCP/IP protocols—through a direct connection via a local area network (LAN), cable modem, or DSL line; or by dialing in using a modem. To connect via LAN, cable modem, or DSL line, a computer needs a network card. To communicate with the network and the Internet's TCP/IP protocols, the network card requires a hardware driver—software that mediates between the network and the network card. When the computer instead dials in to the Internet using a modem, the computer must use one of two software protocols: either Serial Line Internet Protocol (SLIP) or Point-to-Point Protocol (PPP). These protocols do the job of communicating with the Internet's TCP/IP protocols.

How the Internet's Basic TCP/IP Protocols Work

TCP

1 The Internet is a packet-switched network, which means that when you send information across the Internet from your computer to another computer, the data is broken into small packets. A series of switches called *routers* sends each packet across the Net individually. After all the packets arrive at the receiving computer, they are recombined into their original, unified form. Two protocols do the work of breaking the data into packets, routing the packets across the Internet, and then recombining them on the other end: The Internet Protocol (IP), which routes the data, and the Transmission Control Protocol (TCP), which breaks the data into packets and recombines them on the computer that receives the information.

010010010(
1111011101
0101110101
1110101011
1010100010
0111110110

21,915

01011101011
1110101
10101000
1110011
1001001
11011

14,782

IP

11101101
010111011
1111010101
1010100010
0111100110
0100100100
1111011101
0101110101
1111010101
1010100010
0111100110

0111100110
0100100100
1111011101
0101110101
1110101011
1010100010
0100100100
1111011101
0101110101
1111010101

2 For a number of reasons, including hardware limitations, data sent across the Internet must be broken into packets of fewer than about 1,500 characters each. Each packet is given a header that contains a variety of information, such as the order in which the packets should be assembled with other related packets. As TCP creates each packet, it also calculates and adds to the header a *checksum*, which is a number that TCP uses on the receiving end to determine whether any errors have been introduced into the packet during transmission. The checksum is based on the precise amount of data in the packet.

137.42.6.72

137.42.6.72

137.42 6.72

137 42.6.72

3 Each packet is put into separate IP *envelopes*, which contain addressing information that tells the Internet where to send the data. All the envelopes for a given piece of data have the same addressing information so they can all be sent to the same location to be reassembled. IP envelopes contain headers that include information such as the sender address, the destination address, the amount of time the packet should be kept before discarding it, and many other types of information.

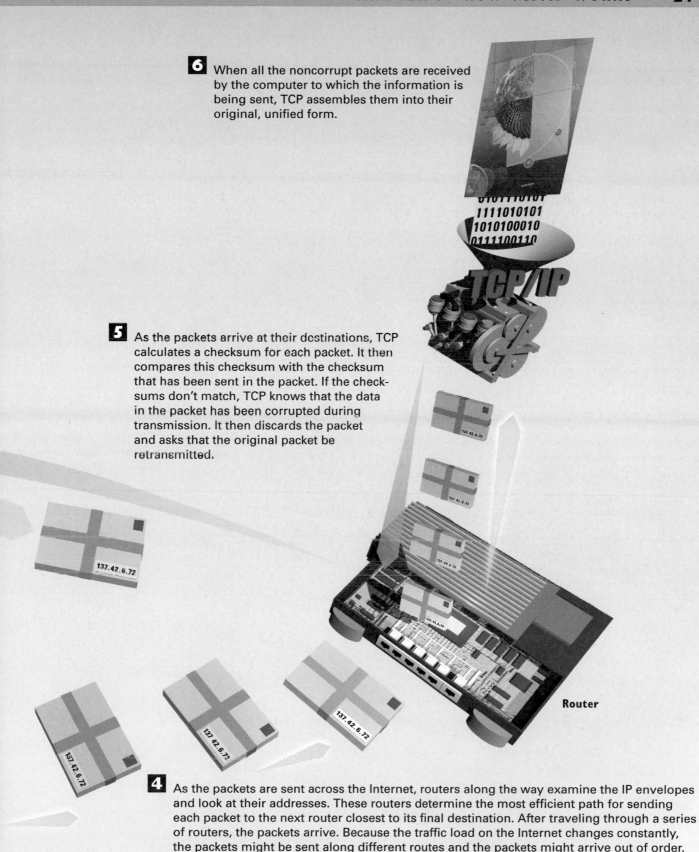

6 When all the noncorrupt packets are received by the computer to which the information is being sent, TCP assembles them into their original, unified form.

5 As the packets arrive at their destinations, TCP calculates a checksum for each packet. It then compares this checksum with the checksum that has been sent in the packet. If the checksums don't match, TCP knows that the data in the packet has been corrupted during transmission. It then discards the packet and asks that the original packet be retransmitted.

Router

4 As the packets are sent across the Internet, routers along the way examine the IP envelopes and look at their addresses. These routers determine the most efficient path for sending each packet to the next router closest to its final destination. After traveling through a series of routers, the packets arrive. Because the traffic load on the Internet changes constantly, the packets might be sent along different routes and the packets might arrive out of order.

How IPv6 Works

◆ 1 Because IPv4 uses only 32 bits for its IP addresses (called its *address space*), the number of total unique IP addresses is limited. IPv4 addresses are four numbers, separated by dots. Each number can only be up to 256. One example of an IPv4 address is 69.37.119.8. When the Internet was first designed, its creators never imagined that the address space would ever fill up, which is why they designed it the way they did.

4,294,967,296 addresses

340,282,366,920,938,463,463,374,607,431,768,211,456 unique addresses

012.345.678.910

2001:0db8:85a3:08d3:1319:8a2e:0370:7334

2 IPv6 dramatically expands the address space, because it uses 128 bits instead of 32. When it is adopted, there will be far more IP addresses available for Internet use.

2001:0db8:85a3:08d3:1319:8a2e:0370:7334

3 IPv6 offers other benefits, in addition to expanding the total number of IP addresses available. It will allow for networks and Internet Service Providers (ISPs) to assure Quality of Service (QOS) for certain applications, such as watching live video or making phone calls using the Voice over Internet Protocol (VoIP). One way it does this is by giving higher priority to certain packets, and lower priority to other packets. IPv6 also offers new security capabilities, by using authentication and encryption, among other features.

4 It will be many years before IPv6 is widely accepted. Until then, some businesses and applications will use IPv6, while the rest of the Internet will use IPv4. A variety of techniques can be used to allow IPv6 to operate with IPv4. In one technique, "dual stack" routers will be used. Routers will be programmed to work with both IPv4 and IPv6, and so will handle each packet differently depending on which version of IP it uses.

5 In another technique, IPv6 *datagrams* (information about how to route packets) will be wrapped inside IPv4 packets, and in this way will be able to tunnel through the Internet.

CHAPTER

4

Understanding the Internet's Software Structure

THE Internet works on the client/server model of information delivery. In a client/server model, the client computer connects to a server computer on which information resides; the client depends on the server to deliver information. In effect, the client requests the services of the server computer. These services can involve searching for information and sending it back to the client, such as when a database on the Web is queried. Other examples of these services are delivering web pages and handling incoming and outgoing email. Whenever you use the Internet, you're connected to a server computer and requesting the use of that server's resources.

Typically, the *client* is a local personal computer or the software that runs on it, and the *server* (also known as the *host*) is usually a more powerful computer that houses the data and/or server software. Hosts and clients can be of many makes and manufacturers and run a wide variety of operating systems.

The connection to the server is made in many ways—via a LAN (local area network), via a phone line, via a cable modem or DSL modem, wirelessly, or any one of other countless ways. A primary reason to set up a client/server network is to allow many clients to access the same applications and files that are stored on a server. These clients can be any one of many types of computers accessing the Internet in many ways.

In the case of the Internet's World Wide Web, the client is actually the browser on your PC and the server is a host computer located somewhere on the Internet. Typically, the browser sends the server a request for a specific web page. The server processes that request and sends an answer back to the browser (again, most often in the form of a web page).

The connection between the client and server is maintained only during the actual exchange of information. Thus, after a web page is transferred from the host (or server) computer, the HTTP connection between that computer and the client is broken. (HTTP stands for Hypertext Transfer Protocol; it's the protocol used by the World Wide Web.) Even though the HTTP connection is closed, the ISP maintains the TCP/IP connection to the Internet.

The client/server model enables the desktop PC to run the browser software to search the Web, yet still access host servers around the Internet to execute search and retrieval functions. Many of these functions are accomplished through technology called the Common Gateway Interface (CGI). For more information about how CGI works, see Chapter 35, "How CGI Scripting Works." In essence, this architecture enables the Web to be conceived of as a limitless file storage medium and database, distributed among thousands of host computers, all accessible by any individual device with Internet access.

The following illustration shows how the Web runs on client/server architecture. Keep in mind that all other resources on the Internet run on the client/server model as well. For example, in email transactions the client would be the email software on your computer, whereas the server would be the email server to which you connect.

How Client/Server Architecture Works

2 The host computer runs the server software that enables the host to separate the actual request from the packets and perform the asked-for services. This will involve either retrieving and sending back the specified web page to the client PC or executing a database search and sending back to the client the result in the form of a web page.

1 The PC-based browser software controls the client end of the Web application. Using TCP/IP, the browser issues HTTP requests to the host server. The browser can request a specific web page, or it can ask the host server to perform a database query. In either instance, the request is broken into HTTP packets that are sent across the Internet's TCP/IP communications infrastructure to the host computer.

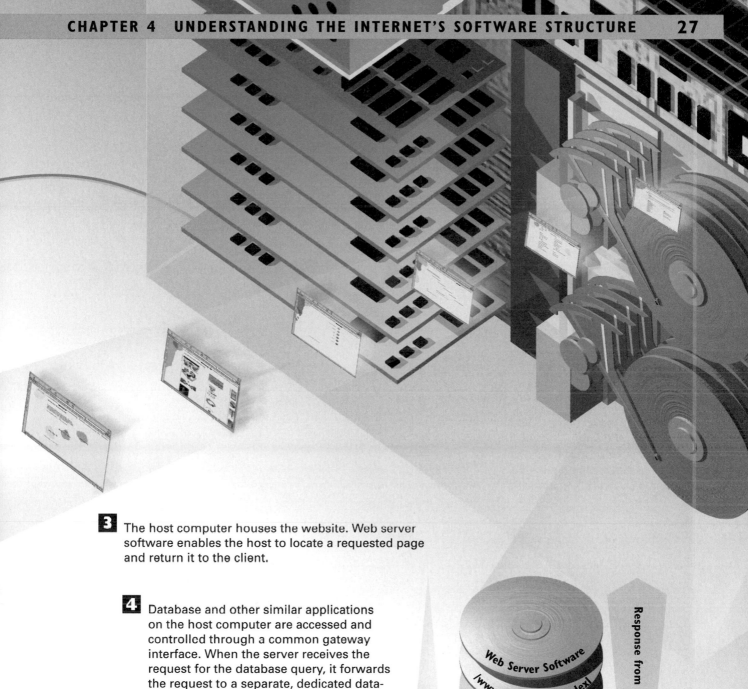

3 The host computer houses the website. Web server software enables the host to locate a requested page and return it to the client.

4 Database and other similar applications on the host computer are accessed and controlled through a common gateway interface. When the server receives the request for the database query, it forwards the request to a separate, dedicated database server or application for processing via the CGI.

Web Server Software

/www.zdpress.com/index/

/toc/chapter7.html

/toc/illustration/chap7.gif

CGI Application

Database Index

Data

Database Application

CGI Request

Response from Database

CHAPTER

5

How Internet Addresses and Domains Work

THE heart of how the Internet works is the Domain Name System (DNS), the way in which computers can contact each other and do things such as exchange email or display web pages. When someone on the Internet wants to contact a location—for example, to visit a website—he types in an address, such as www.metahouse.com. (A specific location on the Internet is also referred to as a *uniform resource locator*, or *URL*.) The DNS translates the plain English address, www.metahouse.com, into a series of numbers called an IP (for Internet Protocol) address. An IP address, such as 123.23.43.121, marks the location of a computer on the Internet similar to the way a house number and street mark the location of where you live.

In this example, metahouse.com is called a *domain*. To work most efficiently, the Internet has been organized into a number of major domains. *Major domains* refer to the letters at the end of a plain English address, such as .com. A number of common domains are .com (commercial), .edu (education), .gov (government), .mil (military), .net (Internet service providers and networks—companies and groups concerned with the organization of the Internet), and .org (organization).

Domains are organized in a hierarchical manner, so that beneath major domains are many minor domains. As an example of how the DNS and domains work, look at NASA's SPACElink Internet address: spacelink.nasa.gov. The top domain is .gov, which stands for government. The domain just below that is .nasa, which is the NASA domain. Then, spacelink identifies the NASA computer that runs the SPACElink program. SPACElink's numeric IP address has changed through the years, but its Internet address has stayed the same.

Computers called *name servers* are responsible for keeping track of such changes and translating them between IP addresses and domain addresses. The Internet can't understand alphanumeric Internet addresses, such as ziffdavis.com, so name servers translate those addresses into their proper numeric IP addresses, such as 163.52.128.72. Name servers contain tables that match alphanumeric Internet addresses to numeric IP addresses.

When you connect your computer to the Internet, your computer needs to have an IP address assigned to it to do common things, such as browsing the Web. Depending on how your computer is set up and how your service provider operates, you might have a static address or a dynamic address. A *static* IP address never changes, so if you have one, you will have the same IP address every time you connect to the Internet. However, because the Internet has only a limited number of IP addresses, many ISPs use dynamic addresses. With a *dynamic* IP address, you are given an IP address from a limited block of IP addresses every time you connect. In this way, ISPs don't have to have an individual address for every subscriber. Instead, they can share their pool of addresses among all subscribers.

Understanding Internet Addresses and Domains

1 The Internet Protocol (IP) delivers mail based on the specific email address. The domain of the address is expressed as four numbers, separated by periods (called dots), such as 163.52.128.72. However, because it would be difficult to remember such complex addresses, you can instead use Internet addresses made up of words, letters, and numbers. Computers called domain name servers translate the alphanumeric address into a numerical address, so email can be sent to the proper location.

2 An email address is made up of two major parts separated by an @ (at) sign. The address can tell you a good deal of information about the person who owns the address. The first part of the address (to the left of the @ sign) is the username, which usually refers to the person who holds the Internet account and is often that person's login name or in some way identifies her. The second part of the address (to the right of the @ sign) contains the hostname (which can refer to a specific server on a network), followed by the Internet address, which together identify the specific computer on which the person has an Internet email account.

Name Server

preston@biz.zd.com

Username Hostname Domain Name

3 When you send email, the Internet must know the numeric IP address, such as 163.52.128.72. Name servers look up the alphanumeric address and substitute the numeric IP address for it so the email can be delivered properly.

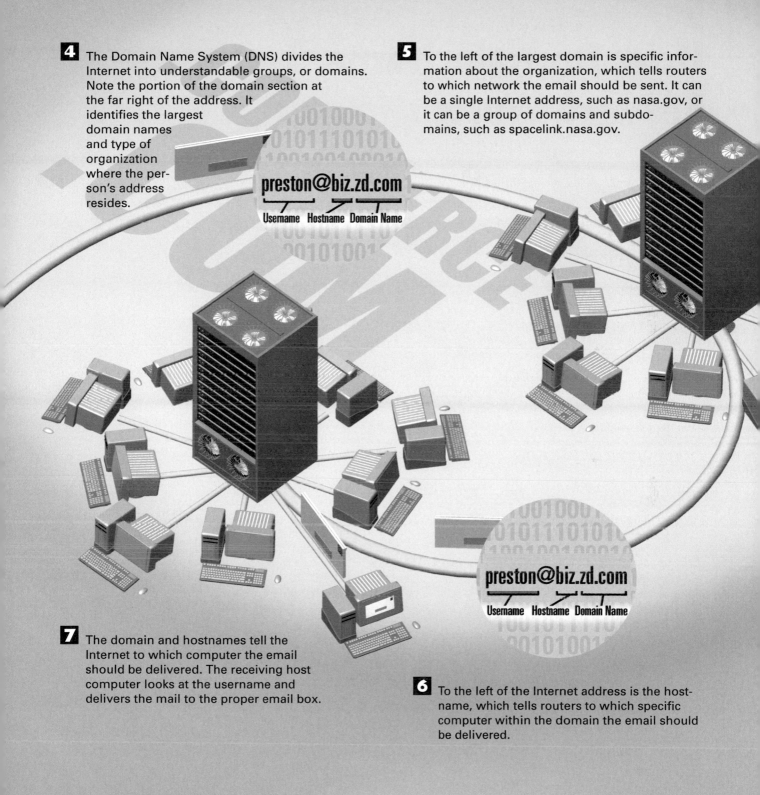

4 The Domain Name System (DNS) divides the Internet into understandable groups, or domains. Note the portion of the domain section at the far right of the address. It identifies the largest domain names and type of organization where the person's address resides.

5 To the left of the largest domain is specific information about the organization, which tells routers to which network the email should be sent. It can be a single Internet address, such as nasa.gov, or it can be a group of domains and subdomains, such as spacelink.nasa.gov.

preston@biz.zd.com
Username   Hostname   Domain Name

preston@biz.zd.com
Username   Hostname   Domain Name

7 The domain and hostnames tell the Internet to which computer the email should be delivered. The receiving host computer looks at the username and delivers the mail to the proper email box.

6 To the left of the Internet address is the hostname, which tells routers to which specific computer within the domain the email should be delivered.

How Domain Name System Servers Work

www.zdp.com

1 When a particular uniform resource locator (URL) needs to be contacted, the address with the URL must be matched to the true IP address. Your web browser first goes to a local name server maintained by your ISP, online service, or company to get this information. If the IP address is a local one—on the same network as the one you are on—the name server can resolve the URL with the IP address. It will send the true IP address to your computer.

Web Browser

3 If the information you have requested isn't on a local network, the local name server might not have the address you're looking for. In that instance, the local name server must get the information from a name server on the Internet. The local name server contacts the root domain server. The root domain server tells the local server which primary name server and secondary name server have the information about the requested URL.

www.zdp.com

Yes www.zpd.com
123.333.29.8

**InterNIC
Internet
Name Server**

InterNIC

**Intranet
Name Server**

www.zdp.com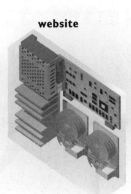

website

2 Your web browser now has the true IP
address of the place you're trying to
locate. It uses that IP address and contacts the site. The site sends you the
information you've requested.

www.zpd.com
123.333.29.8

4 The local name server now contacts the primary
name server. If the information cannot be found in
the primary name server, the local name server contacts the secondary name server. One of those name
servers will have the proper information. It then
passes the information back to the local name server.

Send it.

www.zpd.com
123.333.29.8

**Intranet
Name Server**

5 The local name server
sends the information
back to you. Your web
browser now uses the
IP address to contact
the proper site.

Root

How Static and Dynamic IP Addresses Work

1 When you connect to the Internet, your computer must be identified by a number called an IP address. There are two different methods for assigning IP addresses, statically or dynamically. When you have a static IP address, your computer keeps the same IP address every time you connect to the Internet. Dynamic addresses, on the other hand, are assigned every time you connect to the Internet.

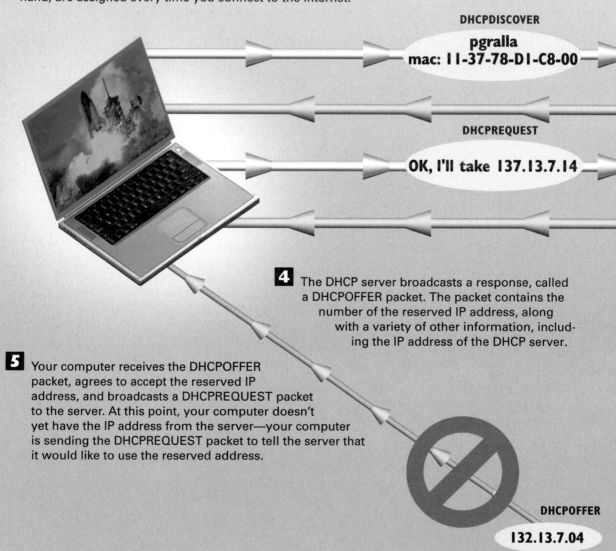

DHCPDISCOVER

pgralla
mac: 11-37-78-D1-C8-00

DHCPREQUEST

OK, I'll take 137.13.7.14

4 The DHCP server broadcasts a response, called a DHCPOFFER packet. The packet contains the number of the reserved IP address, along with a variety of other information, including the IP address of the DHCP server.

5 Your computer receives the DHCPOFFER packet, agrees to accept the reserved IP address, and broadcasts a DHCPREQUEST packet to the server. At this point, your computer doesn't yet have the IP address from the server—your computer is sending the DHCPREQUEST packet to tell the server that it would like to use the reserved address.

DHCPOFFER

132.13.7.04

**DHCP
Server**

2 To obtain a dynamic IP address, your computer sends a broadcast message called a DHCPDISCOVER packet to the network or ISP to which you're connecting. This packet contains identifying information about your computer, including its name.

3 The packet is broadcast throughout the receiving network. It's received by a DHCP server. The DHCP server checks the list of available IP addresses and reserves one for your computer so that no other computer can be assigned that address.

DHCPOFFER

137.13.7.14

reserved	137.13.7.13
OK	137.13.7.14
reserved	137.13.7.15
	137.13.7.16
	137.13.7.17
reserved	137.13.7.18

DHCPPACK

137.13.7.14 is yours

6 If there is more than one DHCP server on the network, your computer might receive more than one DHCPOFFER packet, offering an IP address. Your computer chooses just one DHCPOFFER packet and discards and ignores the rest.

7 The accepted DHCPREQUEST packet is received by the DHCP server. In response, the server sends a DHCPPACK packet to your computer. This packet gives your computer a "lease" on the IP address. Your computer now has full use of that IP address and can use the Internet.

8 The DHCP server and all other DHCP servers note that your computer is using the IP address, so the address is no longer available to be used by other computers. When you disconnect from the Internet, your IP address is released, and DHCP servers can use the address for someone else who connects to the network needing an IP address.

DHCP Server

**reserve
137.13.7.14**

How Network Address Translation Works

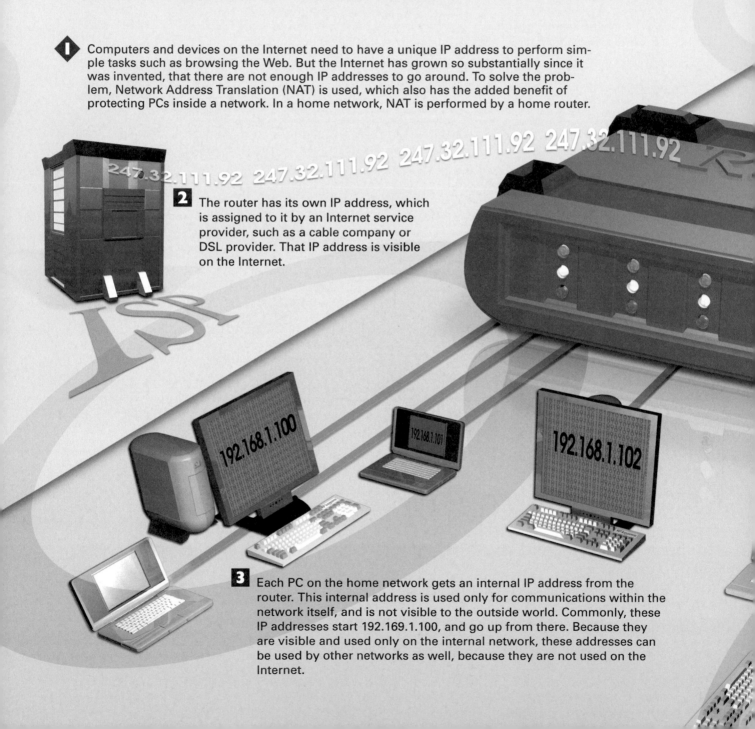

1 Computers and devices on the Internet need to have a unique IP address to perform simple tasks such as browsing the Web. But the Internet has grown so substantially since it was invented, that there are not enough IP addresses to go around. To solve the problem, Network Address Translation (NAT) is used, which also has the added benefit of protecting PCs inside a network. In a home network, NAT is performed by a home router.

2 The router has its own IP address, which is assigned to it by an Internet service provider, such as a cable company or DSL provider. That IP address is visible on the Internet.

3 Each PC on the home network gets an internal IP address from the router. This internal address is used only for communications within the network itself, and is not visible to the outside world. Commonly, these IP addresses start 192.169.1.100, and go up from there. Because they are visible and used only on the internal network, these addresses can be used by other networks as well, because they are not used on the Internet.

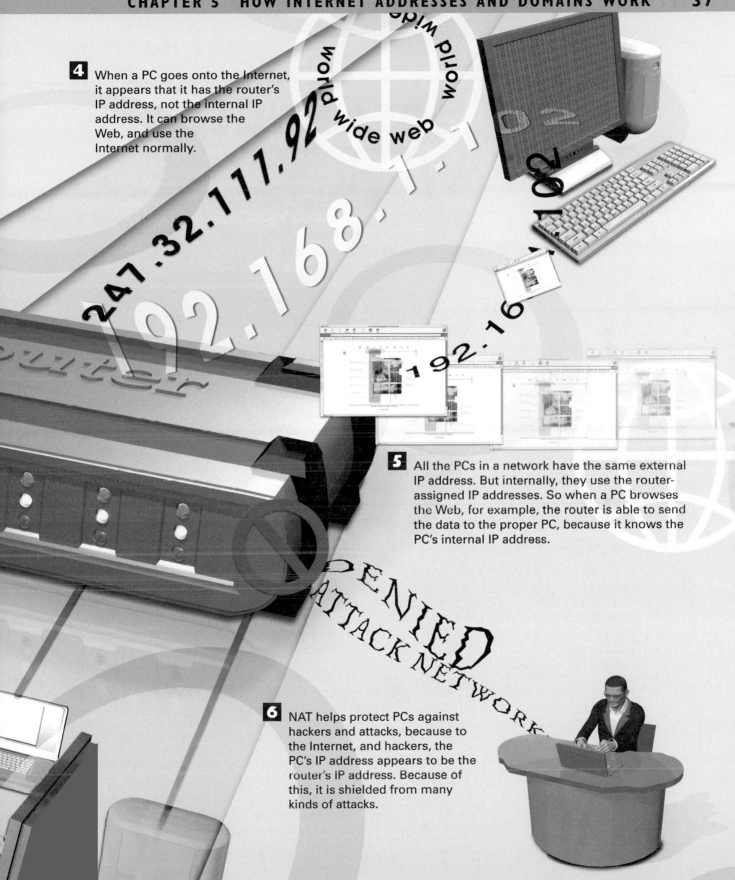

4 When a PC goes onto the Internet, it appears that it has the router's IP address, not the internal IP address. It can browse the Web, and use the Internet normally.

world wide web

world wide web

247.32.111.92

192.168.1.1

192.16...1.102

192.16...

router

5 All the PCs in a network have the same external IP address. But internally, they use the router-assigned IP addresses. So when a PC browses the Web, for example, the router is able to send the data to the proper PC, because it knows the PC's internal IP address.

DENIED

ATTACK NETWORK

6 NAT helps protect PCs against hackers and attacks, because to the Internet, and hackers, the PC's IP address appears to be the router's IP address. Because of this, it is shielded from many kinds of attacks.

CHAPTER
6

How Routers Work

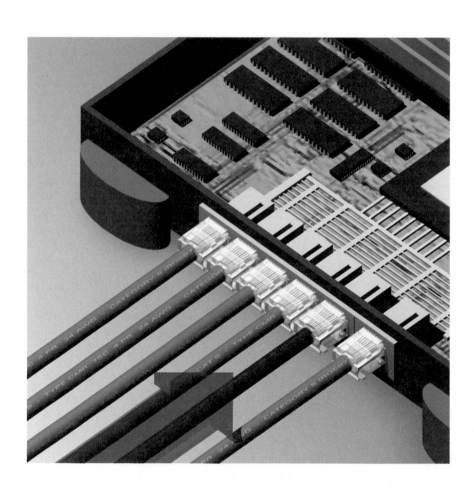

ROUTERS are the traffic cops of the Internet. They ensure that all data gets sent to where it's supposed to go via the most efficient route. When you sit down at your computer and connect to the Internet and send or receive data, generally that information first must go through at least one router—and often more than one router—before it reaches its final destination.

Routers open the IP packets of data to read the destination address, calculate the best route, and then send the packet toward its final destination. If the destination is on the same network as the sending computer, such as within a corporation, the router sends the packet directly to the destination computer. If the packet is going to a destination outside the local network, the router instead sends the packet to another router closer to the destination. That router in turn sends the packet to a yet-closer router, and so on, until the packet reaches its final destination.

When routers determine the next router to receive packets, factors such as traffic congestion and the number of *hops* (routers or gateways on any given path) come into play. The IP packet carries a segment that holds the maximum hop counts it can travel, and a router will not use a path that would exceed that predefined number of hops.

Routers have two or more physical ports: receiving (input) ports and sending (output) ports. When an input port receives a packet, a software routine called a *routing process* is run. This process looks inside the header information in the IP packet and finds the address to which the data is being sent. It then compares this address against an internal database called a *routing table*. The routing table has detailed information about the ports to which packets with various IP addresses should be sent. Based on what it finds in the routing table, the router sends the packet to a specific output port. This output port then sends the data to the next router or to the destination itself.

There are two kinds of routing tables: *static routing tables* and *dynamic routing tables*. The static table is simpler, and specifies specific paths for packets to use to get to their final destination. The dynamic table allows a packet to have multiple routes to get to its destination.

At times, packets are sent to a router's input port faster than the port can process them. When this happens, the packets are sent to a special holding area called an *input queue*, which is an area of RAM on the router. That specific input queue is associated with a specific input port. A router can have more than one input queue. Each input port processes packets from the queue in the order in which they were received, so the first packets sent in are the first to get processed and sent out.

If the number of packets received exceeds the capacity of the queue (called the *length* of the queue), packets might be lost. When this occurs, the TCP protocol on the sending and receiving computers have the packets re-sent.

Note that the router in the following illustration is of the type that routes data throughout the Internet, and isn't the same as a home router that forms the basis of a home network. For information about how a home router works, see Chapter 10, "How Home Networks Work."

How Routers Send Data to Their Destination

1 A router has input ports for receiving IP packets and output ports for sending those packets toward their destinations. When a packet comes to an input port, the router examines the packet header and checks the destination in it against a routing table—a database that tells the router how to send packets to various destinations.

Dynamic Routing Table

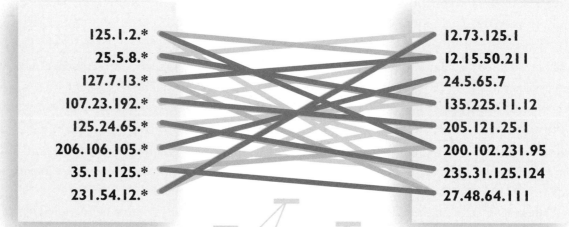

125.1.2.*	12.73.125.1
25.5.8.*	12.15.50.211
127.7.13.*	24.5.65.7
107.23.192.*	135.225.11.12
125.24.65.*	205.121.25.1
206.106.105.*	200.102.231.95
35.11.125.*	235.31.125.124
231.54.12.*	27.48.64.111

5 Dynamic routing is more useful than static routing. It allows a packet to have multiple routes to reach its final destination. Dynamic routing also enables routers to change the way they route information based on the amount of network traffic on some paths and routers. In dynamic routing, the routing table is called a *dynamic* routing table and changes as network conditions change. The tables are built dynamically by routing protocols, constantly changing according to network traffic and conditions.

6 Two broad types of routing protocols exist: interior and exterior. *Interior* routing protocols are typically used only on routers in a company's intranet, or internal network. These interior routing protocols route traffic bound only for inside the intranet. A common interior routing protocol is the Routing Information Protocol (RIP). *Exterior* protocols typically are used for routers located on the Internet. A common exterior routing protocol is the Exterior Gateway Protocol (EGP).

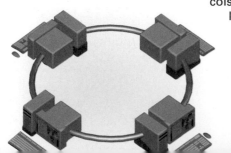

Router

2 Based on the information in the routing table, the packet is sent to a particular output port, which sends the packet to a router that is one step closer to the packet's destination.

Input Port

Output Port

Input Queue

4 A simple type of routing table is called a *static routing table*. In static routing, the routing table has specific ways of routing data to other networks. Only those pathways can be used. New routes can be added to the routing table; however, static routing can't adjust routes as network traffic changes, so it isn't an optimal alternative for many routers.

3 If packets come to the input port more quickly than the router can process them, they are sent to a holding area called an *input queue*. The router then processes packets from the queue in the order they were received. If the number of packets received exceeds the length of the queue, packets might be lost. When this occurs, the TCP protocol on the sending and receiving computers will have the packets re-sent.

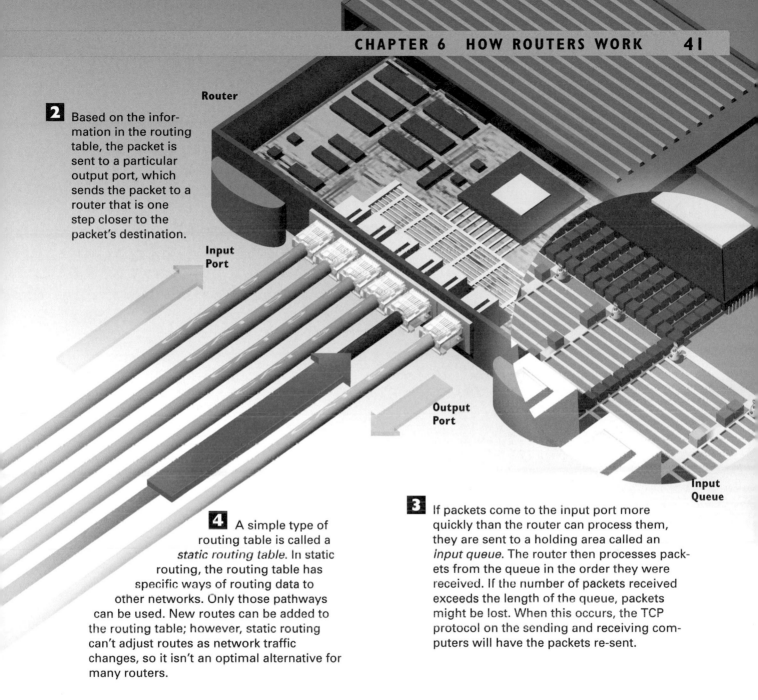

Static Routing Table

125.1.2.*	12.73.125.1
25.5.8.*	12.15.50.211
127.7.13.*	24.5.65.7
107.23.192.*	135.225.11.12
125.24.65.*	205.121.25.1
206.106.105.*	200.102.231.95
35.11.125.*	235.31.125.124
231.54.12.*	27.48.64.111

P A R T

CONNECTING TO THE INTERNET

YOU can connect to the Internet in many ways—and many more ways pop up practically every day. They range from simple telephone dial-in connections to high-speed cable and digital subscriber lines (DSL) to satellite connections, TV connections, wireless connections, connections at work and home via local area networks (LANs), and even connections via cellular telephones. This part of the book looks at the myriad ways people and computers gain access to the Internet.

One general rule is true about Internet connections: the faster, the better. People want the fastest connection possible because many pictures, sounds, and videos are available on the Internet. Today, the three most common ways you can connect to the Internet are through a corporate or university LAN, at home via a cable modem or DSL modem, or over telephone lines. Increasingly important, though, are wireless connections via the WiFi networking standard. Direct connections over LANs are generally the fastest connection, cable modems and DSL modems are the second fastest, and telephone-line connections the slowest. Cable modems, DSL modems, and LAN connections are all very high-speed connections, and are known as broadband connections.

This section looks at the ways computers can connect to the Internet. Chapter 7, "How Computers Connect to the Internet," provides an overview of the types of Internet connections that are possible. Not only will you examine various kinds of network connections and phone-line connections, but you'll also look at newer, high-speed DSL connections as well.

Chapter 8, "How Internet/Television Connections Work," looks at what might become one of the primary ways many of us connect to the Internet—through some type of television connection. This chapter looks at how cable modems work, and peers inside a newer technology—Internet-enhanced TV—that adds interactivity to your television set and makes your Internet experience more compelling. It also looks at what some believe is the future of the Internet and television, IPTV.

Chapter 9, "How Wireless Connections and WiFi Work," looks at how you can make an Internet connection without wires. Some common ones include using a satellite dish, much like the one now used for satellite TV, and using cell phones. But the most common wireless connection of all is known as WiFi, a standard that allows you to hook up without wires to the Internet at home, at work, or at many public hot spots. A laptop or PC equipped with a wireless network adapter can access the Internet without being physically connected to a network—WiFi routers connect you. In addition, a newer technology called WiMax allows anyone in a metropolitan region to connect as well.

Chapter 10, "How Home Networks Work," examines a fast-growing phenomenon—using networks at home to connect to the Internet. Many homes have more than one computer, and users want to be able to share a high-speed connection, such as a cable or DSL modem. Home networks make that possible. And increasingly, other devices at home will be connected to the Internet, not just PCs—and this chapter looks at them as well.

As you'll see in this part of the book, connecting to the Internet will become increasingly easy—and at increasingly higher speeds. Not only can you do things more quickly on the Internet, but you can access entirely new services that contain video, animation, and other high-bandwidth content. And as more places install wireless hardware, the Internet can be accessed anywhere—not just when you happen to be sitting in front of a PC connected to a network or phone line.

C H A P T E R

7

How Computers Connect to the Internet

THERE are many different ways your computer can connect to the Internet, ranging from dial-in connections to LANs (local area networks) to wireless connections to connections over cable TV wires, to DSL connections that use phone wires but connect you at high speed.

At one time, most people connected to the Internet via what is becoming an increasingly antiquated way—using a dial-up modem. Typically, when you use your modem to connect to the Internet, you dial in to an Internet service provider (ISP), for example EarthLink or America Online. When you dial in to and connect to your ISP, you're in fact connecting to a modem attached to a more powerful computer called a server. ISPs typically have banks of hundreds or thousands of modems that accept dial-ins from subscribers trying to connect. Modems are controlled by your computer and communications software by a set of commands called the AT command set (also known as the Hayes command set, named after one of the original modem manufacturers, Hayes). It's a language that instructs the modem on what to do at various points during a communications session, such as opening up a line and sending out tones that the telephone system can understand.

But there's a major problem with connecting this way—it's too slow to be of much use. Websites use many graphics and multimedia features, and dial-up connections are so slow that the Web can seem unusable.

Much faster than dial-up are so-called broadband connections. A broadband connection is a generic name for a high-speed connection to the Internet, most notably cable modems and Digital Subscriber Line (DSL) connections. (For a look at how cable modems work, see "How Cable Modems Work," in Chapter 8, "How Internet/Television Connections Work.")

Several types of DSL technologies are available, but they all work on the same principles. They enable you to use your existing telephone lines to access the Internet at very high speeds.

DSL technologies require that DSL modems be used on each end of the phone line. In fact, the term *DSL* doesn't really refer to a phone line because an ordinary, existing copper phone line can be used for DSL. Instead, it refers to the DSL modems themselves. More confusing still, DSL modems aren't really traditional modems at all. They don't attach to a serial port, as do traditional modems. And they don't dial your telephone, as do traditional modems. Instead, they connect to your computer via a much higher-speed port, either an Ethernet port or a USB port, and they maintain an always-on connection over your phone line. So, you always have an Internet connection when they are plugged into your PC and turned on.

DSL technology has one drawback; it requires that your house (and DSL modem) be located within a certain distance from the telephone company office and its DSL modem. In cities, this should not be a major problem, but it could be a problem in rural areas. The exact distance required depends on the type and speed of DSL service you use. Higher speeds require that you be closer to the phone company office.

How America Online Connects to the Internet

1 Online services such as America Online provide a very convenient way to use Internet resources. These services have their own software that makes accessing Internet resources such as Telnet and FTP easy. They also allow you to use your own Telnet, FTP, newsgroup reader, or other software instead of theirs. Using these resources, you can browse the World Wide Web, either with their own proprietary web browser or by using any other web browser. Finally, some services let you use special software required to access Internet resources such as Internet Relay Chat (IRC).

2 Each online service has a great deal of resources, content, and special areas that are not available to anyone except people who subscribe to that particular service. You dial directly into the online service to get at these resources.

3 When you use the resources of an online service, you don't go outside the service to the Internet—instead, you stay behind a firewall. A *firewall* is a security system of accepting or blocking packets as they are transmitted across a network. Individual online services establish firewalls that let only subscribers into the service.

4 Online services often use their own proprietary software and interfaces to give you access to many common Internet resources, such as Usenet newsgroups, Telnet, and FTP. You issue a command using the online service's own software. The online service then sends the command out over the Internet via a gateway to retrieve the information. The information is sent back via a gateway, through the online service's own software, and then to your computer. In some cases, such as MSN, the online service is TCP/IP-based.

Request
Reply

Search: pets
Found: 3127 pets

Firewall

Online Service A

7 Some online services let you use any web browser you want to browse the World Wide Web. In that instance, you can click an icon on the online service, go into a special area of the online service, or simply launch your web browser on your own computer, and then begin browsing the Web.

6 Online services also let you browse the World Wide Web. One way to browse the Web is to use the online service's own web browser. Typically, you can launch a browser by clicking an icon or going into a special area of the online service. And some services, such as MSN, are browser-based, so the browser is launched as soon as you start the service.

5 The services also let you use your own client software to access Internet resources such as Telnet, FTP, and IRC that the services do not have proprietary software for. To do this, you dial into the online service and establish a TCP/IP connection. You can then get directly onto the Internet using your own client software.

Request

Reply

Other Web Browsers

Request

Reply

FTP

Reply

Email

Firewall

Online Service B

Browse Web

Browse Web

Connecting Your Computer to the Internet

1

Dumb terminal A terminal connected to a mainframe, minicomputer, or other kind of large computer. This type of connection often can be found in libraries or universities, although those institutions are moving toward offering fuller Internet access than dumb terminals provide.

RS-232C

802.11 (WiFi) Digital Radio

3 **Wireless access** Laptops equipped with wireless network cards that adhere to the WiFi (802.11) standard can get high-speed access at public hot spots such as airports, hotels, and some coffee shops.

4 **Direct connection** LANs or large computers such as mainframes can be directly connected to the Internet. When a LAN is connected to the Internet, all the computers on the network can have full access to the Net. This type of access is common inside corporations.

Fiber Optic

LAN Router

Ethernet

2 **Cellular access** Cellular telephones and palmtops can send and receive email and browse the Web. They do this at lower speeds than regular dial-up modems, but the connections are available all the time.

Cellular Radio Link

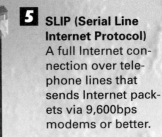

5 **SLIP (Serial Line Internet Protocol)** A full Internet connection over telephone lines that sends Internet packets via 9,600bps modems or better.

Phone Line

Phone Line

Phone Line

7

DSL lines Special digital telephone connections, called DSL, can be used to connect to the Internet at very high speeds. DSL modems are required for DSL connections.

9 **WebTV** You also can access the Internet directly on your television set by using a set-top box that dials in to the Internet and then displays web pages on your television set. The best known of these is the WebTV set-top box and network. You also can use satellite dishes that are similar to television satellite dishes to access the Internet.

TV

6

PPP (Point-to-Point Protocol) Similar to SLIP, this is a full Internet connection over telephone lines via modem. It is more reliable than SLIP because it double-checks to ensure that Internet packets arrive intact. It re-sends any damaged packets.

8 **Cable modem** The Internet can be accessed over some cable TV systems using the coaxial cable that carries television signals. A special cable modem must be used. Cable modems might be capable of sending and receiving data at speeds 20–100 times as fast as conventional modems.

10 **Online services** All the major online services allow you to tap the full power of the Internet. No special setup is required. When you dial in to the online service, you can use the Internet's resources, including browsing the World Wide Web.

Phone Line

Coaxial Cable

Online Service

Phone Line

How a Modem Makes Its Connection

2 The modem dials a number, and a modem on the other end answers the call. When the receiving modem answers the call, your modem sends out a tone to inform the receiving modem that another modem is doing the calling.

I'm a modem.

1 Modems are controlled by software on your PC using a language called the Hayes command set or AT command set. When a modem is to be dialed, the first command given it is to tell it to go *off hook*—in other words, to open a connection with the phone line. After that, a command tells the modem to dial a telephone number to make a connection.

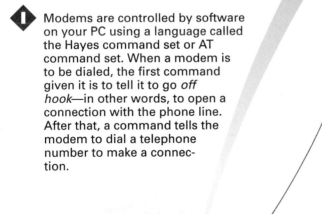

Modem

3 The receiving modem in turn answers with its own tones, and a basic connection is established. The modems now exchange information about how they are going to send data to each other—a process known as a *handshake*. In this handshake process, the modems agree on things such as the communication speed as well as whether they will use what is called a parity bit to check for errors during communications.

So am I!

Connect!

Modem

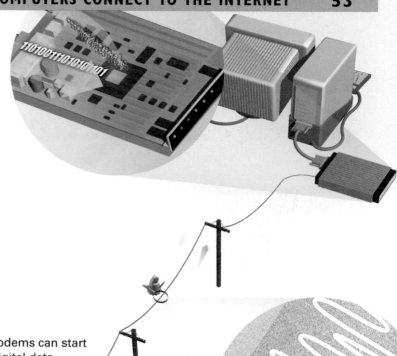

6 The analog signals reach the receiving modem where they are changed by the receiving modem—demodulated—from analog data back to digital data and sent into the computer via the serial port. This modulating and demodulating of data is what gives the modem its name: MOdulating/DEModulating.

4 Now that the connection is established, the modems can start exchanging data. Your computer works with digital data—binary bits of information that are either on or off. Your PC sends this binary data to be communicated to the modem.

5 The telephone system, unlike a computer, works with analog information—streams of continuous electric current that vary in frequency and strength. The digital data in your computer must be changed to analog information so it can be sent via the telephone system. The modem takes the digital information and changes it—modulates it—into analog signals. The information travels along the telephone system as analog data.

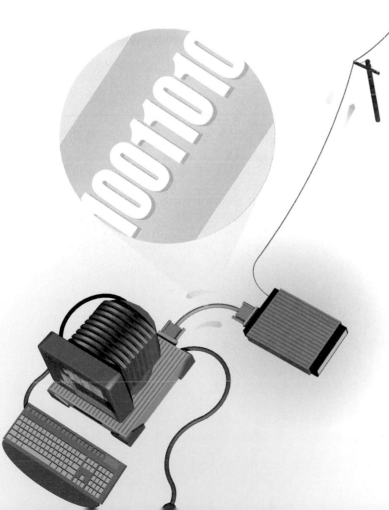

How DSL Makes Its High-Speed Connection

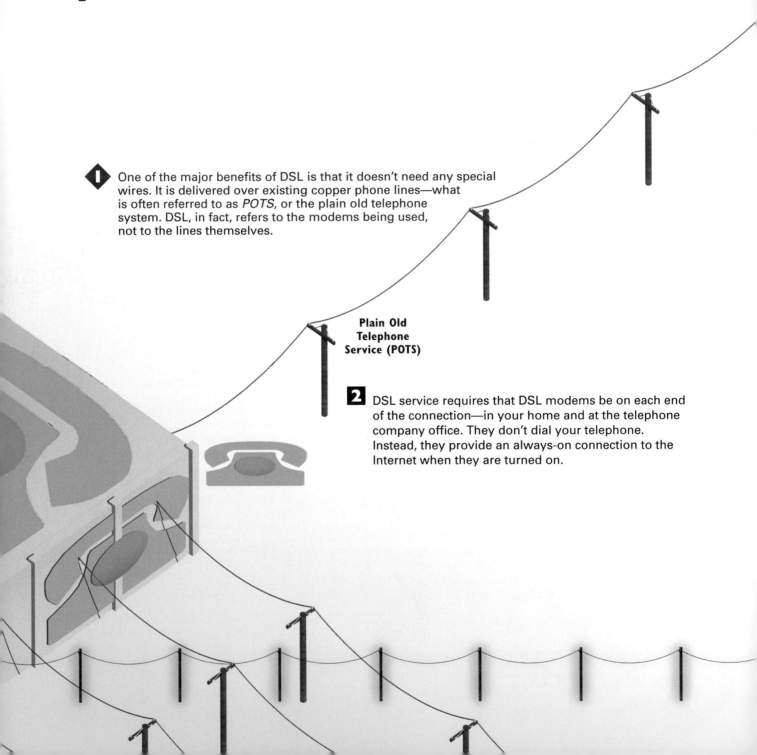

1 One of the major benefits of DSL is that it doesn't need any special wires. It is delivered over existing copper phone lines—what is often referred to as *POTS*, or the plain old telephone system. DSL, in fact, refers to the modems being used, not to the lines themselves.

Plain Old Telephone Service (POTS)

2 DSL service requires that DSL modems be on each end of the connection—in your home and at the telephone company office. They don't dial your telephone. Instead, they provide an always-on connection to the Internet when they are turned on.

Copper Phone Line

128 to 640 kilobits

.5 to 5 megabits

voice channel

3 Traditional analog transmissions and voice calls sent over copper telephone wires use only a small portion of the potential bandwidth that can be transmitted over copper telephone wires. DSL enables people to talk on the telephone and use the Internet at high speeds simultaneously—all over a single phone line.

ADSL 'modem'

4 DSL divides the phone line into three channels: one for receiving data, one for sending data, and one for talking over the telephone. Therefore, a single phone line can be used for browsing the Internet and talking over the telephone simultaneously. The phone line is not always physically separated into these channels. Rather, modulation techniques can be used to separate the three types of signals: voice, sending, and receiving. The sending and receiving channels can be divided into a variety of speeds. One form of ADSL might be able to receive data at 1.5Mbps, for example, and send it at 640Kbps.

5 To work properly, your DSL modem must be located within a certain distance from the phone company's answering DSL modem. The exact distance varies according to the precise DSL service and speed being offered, and even according to the gauge of the copper telephone wire. For an 8.448Mbps service, for example, the phone company's DSL modem needs to be within 9,000 feet of your modem. At 2.048Mbps, on the other hand, the modem can be located 16,000 feet away.

<9,000 Feet (DSL OK) **>10,000 Feet (no DSL connection)**

CHAPTER

8

How Internet/ Television Connections Work

WHEN people first began talking about the "information superhighway" several years ago, it wasn't the Internet they were talking about. Instead, it was television—and specifically cable television—that they believed would change the way we lived and worked. There were visions of 500 TV channels, "interactive television," shopping from home, and customized news available whenever you wanted it. This information superhighway was going to hook us all together electronically so we could more easily communicate and get information, services, goods, and entertainment. It didn't pan out that way. Instead, the Internet has become an information superhighway that can do almost everything people imagined could be done by using cable TV.

But the Internet is no longer the sole driving force behind the information superhighway. Every day, TV and the Internet are drawing closer to each other. The Internet is gaining more TV-like qualities, such as playing videos and music, to broadcasting live video feeds. Television technology is starting to use the Internet to add interactivity to the television experience.

In fact, television and the Internet are already merging. Soon you'll be able to watch a sporting event and simultaneously chat with others while you're watching—all on the same screen. Furthermore, when a batter comes up to bat during a baseball game, you'll be able to use the Net to get detailed statistics about the batter, and even past videos and highlights of his career.

Television and the Internet have already begun to merge in very real ways, notably through cable modems, interactive TV (which uses the Internet to deliver information to people on their TV screens), and IPTV, which uses the Internet's underlying protocols to deliver TV signals to people's homes over telephone lines.

Cable modems offer extremely high-speed access to the Internet. They enable you to access the Net using the existing coaxial TV cable that comes into your house. Cable modems offer T1-like and faster speeds, but at a fraction of the cost of T1 lines. They can deliver these high speeds because they are sent through high-capacity cable lines. Because Internet data and the normal cable signal coexist on the same lines, you can access the Net and watch TV simultaneously.

A different technology enables you to browse the Web using your television set. A *set-top box* connects your TV to the Net via a modem, takes the signal from the modem, and sends it to the TV. A remote control-like device enables you to browse the Web while watching TV at the same time. Interactive TV goes a step further and uses a set-top box to enable interactivity with your PC, using Internet technologies. At this point, no single standard exists for how Internet-enhanced TV works, nor even an agreement on which features such a service should have. The illustration in this chapter shows some of the common ways that such a service will most likely work.

Finally, telephone companies are getting into the business of delivering TV signals into people's homes over fiber-optic lines. They do this using IPTV, which uses the Internet's underlying protocols to deliver TV.

How Cable Modems Work

1 The coaxial cable—sometimes called a *broadband wire*—that comes into a home from a pole is divided into two connections by a splitter inside the home. One part of the wire goes to the normal set-top box that provides cable TV access. The other part of the wire goes to a cable modem, sometimes called a *broadband modem*.

2 The cable modem attaches to an Ethernet network card inside the computer. The network card is configured the same as any other network card on a computer that is attached to the Internet and has a network address.

3 The signals for sending and receiving data to and from the Internet travel through the coaxial cable, through the cable modem, and into your computer through the network card. The coaxial cable carries television and computer signals simultaneously. The computer signals travel on a 6MHz channel within the broadband spectrum on the coaxial cable.

RECEIVED

PC

Cable Modem

Splitter Splitter

Coaxial Cable

cable TV signal

Cable TV Converter

TV

1010110100101001001001001001
01010101110000110110110101
010101010101010100100101001001001
0101011010000110110

7 The head end also has high-speed Internet servers. A news server offers access to Internet Usenet newsgroups at a high speed because people access the server via the high-speed fiber-optic wires and coaxial cables instead of having to go out over the slower Internet. Additionally, *proxy servers* cache in their memory the most current versions of the more frequently accessed sites on the Internet. In that way, cable modem customers can get high-speed access to the sites because they get them via high-speed fiber-optic wires and coaxial cables instead of having to go out over the slower Internet.

4 The cable company divides each town or city into neighborhoods of about 500 homes, all of which are located on a single local area network, or *node*. All those 500 homes share the node. Both television and Internet data travel to and from those 500 homes to the node over coaxial cables. If many people simultaneously access the Internet on a single node, access is slower than if only a few people simultaneously access the Internet.

5 The nodes are connected via high-speed fiber optic lines to a head end cable facility. A single head end typically handles all the nodes for 4–10 towns. The head end is responsible for delivering television programming and Internet access to the cable customers.

6 The head end receives television transmissions from satellites and has Internet access via high-speed links to the Internet. These feeds provide the cable programming and Internet access to cable customers.

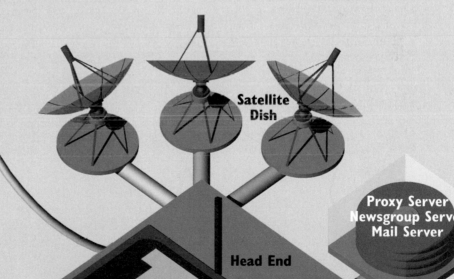

Node

Satellite Dish

Proxy Server
Newsgroup Server
Mail Server

Head End

High-Speed Internet Access

How Internet-Enhanced TV Works

1 To receive Internet-enhanced TV, a television set requires a special set-top box that can receive and deliver the Internet-enhanced services. The set-top box has a powerful processor and a hard disk inside it.

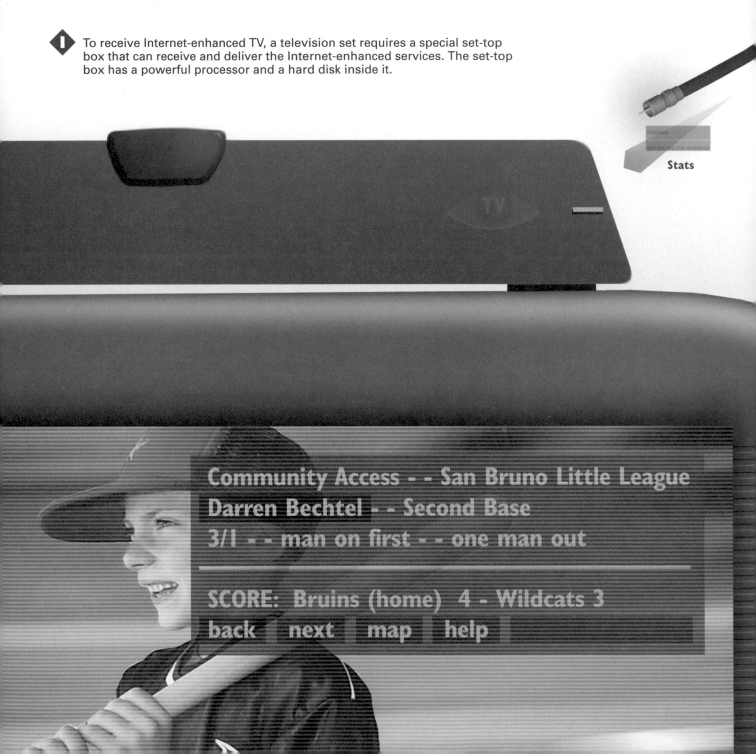

Stats

Community Access - - San Bruno Little League
Darren Bechtel - - Second Base
3/1 - - man on first - - one man out

SCORE: Bruins (home) 4 - Wildcats 3
back   next   map   help

Get Stats

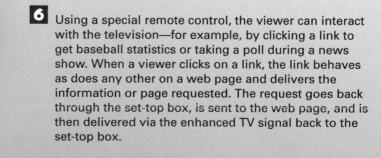

2 Internet-enhanced TV can work with many types of TV connections, including cable connections, satellite connections, and possibly DSL connections as well. The connection, such as the cable connection shown here, connects directly to the set-top box, not to the television itself.

3 When a TV station sends out a broadcast, it contains the normal TV broadcast, as well as an accompanying enhanced TV signal with Internet-related information. Televisions without the special set-top box display the normal TV broadcast and ignore the enhanced signal.

4 The enhanced signal can contain a variety of extra information, and it can be sent using Hypertext Markup Language (HTML), the language of the Web. For example, the information might contain statistics about a batter during a baseball broadcast, or it could allow viewers to answer questions during a quiz show. The HTML pages also could contain TV-specific HTML commands that can be displayed only via set-top boxes and not with web browsers.

```
<body style="background: url(t
<a href="tv:">back</a>
<a href="tv:">next</a>
```

5 The set-top box interprets the HTML information and formats it in a way that can be displayed on a TV set. This information can be overlaid on the regular TV show so that you can see the information at the same time that you're watching the show.

6 Using a special remote control, the viewer can interact with the television—for example, by clicking a link to get baseball statistics or taking a poll during a news show. When a viewer clicks on a link, the link behaves as does any other on a web page and delivers the information or page requested. The request goes back through the set-top box, is sent to the web page, and is then delivered via the enhanced TV signal back to the set-top box.

How IPTV Works

1 Video signals are received by the telephone company's national head end, which pulls in video feeds from satellites.

2 The feeds are usually received in digital format, usually MPEG-2, although sometimes in H.264 and Windows Media formats as well. If the signals are not received as digital feeds, they are encoded into a digital format, most often MPEG-2.

3 The video streams are broken into IP packets, and sent into the telephone company's core network, a massive network that handles data, voice, and other traffic in addition to TV feeds.

Because the network is internal and controlled by the telephone company, rather than the external network, the telephone can use tools to enhance the quality of the video signal, or make sure that its packets are given the highest priority possible, using Quality of Service (QoS).

4 The video streams travel over the network to local offices throughout the country. Local offices integrate the feeds with local programming, such as local stations, local advertising, and services such as pay per view. In addition, local offices have the "middleware" software that handles billing and similar tasks.

5 IPTV is designed to be used by telephone companies to deliver TV signals into home via fiber-optic connections. In order for a house to receive IPTV, it needs to have a fiber-optic connection, which can carry much more data than can normal, copper telephone lines.

CHANNEL 17 Local Sports

6 Unlike with cable TV, not all channels are simultaneously sent from local offices to individual houses, because of bandwidth constraints. Instead, only several are sent at a time, in a multicast group. When someone wants to change their channel, an IPTV box in their home switches the channel using the IP Group Membership Protocol (IGMP), which attempts to connect to the multicast group that holds the new channel.

Group1
Group 2   **Group 3**
Group 4

Approved

7 The local office receives the request to join the new multicast group, and its middleware checks to make sure that the person is authorized to watch the channel.

OK to switch user 856.213.852.301 to IGMP channel #37?

CHANNEL 43 Tennis Forever

8 If the person is authorized to view the channel, he is put on the multicast group, and the channel is streamed to his TV.

INTERNET PROTOCOL TV

CHAPTER
9

How Wireless Connections and WiFi Work

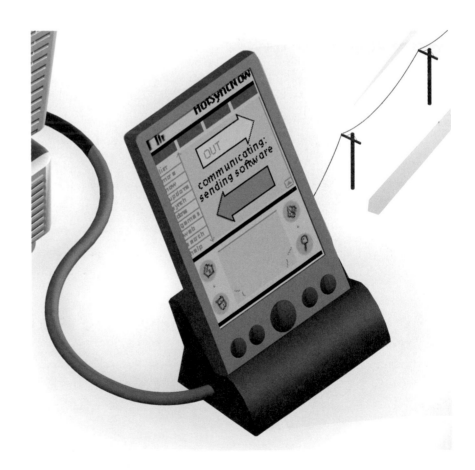

THE wired world created a revolution of allowing people to connect to the Internet. Now the unwired world—the ability to connect to the Internet wirelessly—is bringing just as big a change.

The most popular way of connecting to the Internet wirelessly is via a family of technologies called 802.11 or WiFi. There are several different standards for 802.11, and they connect at different speeds, including 802.11b standard, which operates in the 2.4GHz spectrum and transfers data at a maximum rate of 11Mbps; the 802.11a standard, which operates in the 5GHz spectrum at 54Mbps; and the 802.11g standard, which operates in the 2.4GHz spectrum and transfers data at a maximum rate of 54Mbps. In addition, there are other emerging standards that transfer data at much higher rates, such as the 802.11n, which will transfer data at rates approximately ten times faster than 802.11g.

To connect to the Internet this way, an 802.11 card needs to be used in a computing device such as a laptop or palmtop computer, and it needs to connect to a nearby compatible wireless access point, most often called a router. These routers can be in a home or business. Increasingly there are also public access points, called *hot spots*, which allow you to connect to the Internet from public places such as coffee shops, hotels, and airports.

One problem with WiFi networks is that they can be vulnerable to snoopers and hackers, who can use a technique called *war driving* to get into the network.

There are a variety of other ways to connect wirelessly to the Internet as well, for example by using a satellite connection.

Satellite-access systems are, in a way, odd hybrids. Many, but not all, still require that you use a modem. The modem is used to request information from the Internet, so when you send information through the Internet, it goes at normal modem speeds. However, that requested information is sent back to you at the high satellite transmission speeds, not the slower modem speeds. However, this means that if you're sending email, or transferring a file to someone via FTP, that information is sent at modem speeds, not satellite speeds.

When you access the Internet via satellite, you still use a traditional PC. However, you can also get onto the Web in other ways using new types of digital devices, most notably palmtop devices. These little computers, sometimes called personal digital assistants (PDAs) can literally put the Web in the palm of your hand. You connect a modem to them and can then get onto the Internet and send and receive email and browse the Web with them, although as explained earlier, you can also use them to access the Internet using WiFi technology.

An emerging technology may be the most revolutionary wireless technology of all—WiMax blankets an entire metropolitan area with high-speed Internet access, and so wherever you are, you can be connected to the Internet.

How to Access the Internet via a Satellite Connection

1 Accessing the Internet via a satellite connection delivers information to your computer at much higher speeds than do normal modems—at 400 Kbps. To use it, you need a satellite dish on your home in the same way that you need a satellite dish to get satellite TV.

6 The satellite in turn sends the information at 400Kbps to the satellite dish in your home.

7 The satellite dish sends the information to your PC via a coaxial cable, the same type of cable used by cable TV systems. Coaxial cable can send data at higher speeds than can normal telephone lines. The coaxial cable sends the data to a network card inside your computer. You now can view the web page—and you'll have gotten it at 400 Kbps rather than at 28.8Kbps or 56Kbps.

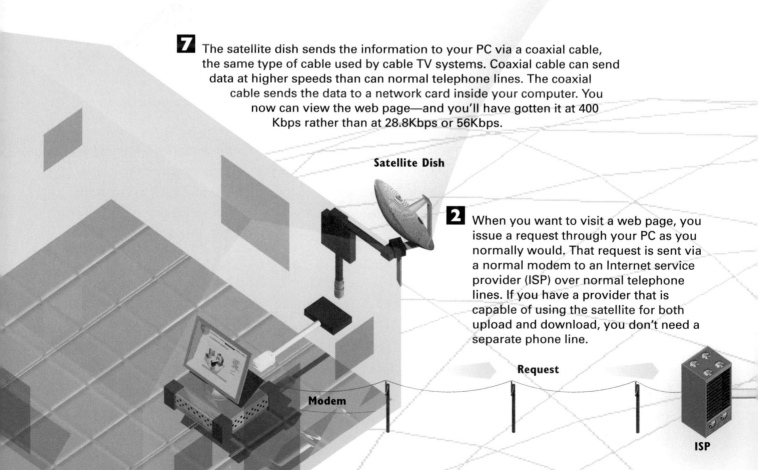

Satellite Dish

2 When you want to visit a web page, you issue a request through your PC as you normally would. That request is sent via a normal modem to an Internet service provider (ISP) over normal telephone lines. If you have a provider that is capable of using the satellite for both upload and download, you don't need a separate phone line.

Request

Modem

ISP

Satellite

5 The NOC sends the information to a satellite above the earth at 400Kbps.

4 Instead of transferring the information directly back to you over telephone lines, the web server sends the information to the satellite company's network operations center (NOC) (also called a satellite ground station) via special high-speed links.

3 Your request to visit the page goes to the web server that houses the site you want to visit.

Web Server

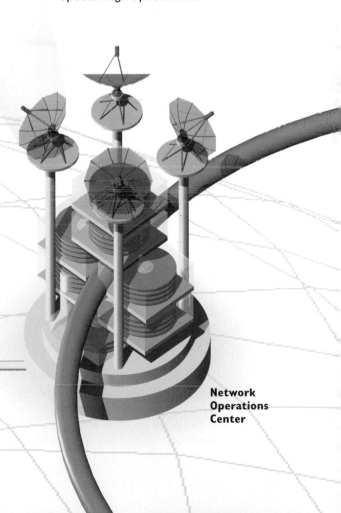

Network Operations Center

How Cell Phones Access the Internet

1 The main way cellular telephones access the Internet is through a protocol called the Wireless Access Protocol (WAP) and its associated markup language, the Wireless Markup Language (WML). To use WAP to access a web page with a cellular telephone, you first need to make a cellular phone call. When you dial a cell phone, it looks for the nearest cellular antenna, called a *base station*, to transmit the call. The phone scans nearby base stations and locks on one that is either the closest or has the most powerful signal.

MSN 13572
ESN 25817

Who are you?   Get
Web
Page

WML

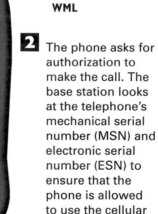

2 The phone asks for authorization to make the call. The base station looks at the telephone's mechanical serial number (MSN) and electronic serial number (ESN) to ensure that the phone is allowed to use the cellular network.

3 The base station sends the call to a telephone–wire-based network (also called a landline) and then to a network server and WAP gateway.

8 You can now read the page on your cellular telephone—it has been specially formatted for its display. However, cellular phones have difficulty handling graphics, so not all web pages will display properly, even after they've been reformatted to WML.

Get Web Page

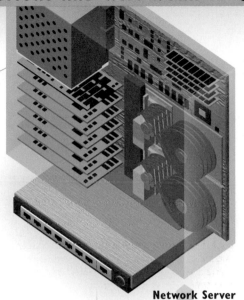

Get Web Page

Network Server

Phone Company

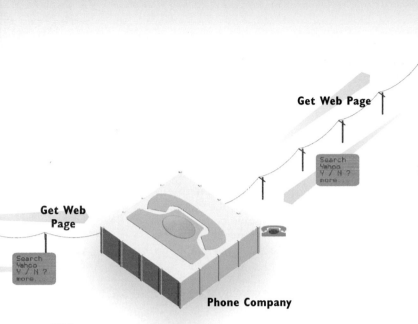

7 The WML page is sent back through the landline to a base station. The base station sends the page to your cellular telephone.

6 If the page is in normal HTML format, the gateway reformats the page in WML, so your cell phone can read the page. If the page is already in WML format, the gateway doesn't need to reformat the page.

Get Web Page

WAP Gateway

4 The gateway sends the request for the web page on to the web server on which the page is located.

Get Web Page

5 The page is sent back to the WAP gateway.

Router

How Bluetooth Works

Notebook PC

3 When a Bluetooth device finds another device, or more than one device, within its range, they go through a series of communications that establish whether they should communicate with one another. Not all devices will communicate—for example, a stereo might not communicate with a telephone. Devices determine whether they should communicate with one another by examining each other's Bluetooth profiles, which are coded into the devices' hardware by the hardware manufacturer. *Profiles* contain information about the device itself, what it is used for, and with which devices it can communicate. If devices determine they should communicate with one another, they establish a connection. The connection of two or more Bluetooth devices is called a *piconet*.

CONNECTED
Files to transfer: 42

2 The Bluetooth device constantly sends out a message, looking for other Bluetooth devices within its range.

1 Bluetooth is a wireless technology that allows computers, telephones, personal data assistants (PDAs), and even home devices such as stereos and TVs to communicate with one another. Each Bluetooth device has a microchip embedded in it that can send and receive radio signals. It can send both data and voice. The radio signals are sent and received in the 2.4GHz radio band, often referred to as the *industrial, scientific, and medical (ISM)* band. Inside the chip is software called a *link controller* that does the actual work of identifying other Bluetooth devices and sending and receiving data.

Bluetooth Chipset

Piconet I

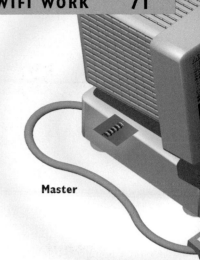

4 After the connection is established, the devices can communicate with one another. You could use a Bluetooth device to access information from the Internet, if the device it's accessing the data from is connected to the Internet. For example, you could have a home network with Bluetooth capability and connect a palmtop computer to the Internet by connecting through the home network.

Master

5 If there are many Bluetooth devices or piconets near each other, their radio signals could conceivably interfere with one another. To ensure that doesn't happen, Bluetooth uses *spread-spectrum frequency hopping*. In this technique, the transmitters change their frequencies constantly—1,600 times per second. In this way, the chance of interference is very small—and if interference does occur, it occurs for only a tiny fraction of a second. When two or more devices are connected in a piconet, one device is the master and determines the frequencies to switch among. It instructs all the other devices on which frequencies to switch to, and when.

Slave

Handheld

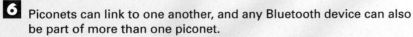

6 Piconets can link to one another, and any Bluetooth device can also be part of more than one piconet.

Slave

Piconet 2

How Wireless (WiFi) Networks Work

Ethernet

Access Point

WiFi Card

1 A key component of an 802.11 network (also called a *WiFi network*) is an *access point* or *router* (also called an *AP*). The access point consists of a radio transmitter and receiver as well as an interface to a wired network such as an Ethernet network, or directly to the Internet. The access point serves as a base station and a bridge between the wireless network and a larger Ethernet network or the Internet.

2 For a computer to become part of the network, it must be equipped with an 802.11-compatible wireless network card so that it can communicate with the access point. Each computer that's part of the network is usually referred to as a *station*. Many stations can communicate with a single access point. An access point and all the stations communicating with it are collectively referred to as a Basic Service Set (BSS).

3 When a station is first turned on or enters an area near the access point, it scans the area to look for an access point by sending out packets of information called *probe request frames* and waiting to see whether there is an answering probe request from a nearby access point. If the station finds more than one access point, it chooses one based on signal strength and error rates.

4 Stations communicate with the access point using a method called *Carrier Sense Multiple Access with Collision Avoidance (CSMA/CA)*. They check to see whether other stations are communicating with the access point, and if they are, wait a specified random amount of time before transmitting information. Waiting a random amount of time ensures that the re-attempts at transmission don't continuously collide with one another.

Probe Request Frame

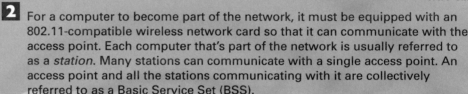

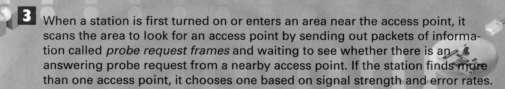

Station 128
Request To Send
12:47:035

Access Point 7
OK Station 128
Clear To Send
12:47:035

Station 42
Request To Send
12:47:035

Station 219
Request To Send
12:47:035

Station 7
Request To Se
12:47:035

Station 67
Request To Send
12:47:035

Station 37
Request To Send

Station 193
Request To Send

5 Before a station transmits information or a request, it first sends a short packet of information called a *Request to Send (RTS)*, which includes information about the request or data to come, such as its source, destination, and how long the transmission will take.

6 If the access point is free, it responds with a short packet of information called a *Clear to Send (CTS)*, telling the station that the access point is ready to receive information or requests.

7 The station sends the packet to the access point. After the packet is received, the access point sends an ACK (Acknowledgment) packet confirming that the data was received. If an ACK packet isn't sent, the station resends the data until it receives an ACK packet.

8 An 802.11 network can have many access points and many stations. Stations can move from access point to access point. Taken together, all the access points and stations are called an *Extended Service Set (ESS)*.

9 The 802.11 standard also allows stations to communicate directly with one another, without a connection to an access point, a network, or the Internet. When stations communicate directly with one another, it's called a *peer-to-peer network*. This allows the stations to do things such as share files.

Peer-to-Peer Network

How Public Wireless Hot Spots Work

1 A wireless WiFi hot spot allows people with laptops, PDAs, or other devices equipped with WiFi network cards to connect to the Internet by connecting to the hot spot. There are thousands of hot spots in coffee shops, fast food restaurants, hotels, and airports, and collections of hot spots cover entire sections of cities. You must pay to connect to many hot spots, although an increasing number are free.

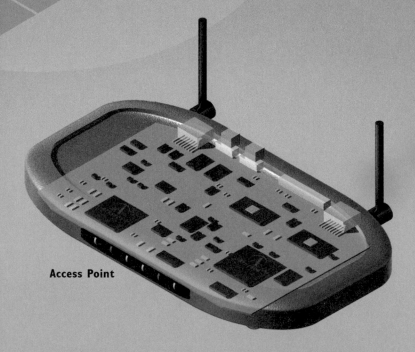

Access Point

2 Each hot spot needs its own connection to the Internet, so that people who connect to the hot spot can in turn connect to the Internet. The connections from the hot spot to the Internet are typically high speed, because all users of that hot spot need to share its bandwidth.

3 Before using for-pay hot spots, users need to sign up, as they do with any other Internet service provider. Payment can be on a monthly or per-use basis. When a hot spot subscriber wants to get Internet access via a hot spot, he uses software built in to the operating system, or software from the hot spot provider. If the hot spot is a for pay hot spot, he'll also have to log in and provide a user name, as a way of providing authentication that he is who he says he is.

4 If the user has signed up for a hot spot network, such as from a large, national provider like T-Mobile, he will be able to connect from any of the hundreds or thousands of hot spots run by the provider. He will not be able to connect to hot spots that aren't run by his provider.

**WiFi Service
Coverage Maps**

5 Some metropolitan areas have established free, public hot spot zones in downtown areas. Anyone can connect to the Internet via hot spots in these areas for free. They are actually more than a single hot spot. Individual hot spots provide overlapping coverage, so that someone can "roam" from one hot spot to another, and never lose an Internet connection.

How WiMax Works

1 WiMax (Worldwide Interoperability for Microwave Access) is similar to WiFi, but broadcasts over an entire metropolitan area, rather than just a single location, using the 802.16 standard. A wireless Internet service provider (WISP) provides WiMax Internet service. The WISP, like other ISPs, needs to connect to the Internet via a high-speed backbone, so that it can provide Internet service to its subscribers.

Internet

Wireless Internet Service Provider (WISP)

Line-of-sight transmission

2 The WISP provides high-speed Internet connections to a WiMax tower via a high-speed wired connection, such as a T1 line. A WiMax tower is like a cell phone tower, except that it provides Internet connections rather than cell phone service. A single tower can broadcast up to 30 miles, compared to 100 feet for WiFi.

3 A high-speed connection to a WiMax tower can also be provided via a line-of-sight microwave link, either directly from the WISP, or from another WiMax tower. In this way, WiMax towers can be strung along a very large area, providing widespread WiMax coverage.

WiMax transmitter

4 There are several ways that a WiMax tower can provide wireless access to WiMax subscribers. It can provide direct line-of-sight access if there is an unimpeded view between the WiMax receiver and a WiMax tower. A home, for example, may have a small receiver dish antenna. That home may have a network installed in the house, which can receive its Internet connection from the WiMax dish. Line-of-sight connections offer the stablest, highest-speed WiMax connection, at up to 70 Mbps.

Non-line-of-sight transmission

5 A WiMax tower can also provide Internet access via non-line-of-sight transmissions, in much the same way that WiFi does. These connections are less stable, and lower speed than line-of-sight WiMax connections.

CHAPTER

10

How Home Networks Work

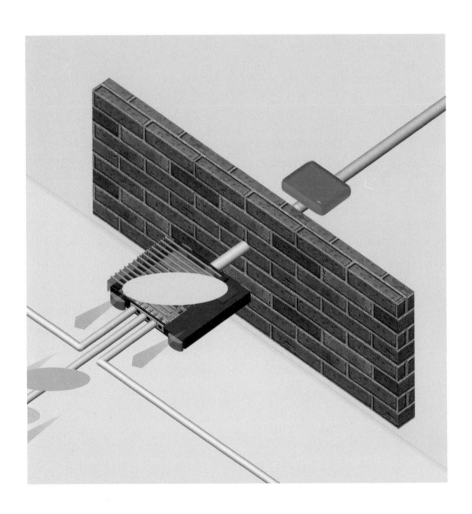

IN today's world, where many households have more than one computer, home networks have become commonplace. Home networks are primarily used to allow multiple computers to share a broadband Internet connection, but also allow those computers to share a printer and exchange files among each other.

The most common networks you'll find at home are wireless networks based on the 802.11 family of protocols called Wi-Fi. (For more details about how Wi-Fi works, see Chapter 9 "How Wireless Connections and WiFi Work.")

Wireless networks, although they got their start in the business world, are now more commonly used at home than at work. There are several reasons for that; a big one has to do with cost. Corporations are located in office buildings that are already wired—the buildings have Ethernet cables strung throughout that connect computers to the network, so building an entirely new wireless network is a very expensive proposition.

By way of contrast, homes don't have Ethernet cables strung throughout the walls. Therefore, to network computers in several rooms—in a study, a home office, and several children's bedrooms, for example—one would have to snake cables throughout the walls, and that costs a significant amount of time and money. With a wireless network, you don't need to spend that time and money.

The other reason that wireless networks have become popular at home is that the simple ones used in homes are very easy to set up, and have become quite inexpensive, in some cases costing less than a hundred dollars for an entire network. To build a wireless network at home, you can buy a network kit with all the required pieces, or you can buy the pieces individually. You'll need a wireless router that connects all the computers to one another and to the Internet. And you'll need to buy wireless network cards for each computer you want to connect to the network. The computers all connect to the wireless router, and the router routes all the traffic among the computers and between the computers and the Internet.

The main reason why people install wireless networks is to share a high-speed Internet connection, such as a cable modem or a DSL modem. But they can use the network for other things as well, notably sharing devices such as printers, sending files back and forth between computers, or playing computer games over the network against other family members. And wireless home networks can also be used to wirelessly stream music and videos to televisions and stereos.

Although today, mainly computers at home are networked wirelessly, in the future other kinds of devices and appliances will be connected to one another as well, such as small, inexpensive email devices that only send and receive email, and even traditional home appliances such as refrigerators, microwave ovens, and alarm clocks. Not only will they connect to one another, they'll connect to the Internet as well.

Connecting these kinds of devices and appliances will make life more convenient—you'll be able to use your refrigerator to automatically generate shopping lists, for example, and send orders directly to grocery stores. And you'll have an alarm clock that can change the time it awakens you based on traffic reports it garners from the Internet. These kinds of devices aren't mere fantasy—they are already being sold or tested. Initially, many will require wires to connect to each other and the Internet, but soon they'll connect wirelessly as well, and some already do.

How Home Networks Let You Share Your Internet Connection

1 The main reason people set up home networks is to share high-speed Internet access, such as via a cable modem or DSL modem, among several computers. To give the home network access to the Internet, an Ethernet cable runs from the cable modem or DSL modem to the networking device, called a *router*.

3 The router does two primary jobs: It connects all the PCs to each other so they can share files and devices such as printers, and it connects all the PCs to the Internet so they can each have a high-speed Internet connection. For the router to do its job, it needs an IP address, which it's given by a server run by the Internet service provider (ISP) that runs the cable or DSL service.

7 In addition to gaining Internet access through the router, the PCs also can share resources such as printers. So, any computer on the network can print to a printer attached to any other computer, as long as the computers are set up to share resources.

6 When a second PC is turned on, it does the same thing the first PC does: It contacts the router and gets a private IP address. This internal IP address will be different from the first—for example, it might be 192.168.1.148. But to the outside world, the IP address looks like the IP address of the router. The PC now has full access to the Internet. Other computers on the home network can get internal IP addresses and access to the Internet in the same way using the home router.

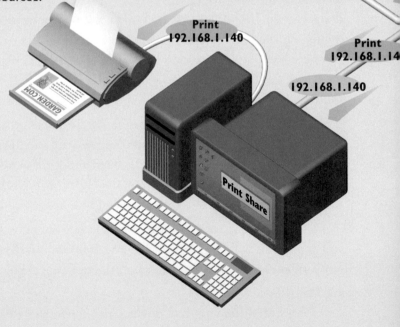

192.168.1.100

Check Mail

Print
192.168.1.140

Print
192.168.1.14

192.168.1.140

Print Share

GARDEN.COM

**ISP Server
(to the Internet)**

137.42.12.12

2 The computers on the network need to be protected against hackers and other dangers on the Internet. A firewall stops hackers from breaking into the home network. (For more information on how firewalls work, turn to Chapter 44, "How Firewalls Work.")

Cable Modem

137.42.12.12
192.168.1.1

Firewall

Hub/Router

4 PCs connect to the router via Ethernet cables. Each PC needs a network card, which is connected via the Ethernet cable to the router.

192.168.1.140

**Print
192.168.1.140**

5 When a PC is turned on, it needs to have an IP address to connect to the Internet. Normally, when a PC is connected directly to a cable modem or DSL modem, the IP address is given to the computer by the ISP that runs the cable modem or DSL service. However, in the case of a home network, the PC instead gets its IP address from the router, which uses a technique known as network address translation (NAT). With NAT, the IP address—such as 192.168.1.100—is a special, private IP address that is used only inside the home network. To the outside world, the IP address looks like the IP address of the router. The PC now has full access to the Internet.

How a Wireless Media and Music Server Works

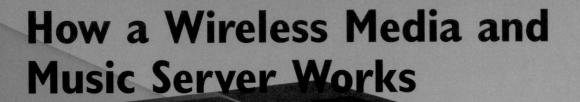

MOVIES.............
Citizen_Kane.WMP
Chinatown.WMP

MUSIC.............
Over_The_Rainbow.MP3
Misty.MP3

Media Server

1 A wireless media and music server includes a hard disk and a central processing unit (CPU), as well as wireless access point and router. It can stream music and video not only to personal computers, but also to television sets and home stereos.

2 For a television, home stereo, or personal computer to play music or video from the server, they each must have a wireless connection to the network. PCs can use their normal wireless adapter. To connect a stereo, a special wireless adapter plugs into the analog-audio port. To connect a television, a special wireless adapter plugs into the composite-video port. Every PC, television, and stereo makes a wireless connection to the media server, so all are on the network.

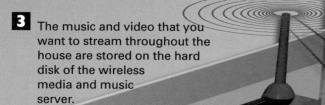

3 The music and video that you want to stream throughout the house are stored on the hard disk of the wireless media and music server.

MOVIES.......
Citizen_Kane.WMP
Chinatown.WMP

MUSIC..........
Over_The_Rainbow.MP3
Misty.MP3

4 When you want to play music or video, you use a remote control. From a menu, you choose what you want to play, for example a video.

KANE

PC

TV

Radio

5 The server uses its CPU to play the video. The video is then streamed wirelessly over the network, for example to a television, where it is displayed.

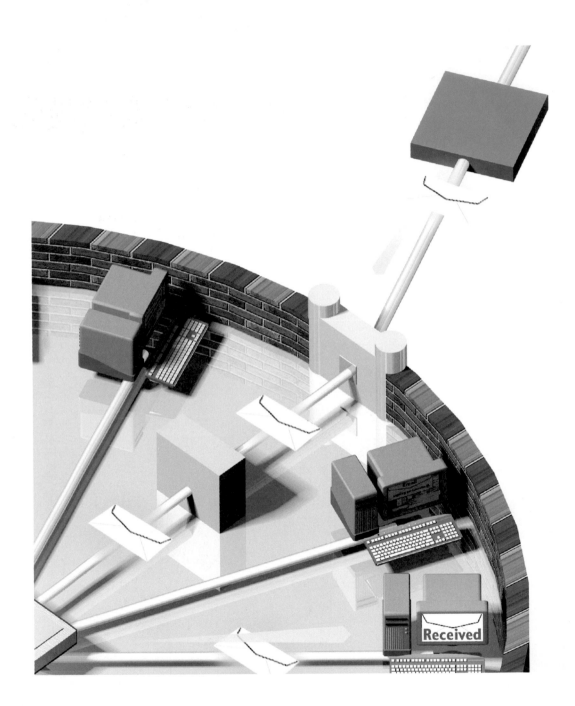

P A R T

COMMUNICATING ON THE INTERNET

SINCE its very earliest days, the Internet has been concerned primarily with one task—making it easier for people to communicate with one another using computers. The Internet was created to enable university researchers to share their thoughts, work, and resources, and for military people to communicate with each other in case of war and even, theoretically, a nuclear attack.

Today, more than two decades after the inception of the first networks that grew into the Internet, it is still primarily a communications medium. Millions of people from all over the world share their thoughts, hopes, work, gossip, and comments on the wires and computers that make up the Internet. Many of the means of communication, such as electronic mail, have changed very little in the past 20 years. Yet other, entirely new ways of communicating have been devised, such as enabling you to use the Internet as your telephone, completely cutting out long-distance charges, even if you're calling to the other side of the world. Some technologies enable people to communicate privately, one on one; others allow for vast discussion groups that span the globe; and still others enable both private communication with one person and public communication with large groups.

This section of the book looks at the main ways people communicate on the Internet.

Chapter 11, "How Email Works," takes a long look at what continues to be the most popular way for people to communicate on the Internet—electronic mail, or email. Email remains possibly the greatest use of the Internet and is used for business and personal communication. You'll see how email gets routed from your computer through the maze of wires that makes up the Internet and then ends up in the proper recipient's inbox. You'll look at all the elements of a mail message and learn how you can send binary files, such as pictures and sounds, through email. You'll also explore mailing lists, where you can subscribe to any one of thousands of public discussions via email or receive what are essentially electronic newsletters delivered to your email inbox. You'll also look at how you can look up anyone's email address using white page directories that use a technology called the Lightweight Access Directory Protocol (LADP). Finally in this chapter, you'll take a look at how email can be encrypted so that snoopers and hackers can't read it as it makes its way across the Internet.

Chapter 12, "How Email Spam Works," covers one of the most controversial modes of communication on the Internet—the use of spam, the equivalent of junk mail via email—that is sent to millions of people each day. Although spam is a problem on newsgroups as well as email, email is the greatest area of controversy. Spam annoys people and wastes their time while they clean out their mailboxes; it clogs the Internet so that other messages might be delivered late (or not at all); and it can be delivered by piggybacking onto other people's email servers, costing them money. The chapter looks at how spam is sent, as well as ways that it can be blocked.

Chapter 13, "How Newsgroups Work," explores Usenet newsgroups—public discussion groups in which anyone can participate. Many thousands of these groups focus on every subject conceivable. You'll see how newsgroups work and how you can decipher their often-arcane names.

Chapter 14, "How Internet Chat and Instant Messaging Work," covers the various ways people can *chat* on the Internet. When people chat on the Internet, they don't actually speak but type comments on their keyboards instead, and then people all over the world can read and respond to them. This chapter closely examines how instant messaging works—a way in which people can chat one on one with others. Two of the most popular pieces of software for communicating on the Internet—using America Online Instant Messenger (AIM) and ICQ—are chat software. This chapter also discusses the first type of Internet chat, called Internet Relay Chat (IRC). Although not as popular as it used to be, it's still a way many people chat with each other online. And it also looks at how chat rooms work, in which groups of people can communicate with each other.

Chapter 15, "How Skype and VoIP Work," details one of the more intriguing uses of the Internet—using it as your telephone. With a microphone and speakers, or a headset, you can make phone calls right from your PC as long as you have an Internet connection. In fact, you can also use the Internet to make phone calls without even using your PC—just plug a phone into your cable modem, DSL modem, or home network router, and use the phone as you would any other. There are a variety of ways to make calls using the Voice over Internet Protocol (VoIP), such as using free software called Skype. With Skype, you can make direct calls to other Skype users all over the world for free, or call regular telephones anywhere in the world for pennies a minute.

Finally, Chapter 16, "How Blogging and RSS Work," covers one of the biggest phenomena to hit the Internet—blogs, also called weblogs. Blogs allow anyone to post their thoughts and insights online, and have become so popular that it has affected the outcome of a presidential campaign, and become one of the most influential technologies on the planet.

CHAPTER

11

How Email Works

ELECTRONIC mail, or email, might be the most heavily used feature of the Internet. You can use it to send messages to anyone who is connected to the Internet or connected to a computer network that has a connection to the Internet, such as an online service. Millions of people send and receive email every day. Email is a great way to keep up with far-flung relatives, friends, co-workers in different branches of your company, and colleagues in your field.

Email messages are sent in the same way as most Internet data. The TCP protocol breaks your messages into packets, the IP protocol delivers the packets to the proper location, and then the TCP reassembles the message on the receiving mail server so it can be read.

You can also attach binary files, such as pictures, videos, sounds, and executable files to your email messages. Because the Internet isn't capable of directly handling binary files in email, the file first must be encoded in one of a variety of encoding schemes. Popular schemes are MIME and uuencode. The person who receives the attached binary file (called an *attachment*) must decode the file with the same scheme that was used to encode the file. Many email software packages do this automatically.

When you send email to someone on the Internet, that message often has to travel through a series of networks before it reaches the recipient—networks that might use different email formats. Gateways perform the job of translating email formats from one network to another so that the messages can make their way through all the networks of the Internet.

A mailing list is one of the most intriguing uses of email. It connects a group of people who are interested in the same topic, such as Japanese cartoons or home schooling. When one person sends email to the mailing list, that message is automatically sent to everyone on the list. You can meet others and talk to them on a regular basis about your shared interests, hobbies, or professions. To get onto a mailing list, you send an email note to the mailing list administrator and include your email address.

Mailing lists can be moderated or unmoderated. A *moderated* mailing list is screened by the list administrator, who might kill duplicate messages or messages not related to the list's theme. An *unmoderated* mailing list is wide open; all mail sent to it is automatically sent to everyone on the list.

Often, when you want to subscribe to a mailing list, you send a message to a computer instead of a person. That computer, known as a *list server* (also called a *listserv*), reads your email and automatically subscribes you to the list. You can unsubscribe from the list in the same way.

In the past, finding the email address of someone was very difficult if you knew only her name. These days, it's not so hard. A variety of "white page" directories have sprung up on the Internet that enables you to easily look up people's email addresses. These sites mainly use a standard called the Lightweight Directory Access Protocol (LDAP), which enables you to find people's email addresses without even having to visit a website. Using the protocol, you can search for email addresses on the Internet from directly within your email program.

One problem with email is that it's not secure—snoopers and hackers can read it as it gets sent along the public wires that make up the Internet. To ensure that no one except the sender and receiver can read it, encryption can be used—software that scrambles the mail so only those with the proper encryption keys can read it.

How Email Is Delivered Over the Internet

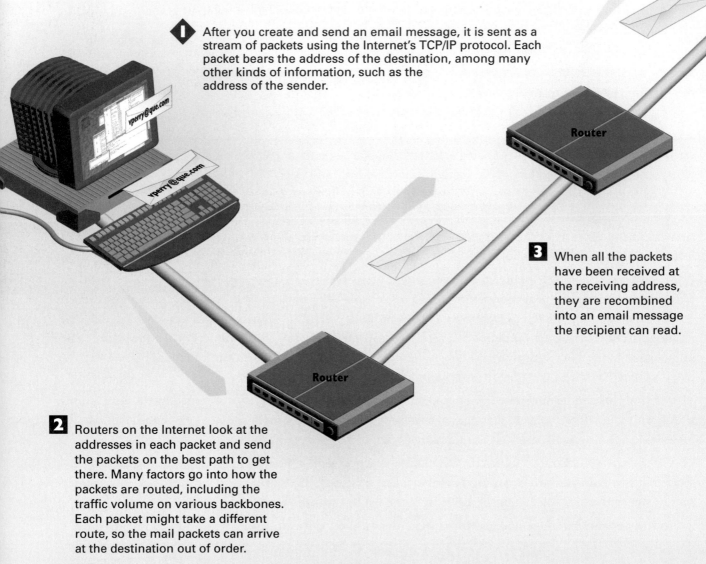

1 After you create and send an email message, it is sent as a stream of packets using the Internet's TCP/IP protocol. Each packet bears the address of the destination, among many other kinds of information, such as the address of the sender.

3 When all the packets have been received at the receiving address, they are recombined into an email message the recipient can read.

2 Routers on the Internet look at the addresses in each packet and send the packets on the best path to get there. Many factors go into how the packets are routed, including the traffic volume on various backbones. Each packet might take a different route, so the mail packets can arrive at the destination out of order.

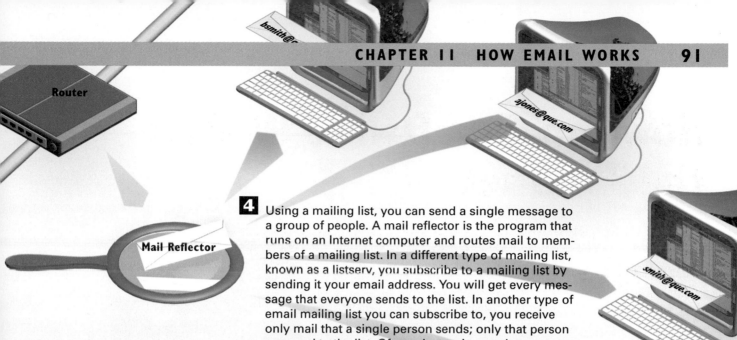

Router

Mail Reflector

4 Using a mailing list, you can send a single message to a group of people. A mail reflector is the program that runs on an Internet computer and routes mail to members of a mailing list. In a different type of mailing list, known as a listserv, you subscribe to a mailing list by sending it your email address. You will get every message that everyone sends to the list. In another type of email mailing list you can subscribe to, you receive only mail that a single person sends; only that person can send to the list. Often, electronic newsletters are distributed in this way.

5 Using the Internet, email can be exchanged among all the major online services, computer bulletin boards, and other networks. From the Internet, you can send email to any of those networks—and from any of those networks, mail can be sent to the Internet. When mail is sent from one of those networks to another, it often must pass through the Internet as a way of routing the mail.

FTP Server

Get me xyz.zip.

xyz.zip

Online Service A

Online Service B

Online Service C

How Email Software Works

Mail Server

1 After the Internet delivers mail to your email box, you need some way to read the mail, compose new mail, and respond to your messages. To do all this, you use email software, sometimes called *mailers* or *readers*.

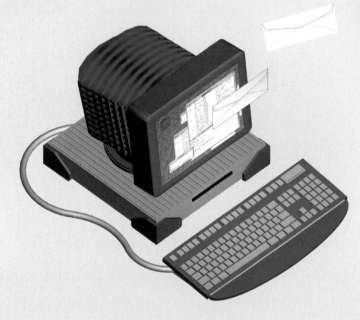

2 When someone sends you an Internet email message, the message isn't delivered straight to your computer. Instead, it gets sent to a mail server. Your email software logs in to the mail server and checks to see whether you have mail.

< new mail from Increase Your ENERGY!!!!!!!!! (spam flag)

< new mail from Que (smcmb@que.publishing.com)

< new mail from Preston (pgralla@gralla.com)

< new mail from Lower Your Monthly Rate!!!

< new mail from Que (smcmb@que.publishing.com)

< new mail from Jeb (jeb132@morenet.com)

-- viewed mail from Michael mt@m-troller.com

-- viewed mail from Que lc31@que.publishing.com

-- viewed mail from Talent Scout judyk@supersniper.com

-- new mail from Preston (pgralla@gralla.com)

3 If you have new mail, you'll see a list of your new mail messages when you log in to the server. You'll often see the name of the sender, the subject of the message, and the date and time the message was sent.

4 When you want to read a mail message, you tell your software to download it to your own computer. There, you read the message using your mail reader, and then you can file it, delete it, or respond to it.

Here it is.

Do I have mail?

5 Email software enables you to do things such as create folders for storing mail, search through your messages, keep an address book of people to whom you send mail, create group mailing lists, create and add a signature file, and more.

OUT

IN

WORK

6 Most email software reads HTML-based pages sent to you so that you can receive, in your mailbox, fully formatted web pages. When you click the links in them, your browser launches and visits the page to which it is linked.

ADDRESS BOOK

<< ADD TO YOUR LIST

Noel Voskuil

Preston Gralla

Michael Troller

Alan Prezeskien

Stephen Collicisan

Laureen Niehoff

patients

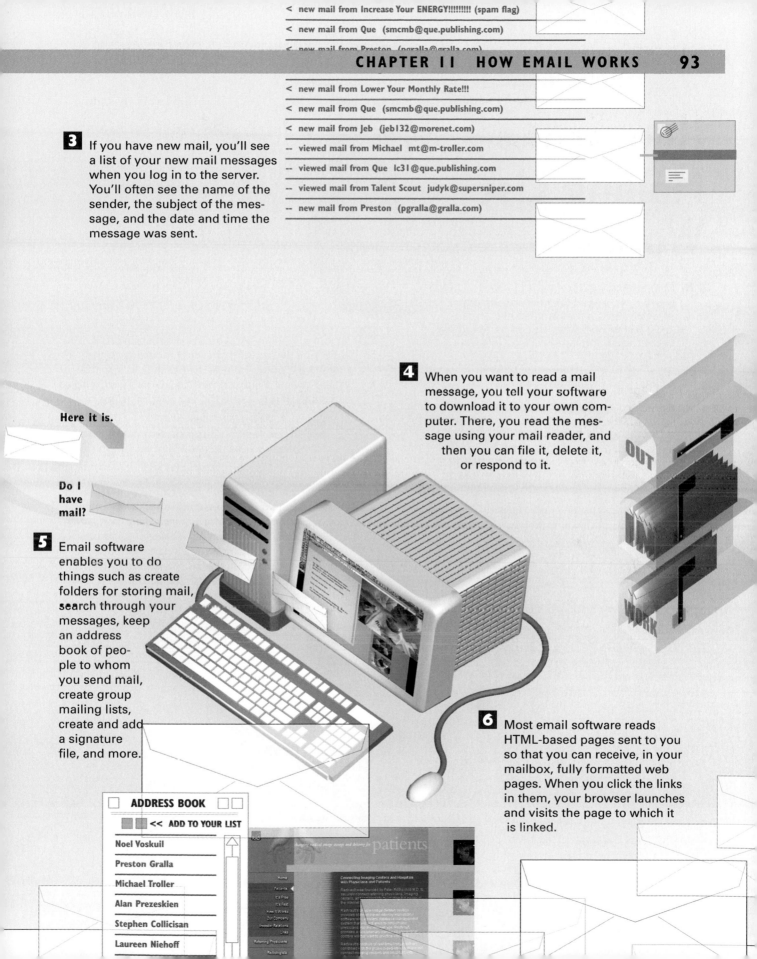

johnp@aoll.com

miagralla@prodigy.com

johnjames@neti.com

billybob@sun.com

jqpublic@usa.gov

asmith@jupiter.com

fredg@tozikal.net

janeq@aoll.com

How a Mailing List Works

1 Mailing lists are a way for groups of people to have public discussions via email. After you join a mailing list, every message you write to the list can be read by everyone on the list.

Join request from:
gabegralla@zdnet.com

2 To join a mailing list, you must subscribe to it. You subscribe by sending an email message to the mailing list administrator and asking to join the list. To cancel a subscription to the list, you send a cancellation request to the list administrator.

3 The mailing list itself is a database of the email addresses of people who have subscribed to it. When you ask to subscribe, you are added to the database.

4 When the computer on which the database resides receives a message to be sent to the mailing list, it automatically mails the message to every address in the mailing list database. Some mailing lists are very active, and people on them can get dozens of messages every day. Because of that, it's a good idea to check your mail frequently and clean out your mailbox. Otherwise, you can bog down your mail server, which can make it difficult for you to read your mail because you'll have so much of it.

miagralla@prodigy.com

johnjames@neti.com

billybob@sun.com

gabegralla@zdnet.com

jqpublic@usa.gov

asmith@jupiter.com

fredg@tozikal.net

janeq@aoll.com

sallyr@goto.com

You are now part of the soccer mailing list.

Ready for soccer season?

Send Message

Send Message

Send Message

Send Message

Send Message

Send Message

Send Message

How Email Is Sent Between Networks

1 When you send an email message, it is first broken up by the Internet's TCP protocol into IP packets. Those packets are then sent to an internal router that examines the address. (An internal router is inside your network, rather than out on the Internet.) Based on the address, the internal router decides whether the mail is sent to someone on the same network or to someone outside the network. If the mail goes to someone on the same network, the mail is delivered to them.

Gateway

Firewall

2 If the mail is addressed to someone outside the network, it might have to pass through a firewall—a computer that shields the network from the broader Internet so intruders can't break into the network. The firewall keeps track of messages and data going into and out of the network, to and from the Internet. It can also prevent certain packets from getting through it.

Internet Router

3 Once out on the Internet, the message is sent to an Internet router. The router examines the address, determines where the message should be sent, and then sends the message on its way.

Firewall

Gateway

4 A gateway at the receiving network gets the email message. This gateway uses TCP to reconstruct the IP packets into a full message. The gateway then translates the message into the protocol the target network uses and sends it on its way. The message also might be required to pass through a firewall on the receiving network.

5 The receiving network examines the email address and sends the message to a specific mailbox.

Received

How BlackBerries Deliver Email

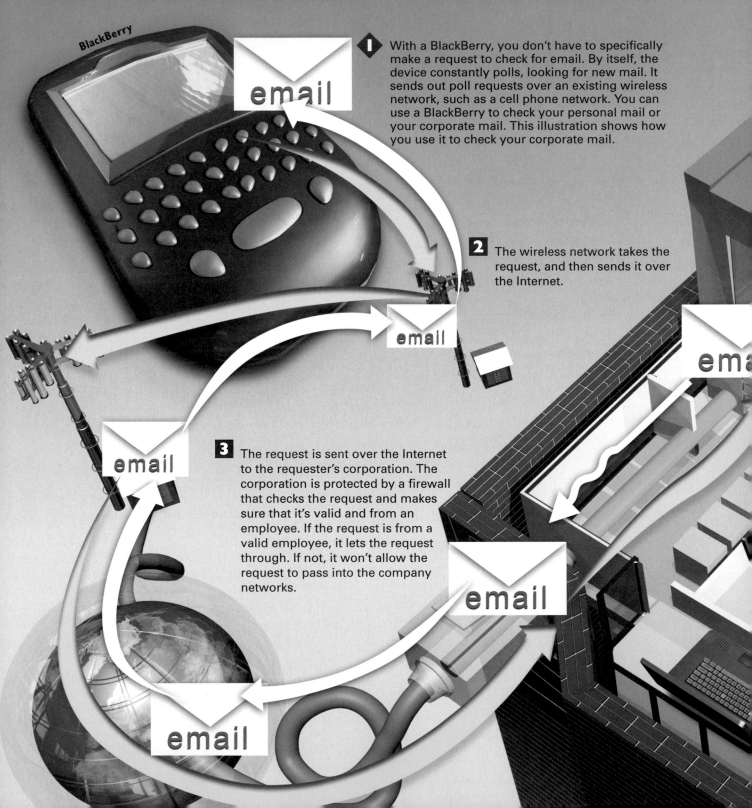

BlackBerry

1 With a BlackBerry, you don't have to specifically make a request to check for email. By itself, the device constantly polls, looking for new mail. It sends out poll requests over an existing wireless network, such as a cell phone network. You can use a BlackBerry to check your personal mail or your corporate mail. This illustration shows how you use it to check your corporate mail.

2 The wireless network takes the request, and then sends it over the Internet.

3 The request is sent over the Internet to the requester's corporation. The corporation is protected by a firewall that checks the request and makes sure that it's valid and from an employee. If the request is from a valid employee, it lets the request through. If not, it won't allow the request to pass into the company networks.

email

email

email

email

email

ema

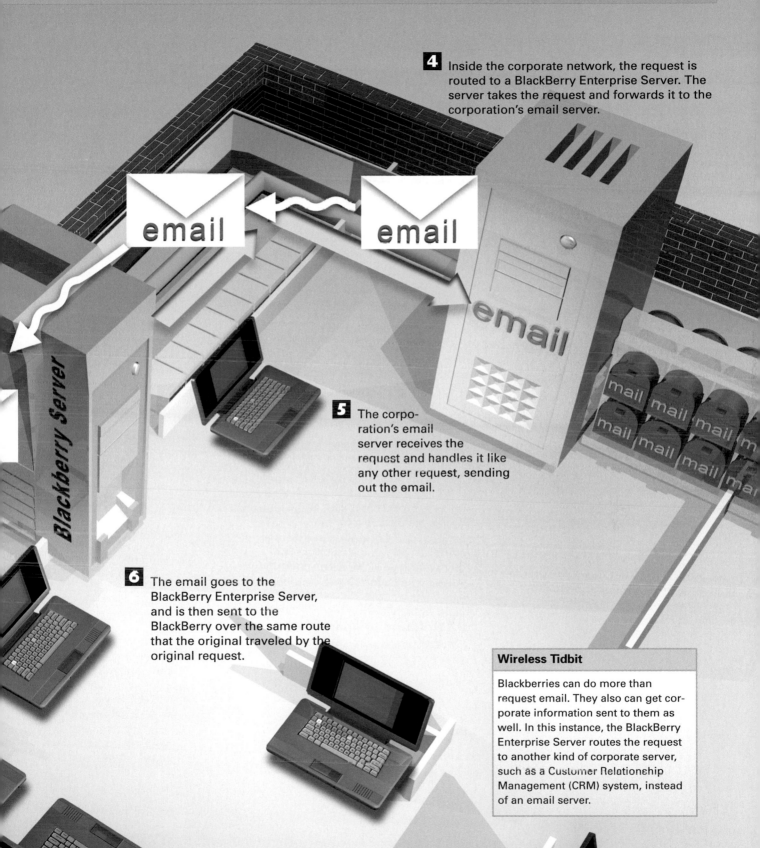

4 Inside the corporate network, the request is routed to a BlackBerry Enterprise Server. The server takes the request and forwards it to the corporation's email server.

Blackberry Server

5 The corporation's email server receives the request and handles it like any other request, sending out the email.

6 The email goes to the BlackBerry Enterprise Server, and is then sent to the BlackBerry over the same route that the original traveled by the original request.

Wireless Tidbit

Blackberries can do more than request email. They also can get corporate information sent to them as well. In this instance, the BlackBerry Enterprise Server routes the request to another kind of corporate server, such as a Customer Relationship Management (CRM) system, instead of an email server.

How White Page Directories (LDAP) Work

I Millions of people have email addresses on the Internet, but finding an email address has always been diffi-cult if you know only a person's name. The Lightweight Directory Access Protocol (LDAP) makes creating white page–style directories easier, so you now can look up people's addresses if you know only their names. An LDAP directory is a database that follows LDAP rules and protocols for organizing its information. It is located on an Internet server. A company or business maintains the server and is responsible for keeping the information on it up to date by adding new names, deleting old names, and updating existing names.

BINDRESPONSE

2 Like much other Internet technology, LDAP works on a client/server model. The client runs on a local computer. Many types of clients are available for many types of computers. To find someone's email address, you run the client on your com-puter and type in the name of the person whose email address you want to find.

Add Name to Address Book

8 Depending on the software you're using, you can now add the name and email address to your local address book, or you can immediately send an email to the person.

3 Before sending the request itself, the client sends an LDAP command, called the BindRequest, to the server. Basically, this is a command telling the server the client wants to make a request.

BINDREQUEST

4 The server answers with a command called the BindResponse, telling the client it can go ahead and make a request.

FIND "GRALLA"

5 The client then sends the request to the server, sending a person's name and asking for his email address.

LDAP
Lightweight Directory Access Protocol

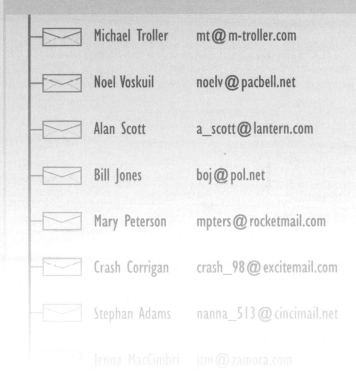

Michael Troller	mt@m-troller.com
Noel Voskuil	noelv@pacbell.net
Alan Scott	a_scott@lantern.com
Bill Jones	boj@pol.net
Mary Peterson	mpters@rocketmail.com
Crash Corrigan	crash_98@excitemail.com
Stephan Adams	nanna_513@cincimail.net
Jenna MacCimbri	jtm@zamora.com

7 The client receives the results and displays them on the local computer.

HERE ARE THE RESULTS

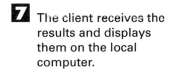

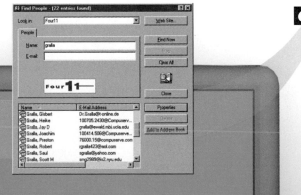

HERE ARE THE RESULTS

6 The LDAP directory performs a search and finds the email address or addresses in its database. It sends the results to the client.

How Encryption Can Keep Email Private

1 Encryption can be used to encode email messages so snoopers and hackers can't read them as they are sent across the Internet. Many types of encryption exist, but in the most common one, keys are used. Everyone gets a public and private key. The *public key* is available for anyone to use to encrypt mail; the *private key* is used only by the recipient to decrypt it. This illustration shows how to encrypt email with the popular encryption program Pretty Good Privacy (PGP). To start using PGP, someone uses her normal email program to compose a piece of mail. After she composes the mail, she decides whether she wants to encrypt the message.

2 When someone decides to encrypt a piece of email, she has to have a copy of the public key of the person to whom she is going to send the message. That key can be obtained a number of ways—from a public Internet site, or the recipient can send it via email. After the person has the key, she stores it in a key ring on her computer and can call it up at any time.

3 After choosing the key of the person who will receive the message, the message is encrypted using that person's public key.

6 The private key decrypts the message, and the person can read it and use it like any other piece of email.

5 The person receives the email as he does any normal piece of email. However, the email is encrypted, and so can't yet be read. So, the person uses his private key to decrypt the message. Before the message can be decrypted, a password for the private key typically must be typed in. However, some email programs and encryption software can be set so that the message is decrypted automatically, as soon as it's received.

4 The encrypted email is sent In the same way that any normal email is sent. The difference is that the email is encrypted so that anyone who reads the mail as it makes its way across the Internet won't be able to understand it—he'll see only seemingly random characters.

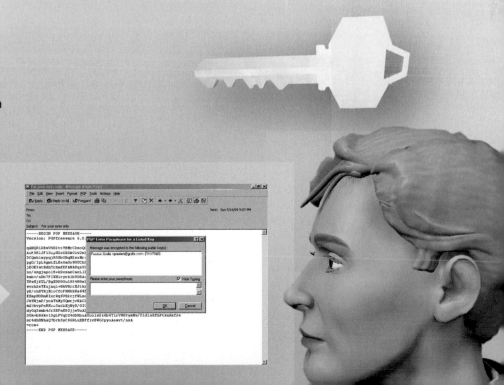

CHAPTER

12

How Email
Spam Works

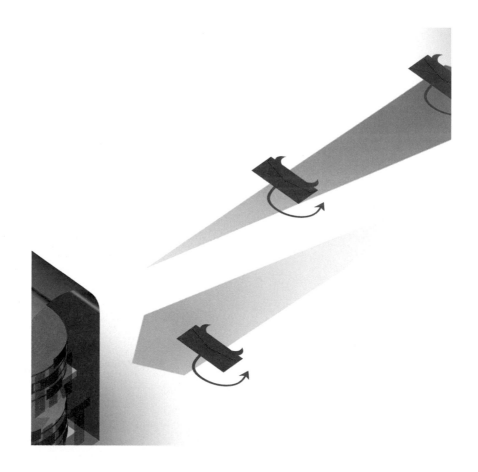

ONE of the most contentious issues to surface on the Internet in the last few years has to do with what Internet users call *spam*. Spam is unsolicited junk email that commercial companies send out, asking you to buy their goods and services. At times it might contain inducements to visit the seller's site. The email usually contains a phone number to call, an address to send money to, or a website to visit to buy the goods and services. Increasingly, spam also contains pornographic content and scams.

The term *spam* comes from a Monty Python skit in which every item on a menu contained Spam luncheon meat. It was originally used to refer to unsolicited postings for commercial products or services on Usenet, especially when they were cross-posted to several newsgroups.

Spam might seem like a minor annoyance, but the truth is that it can cause major problems. Spam floods the Internet with unwanted mail, which can lead to delayed or lost mail. It clogs the Internet pipeline, making other information slower to send. It wastes time for those who have to go through their email boxes deleting unsolicited mail, especially when they pay for their email service by the hour. Additionally, it's fairly common for spammers to hide their real email addresses by forging other people's names onto the From or Sender header of an email message. So, those people whose names were forged might be the target of angry mail. This makes it difficult for webmasters and mail administrators to filter spam messages by From address or domain name. Sometimes spammers even use other people's servers to deliver their bulk email; in essence, forcing someone else to pay the costs of the spammer's mail delivery.

Spam has other dangers as well. Spam is often used to scam unsuspecting victims, for example by sending out false emails claiming someone needs to log in to their bank, and then sending the person to a spoofed bank site. The spammer then steals financial information. This technique, called *phishing*, is covered in Chapter 49, "The Dangers of Spyware and Phishing."

In some ways, spam is not very different from traditional junk mail. Spammers buy or compile massive lists of email addresses, in the same way that junk mailers buy or compile U.S. postal addresses. The spammer then uses special software to send a solicitation to every person on the list—not uncommonly, tens of thousands of pieces of email in a single spam mailing. To hide their true identities, spammers forge names onto the headers of email messages and even "relay" their spam to another mail server on the Internet, so that finding out where the mail comes from is impossible. Often, a user will request to be taken off the list by replying to email addresses the spammers provide. However, this verifies the user's address and he will get even more spam.

A variety of ways have been devised to block spam, including having email filters on email software ignore any mail from known spammers. The software also examines the content of email messages to try and determine whether it is spam. In addition, several states have passed anti-spam legislation, and Congress has also passed a federal law called the Can Spam Act. But the laws are not particularly effective, and the best way to protect yourself is to install anti-spam software.

How Email Spam Is Sent

1 *Spam* is a term used to describe unsolicited email sent to you, often by commercial firms that attempt to sell you goods and services. Spam is sent out as bulk email, often to lists of 10,000 or more people at once. It's inexpensive to send, so its use has exploded on the Internet to the point where it is common for someone to get several dozen of these messages in a single day. Spam has become enough of an annoyance to warrant calls to ban it outright.

2 To send out unsolicited bulk email, a spammer first needs to get a list of email addresses. Often, spammers buy the lists from companies that compile them. These companies use automated software robots to get the email addresses. The robots get the lists from a number of sources. One way is to go into Usenet newsgroups and harvest email addresses by looking inside every message, which usually has in it the email address of the person who posted it.

3 Email addresses also can be harvested from email directories on the websites that allow people to look up others' email addresses. Software robots can go into the directory and grab every address in the directory. Robots also can go into chat areas, such as those on America Online, and gather email addresses.

Get email address.

ADD: all addresses

Get email address.

ADD: all addresses

Bulk Mail List

salmon@earthlink.com

welt@well.com

vegrebski@excite.com

ncsof@webtv.net

johns1739@aol1.com

stevej@apple.com

johnh@liberty.net

alxop1@webtv.net

corpflak@msn.com

sillysam7@kidstoys.net

morm@cheerybar.com

johnqp@prodigy.com

eatright3@heath.com

qwertz@yahoo.com

aiken@unity.net

triweb@li.com

zgooby@znakz.com

joanh@juno.com

hotrod99@fastcar.com

richir@kerbanko.com

morefun@home.com

rebar@builder.org

freddie592@aol1.com

strand@femtonet.com

xtheria@fast.com

george@whths.gov

bigboat@nautilus.com

travelr@trips.fun.com

boffo@snafu.com

yabbadabba@aol1.com

morepower@scottie.com

bigdaddy@lukas.com

4 Some spammers include in the email a return address to which someone who no longer wants to receive spam can send a message and be taken off the spam list. When the remove message is received, a robot automatically takes the person off the list. However, spammers rarely do this because most people would opt not to be on the spam lists.

5 The spammer either buys the resulting email list or compiles one of her own. The spammer uses the list, along with bulk mailing software, and sends a spam message to every person on the list. In the message might be a return address, website, or phone number where the receiver can get more information about the goods and services being sold.

Remove me.

Bulk Emailer

6 Spammers realize that spam offends most people, so the spammers go to great lengths to hide their true email addresses. As one way of hiding their real email addresses, they "forge" parts of the message header in the email address, such as the From, Sender, and Reply fields so it appears that the email has come from someone other than the spammer. Doing this is sometimes called *spamouflage*.

7 As a further way of hiding their true addresses, spammers relay their bulk spam to a server that is not associated with them and then have that server send out the bulk spam. Sometimes spammers have the bulk spam relayed among several different servers to make tracing who really sent the mail even more difficult.

Mail Server

Mail Server

How Email Spam Is Blocked

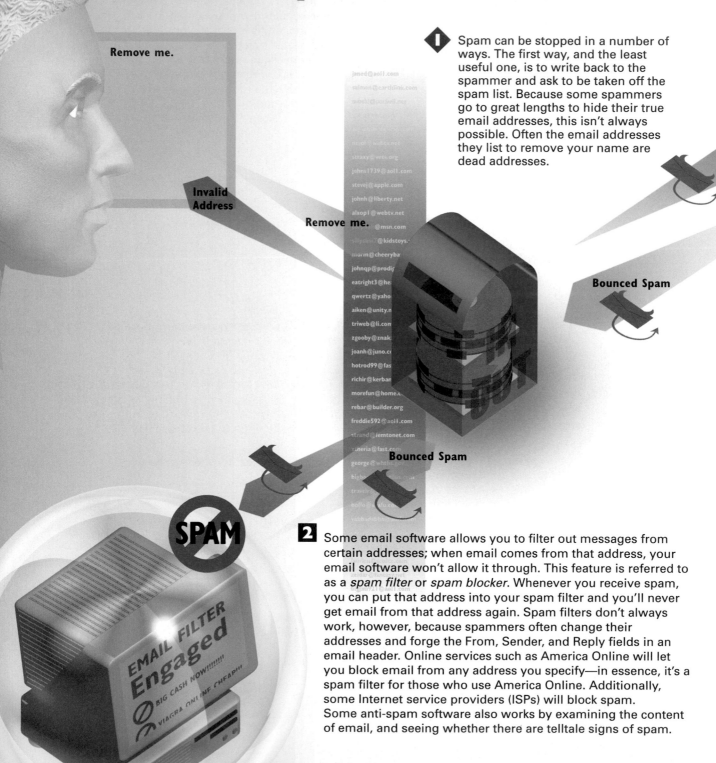

Remove me.

Invalid Address

Remove me.

Bounced Spam

Bounced Spam

janed@aol1.com
salmon@earthlink.com

nicol@webtv.net
straxy@vets.org
johns1739@aol1.com
stevej@apple.com
johnh@liberty.net
alxop1@webtv.net
@msn.com
@kidstoys.
marm@cheeryba
johnqp@prodi
eatright3@he
qwertz@yaho
aiken@unity.n
triweb@li.com
zgooby@znak
joanh@juno.co
hotrod99@fas
richir@kerban
morefun@home.
rebar@builder.org
freddie592@aol1.com
strand@iemtonet.com
neria@fast.com
george@whths.gov

SPAM

EMAIL FILTER Engaged
BIG CASH NOW!!!!!!!!
VIAGRA ONLINE CHEAP!!!

1 Spam can be stopped in a number of ways. The first way, and the least useful one, is to write back to the spammer and ask to be taken off the spam list. Because some spammers go to great lengths to hide their true email addresses, this isn't always possible. Often the email addresses they list to remove your name are dead addresses.

2 Some email software allows you to filter out messages from certain addresses; when email comes from that address, your email software won't allow it through. This feature is referred to as a *spam filter* or *spam blocker*. Whenever you receive spam, you can put that address into your spam filter and you'll never get email from that address again. Spam filters don't always work, however, because spammers often change their addresses and forge the From, Sender, and Reply fields in an email header. Online services such as America Online will let you block email from any address you specify—in essence, it's a spam filter for those who use America Online. Additionally, some Internet service providers (ISPs) will block spam. Some anti-spam software also works by examining the content of email, and seeing whether there are telltale signs of spam.

Routing Table

12.73.125.001	OK
124.5.65.0	OK
135.225.11.12	OK
325.121.25.1	SPAM ●
700.102.231.95	OK
635.31.125.124	SPAM ●
461.48.64.111	SPAM ●

SPAM

3 ISPs and online services such as America Online can block spammers from sending bulk mail to their subscribers. A router examines all incoming mail to the ISP or online service. The router has been told that when email comes from certain addresses, it should block mail from getting into the network. These addresses are put in a routing table that can be changed whenever new spammers are found. ISPs have a variety of other ways for detecting spam as well.

4 Because spammers often change their addresses, using routing tables doesn't always work. Online services and ISPs have gone to court to ban spammers from sending email to their customers. Although the law remains murky, in a number of instances, the courts have decided in favor of online services and the ISPs and have banned spammers from sending mail through them.

I AM SPAM

5 A number of laws and schemes have been proposed to regulate or outlaw spam. In one plan, every piece of spam would have to contain a specific piece of information in the message header, identifying it as unsolicited email. In this way, people could set their spam filters to block every single piece of spam, filtering out that piece of information. Some laws have been proposed that would outlaw spam entirely, in the same way that junk faxes were banned.

6 One way to prevent being spammed is to be sure that your email address isn't added to spam lists. To do this, when posting to Usenet newsgroups, edit your header so that it doesn't contain your email address. You should also notify email directories that you'd like to be taken off their lists. In this way, your email address won't be harvested by robots, and you should get less spam.

USENET
From: No header

CHAPTER

13

How Newsgroups Work

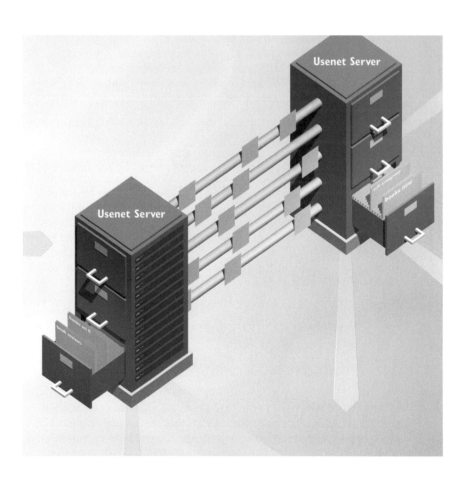

USENET, the world's biggest electronic discussion forum, provides a way for messages to be sent among computers across the entire Internet. People from all over the world participate in discussions on thousands of topics in specific areas of interest called *newsgroups*.

Hundreds of different major hierarchies of newsgroups exist, such as recreation (identified by the letters "rec") and computers (identified by the letters "comp"). Within these major hierarchies are subcategories (such as rec.arts) and further subcategories (such as rec.arts.books). Individual newsgroups can cover anything from movies to parenting, ecology, sports teams, clip art, and news about Usenet itself. Not all Internet sites carry all newsgroups. An administrator at each site decides which newsgroups to carry.

To participate in newsgroups, you need special software to read and respond to them. Readers are available for PC, Macintosh, and Unix computers. America Online also has its own proprietary software that lets you participate in newsgroups. Google Groups lets you read newsgroups straight from the Web at http://groups.google.com.

A good newsgroup reader lets you view the discussions as threads. *Threads* are ongoing conversations grouped by topic. So, for example, the rec.arts.books newsgroup might have many different threads going on at one time, each discussing a different book.

Many newsgroups have a list of Frequently Asked Questions, or FAQs (pronounced "facks"), associated with them. These FAQs answer common questions about the newsgroup. It's a good idea to read the FAQs before submitting questions to the newsgroup as a whole.

You participate in newsgroups by reading the messages and responding to them. There are moderated and unmoderated newsgroups. In a *moderated newsgroup*, each message goes to a human moderator. The moderator looks at the messages, ensuring they're appropriate for the group. If they are appropriate, the messages are posted. All messages sent to an *unmoderated newsgroup* are automatically posted.

When messages are posted, Usenet servers distribute them to other sites that carry the newsgroup. A site usually carries only the most current messages; otherwise, they would soon run out of storage space. Some sites *archive*, or store, old discussions.

A convenient way to check newsgroups is to subscribe to those that interest you. That way, whenever you check the Usenet server, new messages in your subscribed newsgroup will be delivered to you. You can also cancel your subscription to a newsgroup if you are no longer interested in it. You can read newsgroups without subscribing to them; in that case, you must manually ask to read specific newsgroups instead of having it done automatically for you.

Binary files, such as pictures and multimedia, can be posted in newsgroups. These files must be specially encoded for them to be posted. To view them, you must transfer them to your computer and then unencode them with special software. A common encoding scheme used on newsgroups is called uuencode. Most Usenet software readers have unencoding built in.

How Usenet Works

1 Usenet is a global bulletin board and discussion area. It collects messages about many thousands of topics into newsgroups, which are freewheeling discussion areas in which anyone can participate. Newsgroups can be found on many host computers across the Internet. Thousands of newsgroups exist that cover just about every topic you've ever imagined and many you probably haven't thought of.

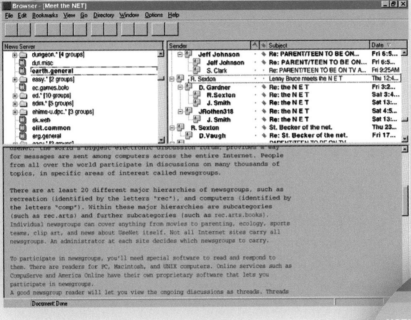

2 To participate, people send and read messages that are posted to the newsgroup. Two kinds of newsgroups exist: moderated newsgroups and unmoderated newsgroups.

3 In a *moderated* newsgroup, a human moderator receives and reads all the messages for the newsgroup. The moderator then decides which messages should be posted. The messages to be posted are put on a newsgroup server. The other messages are discarded. In *unmoderated* newsgroups, all messages are put directly on the server. Newsgroups and all their messages are stored on a Usenet server. They are organized by broad categories and then broken down into specific topics.

USENET.REC.ARTS.BOOKS

POST MESSAGE?

YES   NO

Has anyone here read "Player of Games"? An awesome read IMHO! The Culture universe sounds like a fun place!

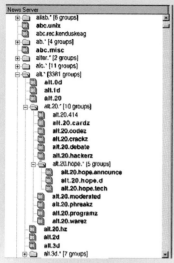

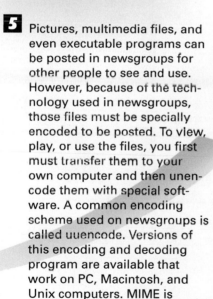

6 Newsgroup reader software lets you read messages and respond to newsgroups. The software gives you ways to manage your newsgroups by also allowing you to subscribe to newsgroups, which means new messages will automatically be delivered to you when you check the server. You'll also be able to cancel your subscription.

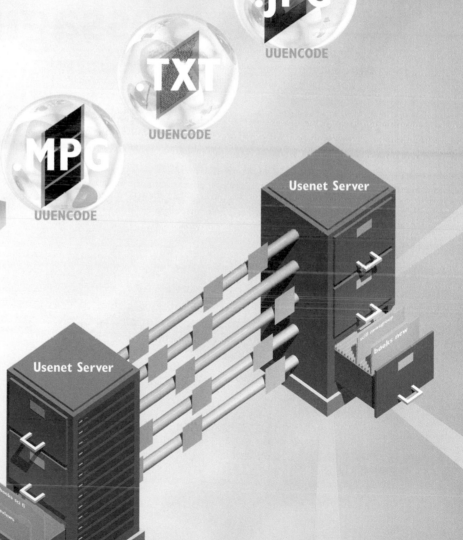

5 Pictures, multimedia files, and even executable programs can be posted in newsgroups for other people to see and use. However, because of the technology used in newsgroups, those files must be specially encoded to be posted. To view, play, or use the files, you first must transfer them to your own computer and then unencode them with special software. A common encoding scheme used on newsgroups is called uuencode. Versions of this encoding and decoding program are available that work on PC, Macintosh, and Unix computers. MIME is another encoding scheme.

4 Usenet servers communicate with one another so that all messages posted on one server are duplicated on the other servers. Although there are many Usenet servers, not all servers carry all newsgroups. Each site decides which newsgroups to carry.

CHAPTER

14

How Internet Chat and Instant Messaging Work

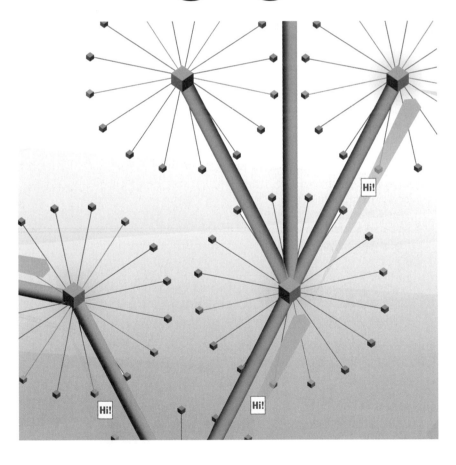

ONE of the most immediate ways to communicate with others via the Internet is to participate in live chat. Chat doesn't refer to people actually talking to each other and hearing each other's voices. Instead, it means that you hold live keyboard "conversations" with other people on the Internet—that is, you type words on your computer and other people on the Internet can see those words on their computers immediately, and vice versa. You can hold chats with many people simultaneously all over the world.

A number of ways are available to chat on the Internet, but one of the most popular ones is called *Internet relay chat (IRC)*. Every day, thousands of people all over the world hold conversations on many topics via IRC. Each topic is called a *channel*. When you join a channel, you can see what other people on the channel type on their keyboards. In turn, everyone in the channel can see whatever you type on your keyboard. You can also hold individual side conversations with someone. Channels live on various servers around the world. Some servers have only a few channels, and others have many of them.

IRC has facilitated communications during natural disasters, wars, and other crises. In 1993, for example, during the attempted Communist coup in Russia when Russian legislators barricaded themselves inside the Parliament building, an IRC "news channel" was set up for relaying real-time, first-person accounts of the events taking place.

IRC follows a client/server model, which means that both client and server software are required to use it. Many IRC clients are available for many types of computers, so whether you have a PC, Macintosh, or Unix workstation, you can use IRC.

Your IRC client communicates with an IRC server on the Internet. You log on to a server using the client and select a channel on which you want to chat. When you type words on your keyboard, they are sent to the server. The server is part of a global IRC server network. The server sends your message to other servers, which, in turn, send your messages to people who are part of your channel. They can then see and respond to your message.

You can chat on the Internet in other ways, as well. Many websites, for example, use proprietary chat software that doesn't use the IRC protocol but enables you to chat when you're on the site.

Another type of chat is called *instant messaging*. In instant messaging, you communicate privately, one on one, with another person. You can create special lists so you're informed when your "buddies" come online ready to chat, and they're informed when you come online.

How IRC Works

1 Internet relay chat (IRC) is a way for people all over the world to "chat" with one another by using their keyboards. The typed words are instantly relayed to computers all over the world, where recipients can read them. This process occurs in real-time, so everyone sees the words as people type them.

2 IRC runs on a client/server model; therefore, to use it, you need client software on your computer. Many IRC clients are available for PCs, Macintoshes, Unix workstations, and other kinds of computers.

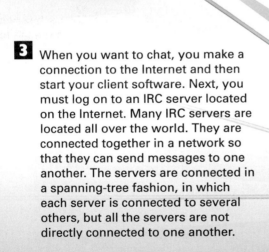

3 When you want to chat, you make a connection to the Internet and then start your client software. Next, you must log on to an IRC server located on the Internet. Many IRC servers are located all over the world. They are connected together in a network so that they can send messages to one another. The servers are connected in a spanning-tree fashion, in which each server is connected to several others, but all the servers are not directly connected to one another.

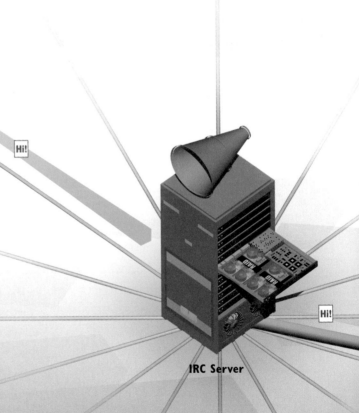

IRC Server

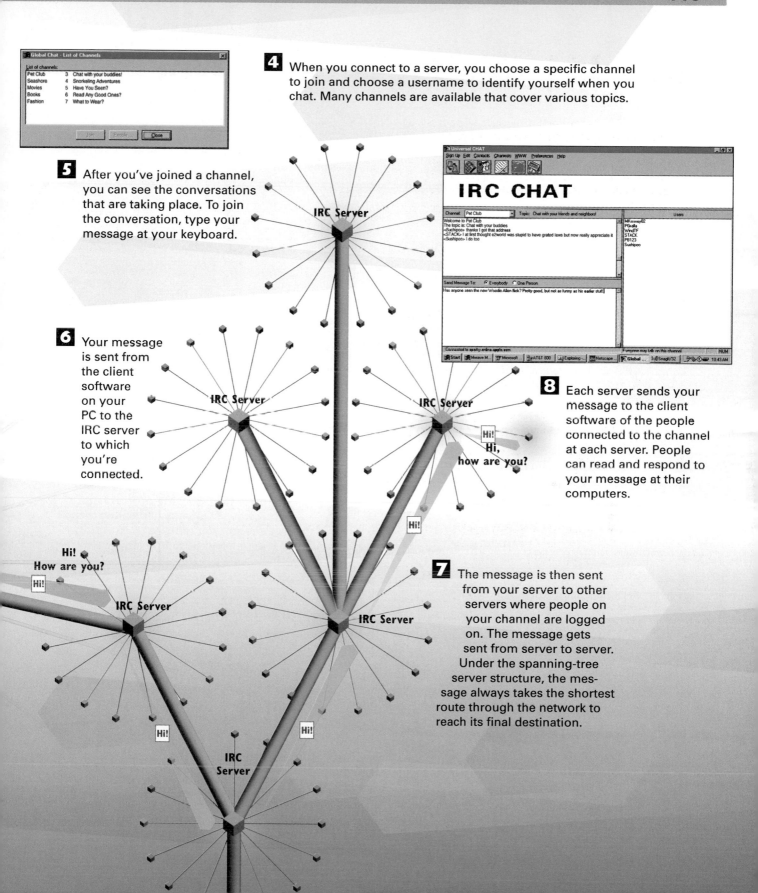

4 When you connect to a server, you choose a specific channel to join and choose a username to identify yourself when you chat. Many channels are available that cover various topics.

5 After you've joined a channel, you can see the conversations that are taking place. To join the conversation, type your message at your keyboard.

6 Your message is sent from the client software on your PC to the IRC server to which you're connected.

8 Each server sends your message to the client software of the people connected to the channel at each server. People can read and respond to your message at their computers.

7 The message is then sent from your server to other servers where people on your channel are logged on. The message gets sent from server to server. Under the spanning-tree server structure, the message always takes the shortest route through the network to reach its final destination.

IRC Server

IRC Server

IRC Server

IRC Server

IRC Server

IRC Server

IRC CHAT

How Instant Messaging Works

1 The Internet version of America Online's Instant Messenger (AIM), one of the most popular instant messaging systems, runs as a piece of client software on your computer. To use it, you must be connected to the Internet. When you run the software, it opens up a TCP connection to an Instant Messenger login server. The software sends your screen name and password over the connection to log you in to the server.

4 When you establish a connection with the AIM server, your client software sends a list of your buddies to the server. The server checks to see whether any of the buddies are online—and it continues to do that for as long as you run the software on your computer. If you change the list of buddies during your session, that information is sent to the server as well so it can keep track of new buddies or ignore buddies you've deleted from your list.

3 Instant message software includes buddy list capabilities. That means you keep a list of people you want to send instant messages to, and when they come online, you are notified so you can send instant messages to and receive instant messages from them. You create a buddy list in your AIM software by adding your buddies' screen names to it.

Cool Lizard is online.

"Hi Mia. Are you interested in getting together next week?"

"Sure. Monday would be best for me. Let's chat later to confirm it."

5 When any of your buddies runs AIM and logs in, your client software is told that he's online, and you get a notice that he's online. You can now send messages to and receive instant messages from him.

2 The server checks the screen name and password. If they're correct, the login server instructs the Instant Messenger software to close the connection to the login server and to open up a new connection to a different AIM server—the one that will handle your instant message session. This connection uses a special communications protocol that allows for AIM functionality, including instant messaging, chatting, transferring files, and video chatting.

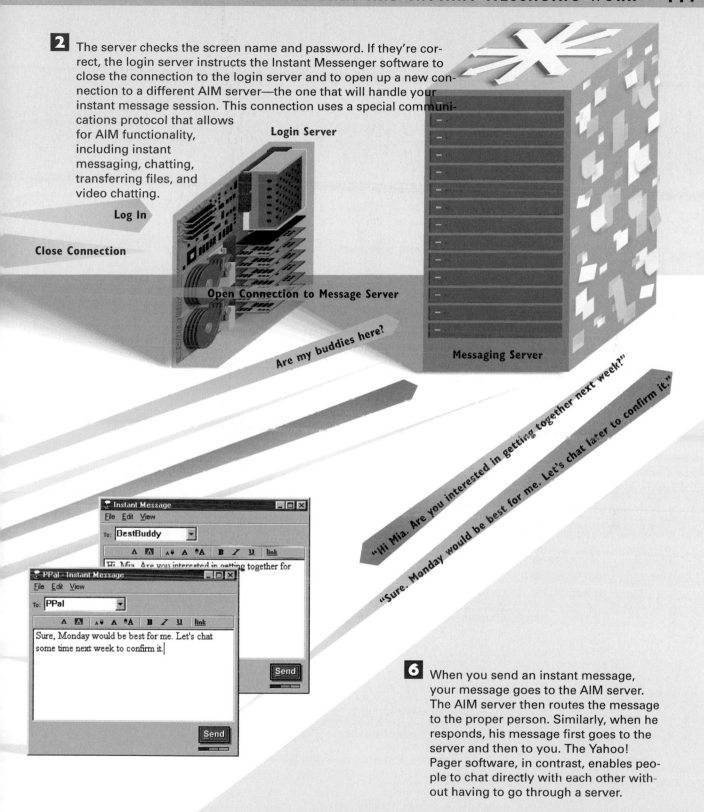

Login Server

Log In

Close Connection

Open Connection to Message Server

Are my buddies here?

Messaging Server

"Hi Mia. Are you interested in getting together next week?"

"Sure. Monday would be best for me. Let's chat later to confirm it."

Instant Message
File Edit View
To: **DestBuddy**
A A A A A **B** *I* U link
Hi Mia. Are you interested in getting together for

PPal - Instant Message
File Edit View
To: **PPal**
A A A A A **B** *I* U link
Sure, Monday would be best for me. Let's chat some time next week to confirm it.

Send

Send

6 When you send an instant message, your message goes to the AIM server. The AIM server then routes the message to the proper person. Similarly, when he responds, his message first goes to the server and then to you. The Yahoo! Pager software, in contrast, enables people to chat directly with each other without having to go through a server.

How Chat Rooms Throw a Party

1 Computers make it hard to be a hermit. At this very moment, there are hundreds of thousands of computer users engaged in friendly chats over the Internet. Chats are held in a chat room, a virtual room that's really software running on an Internet server. The chat software is designed to let several computer users, all online at the same time, type messages that are seen simultaneously by all the other chatters.

2 To join a chat, you first must run a chat client software on your computer. Client programs work over a network with a host program running on a hefty-sized server. The installation, performed by the server software, is barely noticeable. The chat client shown here is for Yahoo!, at chat.yahoo.com.

3 The first time you use a chat program, you set up a screen name, or handle, for yourself. Traditionally, chatters pick a name that's edgy. We'll go with Tabascorow.

4 After you log in under your screen name, you choose which chat room you want to enter. At the same time, thousands of other people are also signing on to the same server. Most of them head for a chat room devoted to a particular subject, such as computer games or politics.

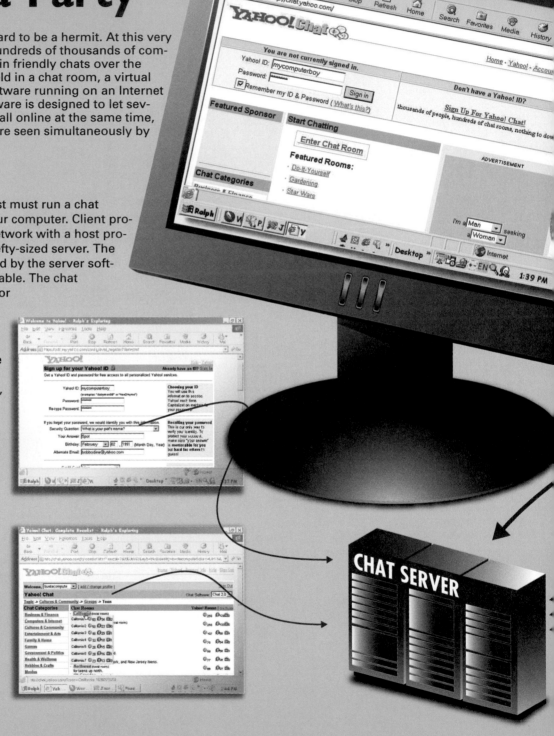

5 When you make your choice, the chat server associates you with the path you took to it so that it will recognize any other messages from you. Then it adds your screen name to a list of other people who are already in the room.

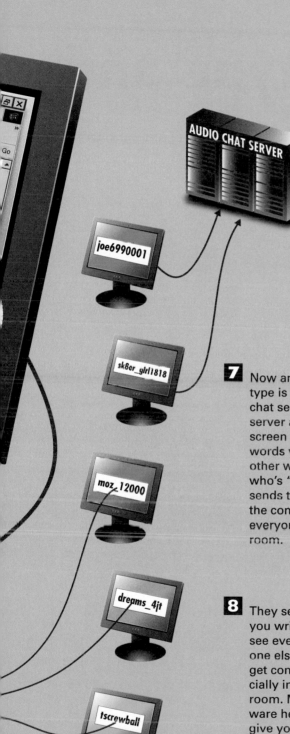

6 Finally it sends a line of text that appears on the screens of everyone in the chat room announcing that Tabascorow has joined the room.

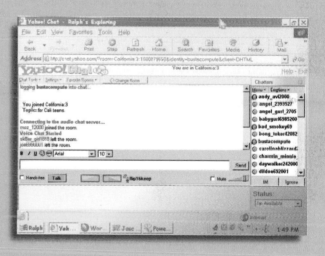

7 Now anything you type is sent to the chat server. The server adds your screen name to the words you typed so other will know who's "talking," and sends them out to the computers of everyone in that chat room.

8 They see everything you write, and you see everything everyone else writes. It can get confusing, especially in a crowded room. Most chat software here lets you give your message a distinctive typeface, size, and color that make it easier for everyone to follow conversation threads.

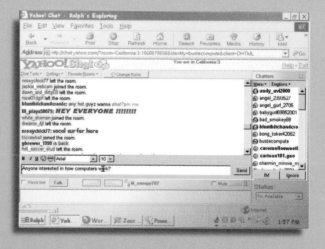

C H A P T E R

15

How Skype and VoIP Work

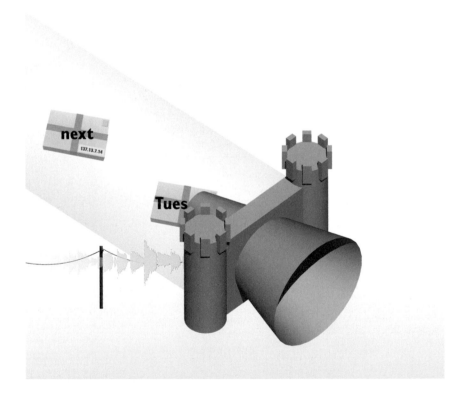

THE Internet has pioneered many new ways to communicate, such as email, live chat, and newsgroups. But it can be used to enable some old-fashioned communication as well: You can make telephone calls using the Internet. When you do so, the sound of your voice and that of the person you're talking to are broken down into packets. Those packets are delivered using the Internet's TCP/IP protocol.

The technique for making a phone call using the Internet is referred to as Voice over Internet Protocol (VoIP), because it uses TCP/IP for delivering voice information.

There are a myriad of ways for using VoIP. In perhaps the most revolutionary technique, you call directly from one computer to another. You don't actually use your telephone with any of them. Instead, you speak into a microphone attached to your computer and listen through speakers and a sound card, or else use a headset or a phone attached to your computer through a USB port.

When you make a computer-to-computer call, you don't actually have to pay for the phone call itself. In addition, you can make calls anywhere in the world, without paying. The only catch is that both parties need to be using the same VoIP software, such as the popular Skype, or VoIP capabilities built into many instant messenger programs such as Yahoo Messenger or America Online Instant Messenger. The software is available for free.

Skype and similar services also allow you to make calls from your PC to landline phones or mobile phones. When you make calls this way, your call mostly travels over the Internet, and only at the end does it enter the normal telephone network. These calls are not free, but they are very inexpensive, especially when compared to international phone rates. Not uncommonly, they are two cents a minute between most places in the world.

VoIP does not have to be used only on computers. Increasingly, the technology is used in concert with special telephone headsets that do not need to be connected to a computer. The popular Vonage service uses this type of technology. With Vonage and similar services, a telephone connects via an Ethernet port to a network connection, such as a cable modem, home router, or corporate network. The call uses TCP/IP to travel over the local network, then through the Internet, and then finally goes to the normal phone network closest to the call location. These calls are less expensive than normal phone calls. Often, a low-cost monthly service includes all phone calls.

VoIP is not only used at home—it increasingly is becoming common at big corporations. The reason is simple—cost. A company need not maintain separate telephone and data networks; a single network can handle all calls. And any calls inside the network, including another company location across the world, can be made for free.

How VoIP (Voice over Internet Protocol) Works

1 There are a variety of ways that VoIP is used to route phone calls over the Internet. This illustration shows a VoIP service such as Vonage that makes calls over the Internet from a home router, Internet cable, or DSL connection. A special VoIP telephone first must be plugged into the router or an Ethernet connection.

2 The VoIP phone converts the voice signal to digital data and compresses it. It compresses it because the data files of an uncompressed voice call could be too large to deliver in a timely fashion across the Internet.

3 The compressed, digitized voice signal is broken up into IP packets.

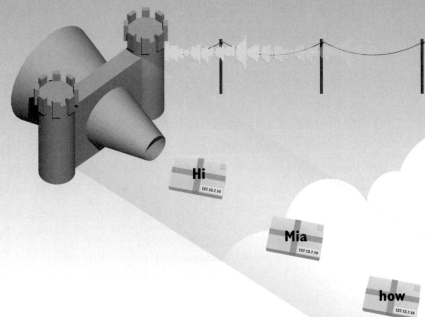

4 The packets are sent out across the Internet the same as any other IP packets, using the Internet's TCP/IP protocol.

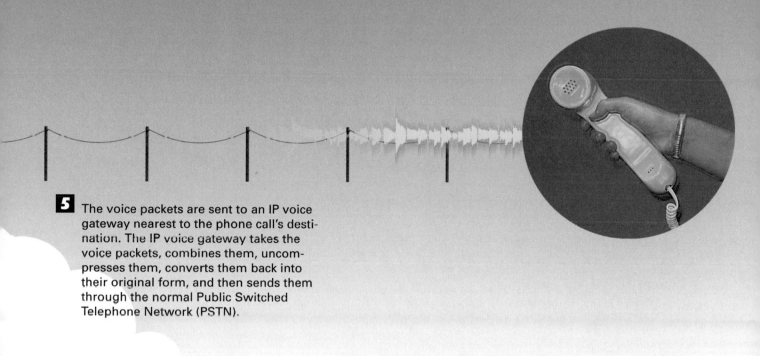

5 The voice packets are sent to an IP voice gateway nearest to the phone call's destination. The IP voice gateway takes the voice packets, combines them, uncompresses them, converts them back into their original form, and then sends them through the normal Public Switched Telephone Network (PSTN).

6 The call goes through the PSTN as does any other call. When the person from the normal telephone speaks, the entire process is reversed—the call is sent to the IP gateway, which compresses it, digitizes it, breaks it into IP packets, and sends it over the Internet back to the caller.

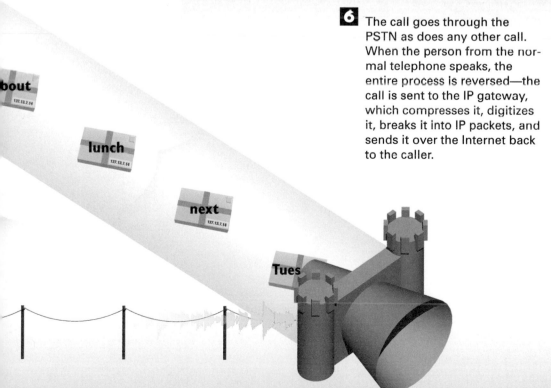

How Skype Works

1 Skype works as a piece of software running on a PC, and requires that the software be downloaded from the Skype site and installed. The software itself is free, as are phone calls made from a PC running Skype to another PC running Skype. PC-to-normal telephone calls, however, cost money, about two cents per minute, even internationally.

2 You use your computer's speakers and microphone to talk, or you can instead install a special headset, or use a phone or headset attached to your computer via its USB port.

3 When you run Skype, you need to log in. Skype is peer-to-peer technology and uses no central server. So when you first log in, you automatically contact a "supernode," which is an ordinary PC running Skype. Any PC running Skype may become a supernode, without the owner's knowledge. The supernode sends you "host cache" information—IP address and port information for supernodes. This lets you connect to supernodes. The host cache information is stored in the Windows Registry.

Supernode

Supernode

Where is user pjoe?

Where is user pjoe?

Supernode

Where is user pjoe?

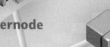

Where is

4 The supernode contacts the login server with your information, logging you in to the Skype network.

5 When you want to call someone you know is on the Skype network, you double-click their name. You make a direct connection to that person, and you can both talk using your PC headphones and speakers.

6 You can also search for people on the Skype network. Search information is sent to a supernode. If the supernode has the person's contact information, including IP address and port, it sends it to you. You can then call the person directly.

7 If the supernode does not have the contact information, it contacts another supernode to get the information. Supernodes continue to contact each other in this way until the information is found.

8 Skype also allows people to make calls to telephones and mobile phones. The call initially goes out over the Internet. Only at the "last mile"—the closest location to the person being called—does the call go over the normal phone network or mobile network. (For more information about how this process works, see "How VoIP Works," in this chapter.)

Where is user pjoe?

Supernode

Where is user pjoe?

Supernode

Where is user pjoe?

Where is user pjoe?

Supernode

Where is user pjoe?

Where is user pjoe?

Where is user pjoe?

Supernode

Where is user pjoe?

Supernode

Where is user pjoe? Supernode

Sup

Supernode

CHAPTER

16

How Blogging and RSS Work

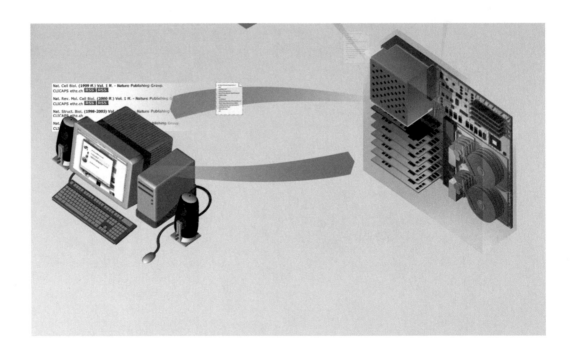

HOW important has the Internet become to the general culture and politics of our time?

Consider this: There are those who believe that the 2004 presidential election between John Kerry and George W. Bush was decided to a great extent by what was then an emerging web technology—blogs. Candidate Kerry was the subject of a well-coordinated attack of numerous blogs, and some people believe that was enough to tip the election in George Bush's favor.

Blogs are no longer "emerging"—propelled by that election, they have become a powerful, cultural force.

So what, exactly, is a blog? To a certain extent, that's open to debate, but generally, most people agree that a blog is made up of individual entries on a web page in diary-like format. Entries can be as short as a single line or a few words, or even a link, or as long as multiple paragraphs. Often, but not always, someone writes a blog about a specific topic, such as Washington politics, or a specific technology. Increasingly, corporations are letting their employees blog as well, as a way to personalize the company. Microsoft, for example, encourages its employees to blog. And Google has a blog that gives the latest company news.

So, what is so revolutionary about blogging? It gave individuals a way to gain an audience for their opinions and writing, without having to work for a newspaper, magazine, TV or radio station, or a media company. The original idea was that individuals could express their opinions without having to go through a media corporation, and could also get information out quickly, because they would not have to go through the procedures normally required by media companies.

Blogging works so well that many bloggers have gone on to join those large media companies they initially disdained or have signed book contracts. Some make a living blogging by selling ads on their blog or joining sites that aggregate blogs and then sell advertising.

In addition, the mainstream media has caught onto blogging, and now many reporters, editors, and writers blog as well.

Not all bloggers write about big things such as politics and technology. Countless people muse about their daily lives and celebrate the simple and the mundane.

One of the earliest problems with blogging spawned a related technology called Really Simple Syndication (RSS). Bloggers faced a major problem—how to get people to visit their websites whenever they post a new blog entry? Some bloggers post multiple times a day, and even if they only post once a day, it was difficult to convince people to spend the time to visit their blog.

The answer, RSS, allows the blog, or portions of the blog, to be automatically fed to anyone without that person actually having to visit the blog itself. Instead, the entry, or portions of the entry, is read in a special RSS reader that automatically goes out and grabs new blog entries on its own.

This not only makes it easy for bloggers to get a new audience, but it makes it easier for people to visit multiple blogs in a day. Rather than having to visit a dozen or more blog sites, which could take a substantial amount of time, a person need only run an RSS reader, which automatically grabs all the different blog entries from many different sites, and lets them be read right in the reader itself.

RSS can be used for keeping up to date with news stories as well, although its primary use remains for reading blogs.

How Blogging Works

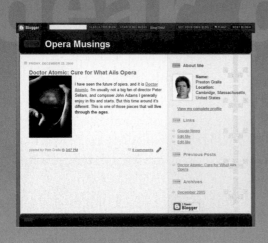

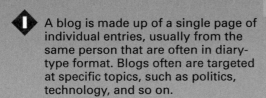

1 A blog is made up of a single page of individual entries, usually from the same person that are often in diary-type format. Blogs often are targeted at specific topics, such as politics, technology, and so on.

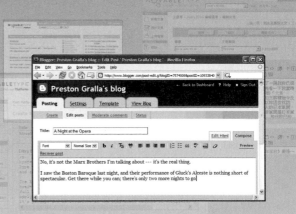

2 Typically, special software or websites are used to create a blog. Movable Type is a common piece of software used to create blogs. It needs to be installed and maintained on a server. Many corporations and publishers use Movable Type to let their employee or writers create blogs.

3 Most individuals create blogs by going to a free website, such as www.blogger.com. The site has simple-to-use forms that help people create their own blogs.

4 Blogs can be read in the traditional way, by having people visit the site, but frequently blogs are read using an RSS reader. RSS is a format that helps people easily read blogs without having to visit the blog on the Web itself. (For details, see the next illustration, "How RSS Works.")

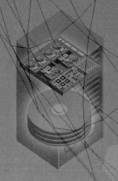

5 When someone updates his blog, the software or website used to create the blog "pings" various RSS syndication servers to alert them there is a new entry in the blog.

6 Syndication servers alert search websites that there is new information on the blog, making it more likely that people will find the blog and read it.

How RSS Works

1 Before an RSS feed can be created, content that is going to be the subject of the feed needs to be put on a web page. Blogs are frequently fed via RSS, but any information put in the Web (such as news articles) can be sent via RSS feeds as well. The page or blog is created as it is normally.

```
<rss version="2.0" xmlns:dc="http://purl.org/dc/elements/1.1/">

  <channel>

  <title>Preston's Picks</title>

  <link>http://www.prestonspicks.com/</link>

  <description>The latest news from Preston, straight toyhou..</description>

  <language>en-us</language>

  <item>

    <title>Black Dogs</title>

    <link>http://www.prestonspicks.com/pub/a/2006/12/04/blackdogs.html</link>

    <description>I recently came across this early novel by Ian McEwan,

      and don't know why I overlooked it –it's one of his best..</description>

    <dc:creator>Preston Gralla</dc:creator>

    <dc:date>2006-12-04</dc:date>

  </item>
```

2 Information that is going to be fed needs to be put into a special XML format. (For information about XML, see "How XML Works," in Chapter 19, "How Markup Languages Work." There are several different types of RSS formats, notably Atom and RSS, and each require different XML coding. Some blogs and websites use both Atom and RSS, and so create files for each.

The XML coding includes all the information sent in the feed, including the headline, description, a link to the original page for those who want to read the full blog or posting, and more.

3 The XML page is put on a web server.

4 A link is put on a web page that has a link to the XML page. Frequently, the web page also displays an icon that lets visitors know that an RSS feed is available on the page.

Update

Update

5 When someone visits a page with an RSS feed they want to read, they click the icon or copy and paste the link of the feed into a piece of software called an RSS reader, which will get the RSS feeds. In some instances, websites, such as Google Reader (www.google.com/reader) function as RSS readers.

Update

Update

6 After an RSS reader is told to subscribe to an RSS feed, it checks the URL that has been copied into it, and grabs the XML page on it.

7 The reader displays the RSS feed so that it can be read by the user. The user can click the feed to get the full version of the blog or news story in the feed. Feeds often have multiple entries in them, not just one, and RSS readers can read all the entries.

8 Whenever the RSS feed has been updated, it "pings" various RSS syndication servers to alert them there is new information in the feed. These servers contact websites to let them know there is new information in the feed, making it more likely that people will find the feed.

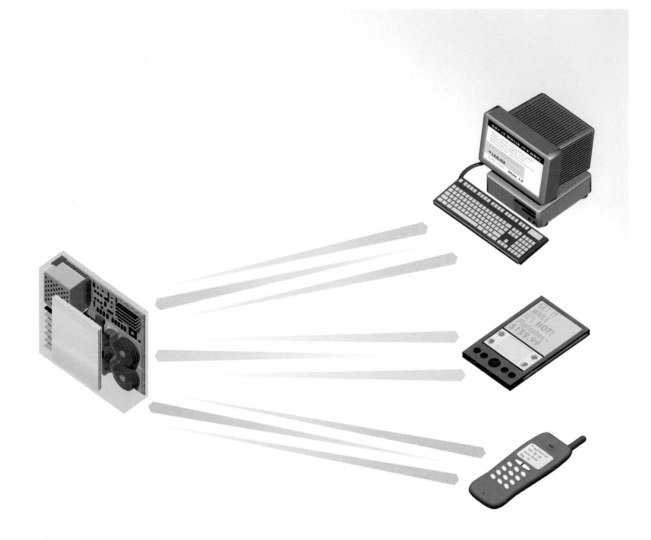

PART 4

HOW THE WORLD WIDE WEB WORKS

WHEN many people use the word "Internet," they are really talking about the World Wide Web. The Web is the most interesting, most innovative, most visible, and fastest growing part of the Internet. To a great degree, the explosive growth of the Web has been what has fueled the enormous amount of interest in the Internet. When people refer to "surfing the Net," they're usually talking about using the World Wide Web.

This section of the book looks in great detail at how the World Wide Web works, from such basic technologies as how web pages work to more advanced features, such as using grid computing to harness and combine the power of hundreds of disparate computers connected to the Internet. You'll learn what the Web is composed of and how a web browser works and thoroughly investigate URLs (uniform resource locators), as well as many other aspects of the Web and web browsers.

Chapter 17, "How Web Pages Work," examines the most basic part of the Web. It starts by covering the general technology of the Web and describes how the Web works. Web pages are, in essence, multimedia publications that can include music, audio, video, and animation, as well as graphics and text. Web pages are connected via hypertext that enables you to jump from any page to any other page, and to graphics, binary files, multimedia files, and other Internet resources. To jump from one page to another, or to another resource, you merely click a hypertext link.

The chapter details how all that works, and looks at the client/server model of the Web. It shows what happens behind the scenes when you type a URL into your browser—how that information gets routed properly so you visit the website that interests you. The chapter also delves into how web pages are organized on a site and how an entire website works as a unit to deliver its information to you.

Chapter 18, "How Web Browsers Work," examines browsers. Web browsers are pieces of software that interpret the language of the Web, Hypertext Markup Language (HTML), and then display those results on your computer. The chapter begins by delving into how browsers do that job.

This chapter also discusses one of the most common, and annoying, facts about the Web—the sometimes incomprehensible error messages you receive when you can't get to a website or web page. You'll see what those messages mean and understand why you can't visit a web page or site when you get one of them.

As mentioned earlier, HTML is the language of the Web. Chapter 19, "How Markup Languages Work," explains how HTML forms the building blocks for creating web pages. The language is an essential set of directions that tells your browser how to display and manage a web document. The chapter shows—in detail—how all that works. It also covers how some of the newer HTML-related technologies—in particular, one called AJAX—are making websites as responsive and interactive as desktop software.

Chapter 20, "How Hypertext Works," looks at hyperlinks, which set the Web apart from most other portions of the Internet. This chapter describes the various ways documents link to each other on the Web and explains concepts such as relative links and absolute links.

Chapter 21, "How URLs Work," looks in great detail at URLs, the addresses you type into your browser to visit a website. You'll look at the underlying structure of a URL and gain a better understanding of how a URL is put together and what it can tell you about the site you're visiting. You'll also see precisely how URLs help retrieve documents from the Web.

Chapter 22, "How Image Maps and Interactive Forms Work," looks at two technologies you use every day on the Web without realizing it: image maps and interactive forms. Image maps aren't maps in a traditional sense. Instead, they're graphics with URLs embedded inside them. When you click one part of the graphic, you're sent to one site, and when you click another, you're sent to a different site. An image map might be a picture of a house, for example, and when you click the living room, you're sent to an entertainment site; when you click a home office, you're sent to a business site.

Interactive forms are the forms you fill out on the Web for doing things such as registering at a site or sending information about yourself before you're allowed to download a particular piece of software free of charge.

Chapter 23, "How Web Host Servers Work," looks at web server software. As mentioned before, the Web works on a client/server model. Your web browser (the client) contacts the web server. This chapter explains how web server software interacts with your browser to deliver web content to you.

Chapter 24, "How Websites Work with Databases," looks at databases. Databases are used on the Web for many things. Web indexes and search sites such as Yahoo! are, in essence, databases that interact with the Web.

Chapter 25, "How .NET and Web Services Work," looks at one of the newer web technologies—and it's a technology that may transform the way that the Web is used, particularly by businesses. Web Services and a related technology from Microsoft, .NET, allow applications and services to be delivered remotely over the Internet, and let businesses tie together their business systems. So, for example, the technology can be used to let you run your business's internal enterprise software when you're anywhere in the world, and you'll be able to run it from your browser and use corporate resources and data you need.

Finally, Chapter 26, "How Grid Computing Works," looks at a remarkable technology that harnesses and combines the CPU power of thousands of disparate computers on the Internet and in essence create a virtual supercomputer. Grid computing has already been used to help in the search for extraterrestrial life by processing radio signals from satellites, and is also being used in medical research.

CHAPTER

17

How Web Pages Work

THE World Wide Web is the fastest growing and, in many ways, the most exciting and intriguing part of the Internet. When people refer to "surfing the Net," more often than not they're talking about using the World Wide Web.

As its name implies, the World Wide Web is a globally connected network. The Web contains many things, but what makes it so fascinating to so many are the web "pages" that incorporate text, graphics, sound, animation, and other multimedia elements. In essence, each page is an interactive multimedia publication that can include videos and music as well as graphics and text.

Pages are connected to one another using *hypertext* that allows you to move from any page to any other page, and to graphics, binary files, multimedia files, as well as any Internet resource. To jump from one page to another, you click a hypertext link—a link that connects web pages and resources.

The Web operates on a client/server model. You run web *client* browser software, such as Netscape Navigator or Microsoft's Internet Explorer, on your computer. That client contacts a web *server* and requests information or resources. The web server locates and then sends the information to the web browser, which displays the results.

Pages on the Web are built using a markup language called Hypertext Markup Language (HTML). The language contains commands that tell your browser how to display text, graphics, and multimedia files. It also contains commands for linking the page to other pages and to other Internet resources.

The term *home page* often is used to refer to the first, or top, page in a collection of pages that make up a website. This is to distinguish it from the many pages collected together as a single "package" of sorts that often make up websites. The home page is similar to a magazine cover or the front page of a newspaper. Usually, it acts as an introduction to the site, explaining its purpose and describing the information found on other pages throughout the site. In this way, the home page often acts as the table of contents for the rest of the site.

In general, websites use three types of organizational structures to organize their pages. In a *tree structure*, a pyramid or an outline format enables users to easily navigate through the site and find the information they want. In a *linear structure*, one page leads to the next, which then leads to the next, and so on, in a straight line. Finally, in a *random structure*, pages are connected to one another seemingly at random.

The last illustration in this chapter shows how someone might build her own pages using an HTML editor. After you create your pages, you use FTP software to post them onto a small portion of a web server. Many Internet service providers (ISP) provide free server space for subscribers, and you can also pay a hosting to host your site as well. Some sites also let you build web pages by using the site's built-in tools. In that case, you wouldn't build a page from scratch and send it via FTP—instead, you'd build the page using online tools provided by the site.

How the World Wide Web Works

1 The World Wide Web is the most innovative and most-used part of the Internet. When you browse the Web, you view multimedia pages composed of text, graphics, sound, and video. The Web uses hypertext links that allow you to jump from one place to another on the Web. The language that enables you to use hypertext links and to view web pages is called *Hypertext Markup Language*, more commonly known as *HTML*.

2 The Web works on a client/server model in which client software—known as a *web browser*—runs on a local computer. The server software runs on a web host. To use the web, you first make an Internet connection and then launch your web browser.

3 In a web browser, you type the URL for a location you want to visit or click a link that sends you to the desired location. The names for web locations are uniform resource locators (URLs). Your web browser sends the URL request using Hypertext Transfer Protocol (HTTP), which defines the way the web browser and web server communicate with each other.

4 When the server finds the requested home page, document, or object, it sends that home page, document, or object back to the web browser client. The information is then displayed on the computer screen in the web browser. When the page is sent from the server, the HTTP connection is closed and can be reopened.

http://www.zdnet.com/downloads

http://www.zdnet.com/downloads

7 URLs contain several parts. The
first part—the http://—details
which Internet protocol to use. The
second part—the part that usually has
a www in it—sometimes indicates which
type of Internet resource is being contacted.
The third part—such as zdnet.com—can vary in
length and identifies the web server to be contacted. The final part identifies a specific directory
on the server and a home page, document, or
other Internet object.

6 The request is sent to the Internet. Internet routers
examine the request to determine which server to
send the request to. The information just to the
right of the http:// in the URL tells the Internet on
which web server the requested information can be
found. Routers send the request to that web server.

Server

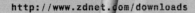

http://www.zdnet.com/downloads

Router

5 The web server receives the request
using the HTTP protocol. The request
tells the server which specific document is being requested and where
that document is located.

How Web Pages Are Organized on a Website

1 The *home page* is the first or top page of any website. A site can be just one page or can be composed of dozens or even hundreds of pages. In the latter case, the home page acts as a table of contents to organize the site and help users find information available on the site.

2 Underlined or highlighted hyperlink text is often embedded in the home page. The hyperlinks serve to connect the top page with other pages throughout the site.

3 Related documents residing together on a web host computer make up a website. However, a single server can host multiple websites, each contained in a separate area or directory, much like a hard drive can accommodate multiple directories. Some websites are so large and heavily trafficked that they can't fit on a single server and require multiple servers.

4 Good web design principles suggest that pages throughout a site link back to the home page. This approach enables users to always find their way back to the top of a site to navigate in other directions.

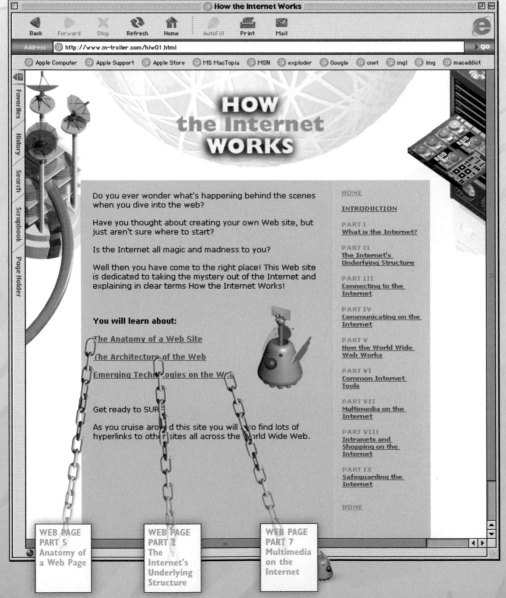

5 Documents within a site can be linked to any other document in the site—and even to documents on other sites. Most websites, however, are designed in a pyramid or an outline structure that gives users a visual model to understand how information is arranged and indicates how to find and navigate through the site's documents.

Linear

6 Websites typically are organized in one of three ways. The first is an outline or a tree structure, which arranges information hierarchically, moving from general information to more specific data.

Tree

7 The second organizational method is linear, in which one page leads to the next, which leads to the next one, and so on.

Random

8 The third organizational structure is really a lack of structure, in which pages are connected to one another seemingly at random. (It's this last structure, though, that makes it clear why the Web is called the Web.)

How Websites Are Constructed

1 First, the raw materials are collected for the web page. Content can be any number of things: family photos, poems, personal opinions, text of any kind, sound clips, and movies. Text can easily be compiled with any word processor, such as Microsoft Word.

Text

Graphics

Multimedia

HTML Page

2 A page can come to life with a few well-chosen images. In designing a family home page, for example, a scanned photo might work well on the web page. Icons or colored bullets spruce up a text list, and navigational icons, such as arrows or pointers, let a user move logically around the site. A whole range of shareware image editors is available on the Internet. *Shareware* is software you can try out for free, and for which you must pay only if you use it after a certain length of time.

3 Software is available that facilitates the arrangement of text, images, and other media without requiring a single line of HTML to be typed; one such program is Microsoft's FrontPage. However, if the pages need to be tweaked, there is no substitute for knowing a little HTML. Before posting new pages, they should be previewed from the hard disk using a web browser. If any changes are necessary, it is easier to make them at this stage. It's best to preview the page with both Internet Explorer and Firefox because the same page can look different in each browser.

Text Editor

Image Editor

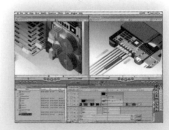

Media Editor

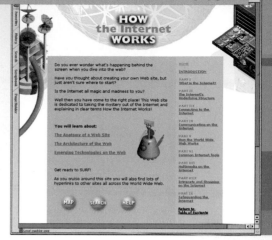

6 An FTP program is used to log on to the ISP's web server; many good FTP programs are available as shareware on the Internet. The ISP issues a username and password at sign-up time, which are used to log on to the directory where the HTML page, graphics, and other media will be placed. After the various elements are put in the correct folder, the "live" pages can be checked on the web using the URL provided by the ISP. In some instances, the software you use to build a website also includes built-in tools for posting the pages.

5 The web page is posted to a hosting service or an ISP that provides the space for doing this free of charge as part of its monthly fee.

HTML Editor

http://www.server.com/yourname

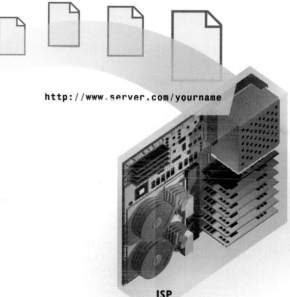

ISP

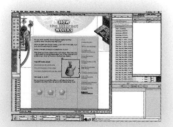

HTML Editor

4 If you want to add other media to your pages, such as digitized sound, music, or video, you need access to the digital files, or you can digitize them yourself with additional computer hardware. When you are dealing with media with large file sizes it will take users a long time to download the file. During editing, try to trim all the fat out of video and audio clips. Also try to scale back the length and resolution of audio and video to decrease file size.

CHAPTER

18

How Web Browsers Work

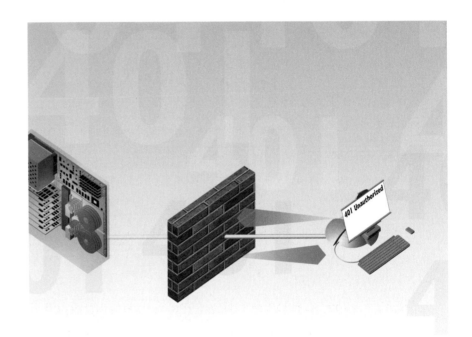

LIKE much of the Internet, the World Wide Web operates on a client/server model. You run a web client on your computer—called a web browser—such as Microsoft's Internet Explorer or Firefox. That client contacts a web server and requests information or resources. The web server locates and then sends the information to the web browser, which displays the results.

When web browsers contact servers, they're asking to be sent pages built with Hypertext Markup Language (HTML). Browsers interpret those pages and display them on your computer. They also can display applications, programs, animations, and similar material created with programming languages such as Java and ActiveX, scripting languages such as JavaScript, and techniques such as AJAX.

Sometimes, home pages contain links to files the web browser can't play or display, such as sound or animation files. In that case, you need a plug-in or a helper application. You configure your web browser or operating system to use the helper application or plug-in whenever it encounters a sound, animation, or other type of file the browser can't run or play.

Over the years, web browsers have become increasingly sophisticated. Browsers are now full-blown software suites that can do everything from videoconferencing to letting you create and publish HTML pages. Browsers now also blur the line between your local computer and the Internet—in essence, they can make your computer and the Internet function as a single computer system.

Increasingly, a browser is not just a single piece of software, but an entire suite. The newest version of Internet Explorer, for example, includes security features such as an anti-phishing filter. The Firefox browser has a companion piece of email software called Thunderbird that can be downloaded as well.

When browsing the Internet, one of the most frustrating experiences is the error messages browsers display when they're having trouble contacting a website. Depending on which browser you use, and which version of the browser you're using, those messages might differ. Sometimes browsers display error messages in plain English—but more often they don't. The final illustration in this chapter lists the most common browser error messages—and what they mean.

How a Web Browser Works

1 Web browsers consist of client software that runs on your computer and displays home pages on the Web. There are clients for a wide variety of devices, including Windows, Macintosh, and Unix computers.

2 A web browser displays information on your computer by interpreting the Hypertext Markup Language (HTML) that is used to build home pages on the Web. Home pages usually display graphics, sound, and multimedia files, as well as links to other pages, files that can be downloaded, and other Internet resources.

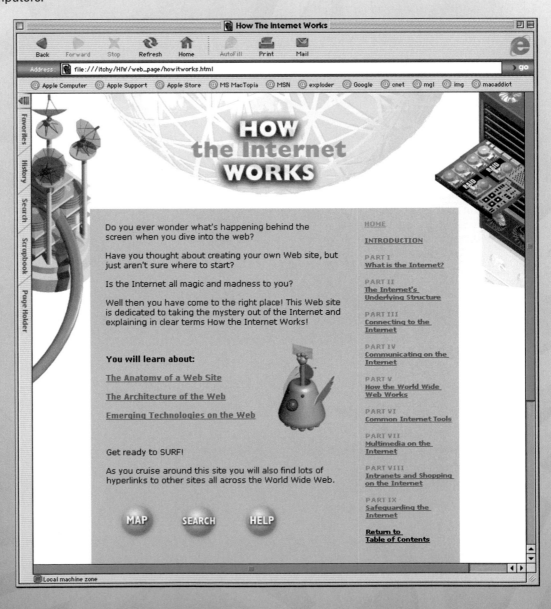

```
<html>         Page Title
<head>
<title>How The Internet Works</title>
<meta http-equiv="Content-Type" content="text/html ...
</head>      Background Color
<body bgcolor="#FFFFFF" link="#6666CC" vlink="...
<div id="Layer1" style="position:absolute; left:...
<div id="Layer2" style="position:absolute; ...
<div id="Layer3" style="position:absolute; ...
          Layer 1
<div id="Layer4" style="position:absolute; ...
<div id="Layer5" style="position:absolute; ...
<div id="Layer6" style="position:absolute; ...
  <p><font size="3" face="Verdana, Arial, Helvet...
    what's happening behind the screens when yo...
  <p><font size="3" face="Verdana, Arial, Helvet...
    about creating your own Web site, but just...
  <p><font size="3" face="Verdana, Arial, Helvet...
    all magic and madness to you?</font></p>
  <p><font size="3" face="Verdana, Arial, Helvet...
    have come to the right place! This Web s...
    out of the Internet and explaining in clear...
  <p> </p>
  <p><font face="Verdana, Arial, Helvetica, ...
    about:</b></font></p>
  <p><b><font face="Verdana, Arial, Helvetica, ...
    Anatomy of a Web Site</a></font></b></p...
  <p><b><font face="Verdana, Arial, Helvetica, ...
    Architecture of the Web</font></a></font...
  <p><b><font face="Verdana, Arial, Helvetica, ...
    Technologies on the Web</font></a></f...
  <p> </p>
  <p><font face="Verdana, Arial, Helvetica, ...
  <p><font face="Verdana, Arial, Helvetica, ...
    site you will also find lots of hyperl...
    Wide Web.</font></p>
</div>
<div id="Layer7" style="position:absolute; ...
  <p><font color="#999999"><b><font size="2" ...
  <p><font color="#9999CC"><a href="intro.h...
  <p><font color="#999999"><b><font size="...
    I<br>
    <a href="pt01start.html">What is the Int...
  <p><font color="#999999"><b><font size="2...
    II<br>  Hyperlink
    <a href="part02start.html">The Internet...
  <p><font color="#999999"><b><font size="...
    III<br>
    <a href="part03start.html">Connecting to t...
  <p><font color="#999999"><b><font size="2...
    IV<br>
    <a href="part04start.html">Communicating...
  <p><font color="#999999"><b><font size="...
    V<br>
    <font color="#6666CC"><a href="part05...
  <p><font color="#999999"><b><font size="...
    VI<br>
    <font color="#6666CC"><a href="part06...
  <p><font color="#999999"><b><font size="...
    VII<br>
    <font color="#6666CC"><a href="part07...
  <p><font color="#999999"><b><font size="...
    VIII<br>
    <font color="#6666CC"><a href="part08start.h...
    the Internet</a></font></font></b></font...
  <p><font color="#999999"><b><font size="...
    IX<br>
    <font color="#6666CC"><a href="part09...
  <p><font color="#999999"><b><font size="2...
    to <br>
    Table of Contents</font></a></font><...
  <p> </p>
  <p> </p>
</div>
<div id="Layer8" style="position:absolute; ...
<img src="bot.gif" width="151" height="1...
<div id="Layer9" style="position:absolute; left:...
<div id="Layer10" style="position:absolute; left:...
<div id="Layer11" style="position:absolute; left:...
</body>
</html>
```

3 The coding in the HTML files tells your browser how to display the text, graphics, links, and multimedia files on the home page. The HTML file your browser loads to display the home page doesn't actually have the graphics, sound, multimedia files, and other resources on it. Instead, it contains HTML references to those graphics and files. Your browser uses those references to find the files on the server and then display them on the home page.

4 The web browser also interprets HTML tags as links to other websites, or to other web resources, such as graphics, multimedia files, newsgroups, or files to download. Depending on the link, it performs different actions. For example, if the HTML code specifies the link as another home page, the browser retrieves the URL specified in the HTML file when the user clicks the underlined link on the page. If the HTML code specifies a file to be downloaded, the browser downloads the file to your computer.

Web browsers can't display some types of files on the Internet, notably some kinds of multimedia files, such as sound, video, and animation files. (A common file type like this is called Flash.) To view or play these files, you need what is called a *helper application* or *plug-in*. You must configure your web browser or operating system to launch these helper applications and plug-ins whenever you click an object that needs them to be viewed. More often than not, when you install the application or plug-in, it will configure itself properly.

The meanings of tags are easily decipherable. Every HTML tag, or instruction, is surrounded by a less-than and a greater-than sign—<P>. Often tags appear in pairs, the beginning tag and the ending tag. They are identical except for a simple slash in the ending tag. So, a paragraph of text frequently is surrounded by tags such as this: <P> Paragraph of text.</P>. Also, tags are not case sensitive. <P> equals <p>.

What Common Browser Error Messages Mean

Server Does Not Have a DNS Entry—When you type a URL in your browser to visit a site, your computer contacts a server called a Domain Name System (DNS) server. The DNS server translates the URL into the IP number that computers can understand—and after it does that, your browser can go to the site. (For more information about DNS servers, see Chapter 5, "How Internet Addresses and Domains Work.") If you get an error message telling you the server doesn't have a DNS entry, it means that the server doesn't have a listing for the URL you typed. This usually means either you typed the URL incorrectly or something is wrong with the DNS server. Check the URL and retype it.

503 Service Unavailable—This is a catch-all error message for a variety of problems, but all of them mean that the website is incapable of contact by your browser. The problem might be the site's server has crashed because of too much traffic or there's network congestion.

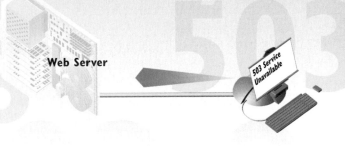

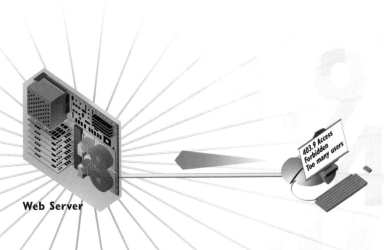

403.9 Access Forbidden. Too Many Users Are Connected—Some websites recognize that if they get too much traffic at once, the entire site can be brought down and no one will be able to visit. Those sites put a limit on the number of people who can come to the site at once—that way, the site is always available, even if not everyone who wants to visit can get in. If you get this "Too Many Users Are Connected" message, it usually means that the website is up and running, but you can't get in because the maximum number of people are already on the site. Keep trying—when one person leaves, another can come in, and it might be you.

404 Not Found—When you get this message, you've arrived at the correct website, but the specific page you're looking for can't be found. That specific page might have been deleted from the site or moved—or you might have typed the location incorrectly.

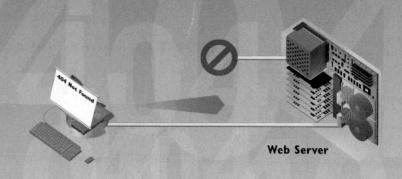

Web Server

Web Server

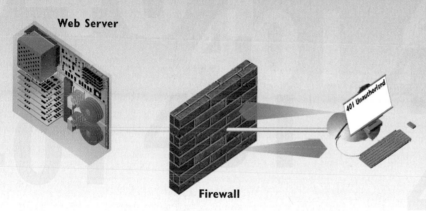

Firewall

401 Unauthorized or 403 Forbidden—If you get either of these error messages, you're trying to enter a website that allows only certain people in—and it's not allowing you to enter. Typically, these types of websites are password protected and also might allow only visitors who are from certain domains, such as zd.com. If you've entered a password, you might have entered it improperly, or you might not be in a domain that's allowed to enter the website.

Spinning hourglass—This isn't an error message your browser displays—instead, your Windows cursor turns into a spinning hourglass. The spinning hourglass tells you that your browser is trying to make a connection to a website. If it keeps spinning and a connection is never made, it can mean that an Internet router someplace between where you are and where you're trying to visit has crashed and you can't make the connection. It can also mean that you've lost your local Internet connection for some reason.

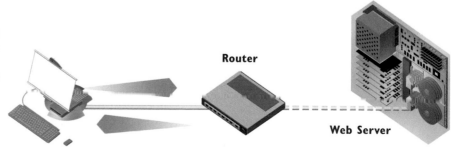

Router

Web Server

CHAPTER

19

How Markup Languages Work

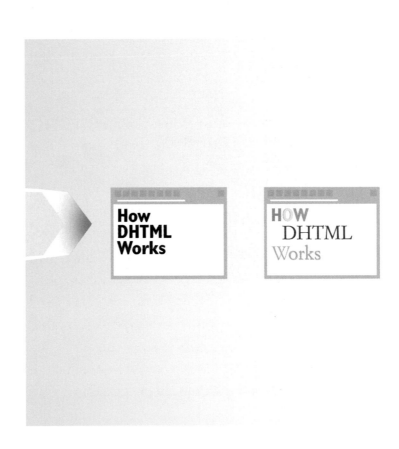

MARKUP languages are the road signs of a web page. They are sets of directions that tell the browser software how to display and manage a web document, much like written music scores are instructions that tell a musician how to play a particular song. These instructions (called *tags* or *markups*) are embedded in the source document that creates the web page.

Tags reference graphic images located in separate files, and they instruct the browser to retrieve and display these images within the page. Tags can also tell a browser to connect a user to another file or URL when he clicks an active hyperlink. So each web page has everything it needs to be displayed on any computer with a browser that can interpret the markup language.

Your original text will probably have headings, multiple paragraphs, and some simple formatting. A web browser will not understand all these layout instructions because the original text isn't formatted with HTML, the language of the Web (discussed later in this chapter). Paragraphs, carriage returns, indents, and multiple spaces will be shown instead as a single space if no HTML markup is added.

Markup languages should not be confused with programming languages, such as C+ or Pascal. Programming languages are used to write complex applications, such as word processors or spreadsheets. Markup languages, in contrast, are much simpler and describe the way information should be displayed—for example, by defining when text should be boldface. In markup languages, tags are embedded within documents to describe how the documents should be formatted and displayed.

Hypertext Markup Language (HTML) is the markup language of the Web. It defines the format of a web document and enables hypertext links to be embedded in the document. You can use any text editor or word processor to add HTML tags to an ASCII text document, although a number of shareware and commercially available HTML editors can assist web page authors as well.

The Web evolves daily, and HTML also expands and changes along with it. A group of technologies that together are termed *Dynamic HTML (DHTML)* have grown out of HTML, and allow HTML to be more than a static language. They enable HTML to perform animations and become more interactive and flexible.

The Extended Markup Language (XML) promises to bring even more significant changes to the Web. It's dramatically different from other markup languages because it separates the content of a page from its presentation. Rather than doing things such as giving instructions on text size, it tags different types of content and then has other technologies such as templates and style sheets determine how that content should look.

XML is at the core of a new technology called Web Services, which allow programs and services to be delivered across the Internet using a web browser. (To see how Web Services work, turn to Chapter 25, "How .NET and Web Services Work.")

The newest XML-related technology is AJAX, which allows websites to function more like desktop programs than websites. It allows for a great deal of interactivity, unlike most web pages, which are slow and static.

How HTML Works

1 To display web pages in any browser, you must add HTML tags to your original text. This process is called *tagging*.

2 Use HTML to give your text structure. All HTML files begin and end with HTML tags. Headings are marked as such, as are paragraphs, line breaks, block quotes, and special character emphasis. Any carriage returns or indentations within the source text do not affect the browser's display of the page. HTML tags need to be put in if they are to be displayed in a browser.

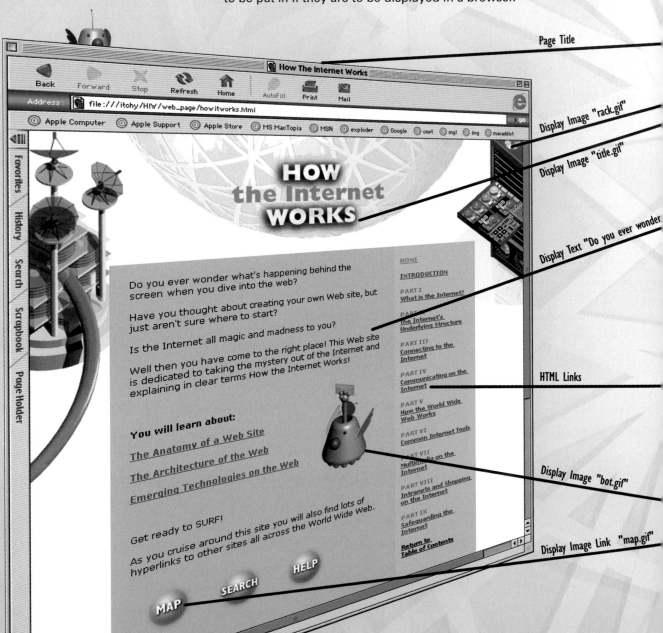

Page Title

Display Image "rack.gif"

Display Image "title.gif"

Display Text "Do you ever wonder

HTML Links

Display Image "bot.gif"

Display Image Link "map.gif"

3 The finished HTML document will be the source page for any browser on any computer. This simplicity of HTML makes cross-platform compatibility easy and reliable. The more complex and specialized the HTML tagging, the longer it will take to download and display the document.

4 Most web browsers enable your document to retain its structural integrity when you display, or *parse*, it. Headings will appear in a larger font size than text within paragraphs, for example, and block quotes will be uniformly indented; however, the look might vary from browser to browser. Note that browsers determine the exact font, size, and color. Also be aware that the relative importance of the elements is always kept intact.

```
<html>
<head>
<title>How The Internet Works</title>
<meta http-equiv="Content-Type" content="text/html; charset=iso-8859-1">
</head>

<body bgcolor="#FFFFFF" link="#6666CC" vlink="#666666">
<div id="Layer1" style="position:absolute; left:581px; top:-66px; width:100px; height:320px; z-index:1"><img src="rack.gif" width="217" height="372"></div>
<div id="Layer2" style="position:absolute; left:0; top:0; width:203px; height:352px; z-index:2"><img src="rtside.gif" width="125" height="450"></div>
<div id="Layer3" style="position:absolute; left:106px; top:0px; width:494px; height:162px; z-index:3"><img src="title.gif" width="545" height="173"></div>
<div id="Layer4" style="position:absolute; left:91px; top:180px; width:502px; height:875px; z-index:4; background-color: #CCCCCC; layer-background-color: #CCCCCC; border: 1px none #
<div id="Layer5" style="position:absolute; left:506px; top:180px; width:156px; height:877px; z-index:5; background-color: #FFCC99; layer-background-color: #FFCC99; border: 1px none #
<div id="Layer6" style="position:absolute; left:115px; top:201px; width:369px; height:604px; z-index:6">
    <p><font size="3" face="Verdana, Arial, Helvetica, sans-serif">Do you ever wonder
    what's happening behind the screen when you dive into the web?</font></p>
    <p><font size="3" face="Verdana, Arial, Helvetica, sans-serif">Have you thought
    about creating your own Web site, but just aren't sure where to start?</font></p>
    <p><font size="3" face="Verdana, Arial, Helvetica, sans-serif">Is the Internet
    all magic and madness to you?</font></p>
    <p><font size="3" face="Verdana, Arial, Helvetica, sans-serif">Well then you
    have come to the right place! This Web site is dedicated to taking the mystery
    out of the Internet and explaining in clear terms How the Internet Works!</font></p>
    <p> </p>
    <p><font face="Verdana, Arial, Helvetica, sans-serif" size="3"><b>You will learn
    about:</font></p>
    <p><b><font face="Verdana, Arial, Helvetica, sans-serif" size="3"><a href="pt05_ch2102.html">The
    Anatomy of a Web Site</a></font></b></p>
    <p><b><font face="Verdana, Arial, Helvetica, sans-serif"><a href="pt01_ch0101.html"><font size="3">The
    Architecture of the Web</font></a></font></b></p>
    <p><b><font face="Verdana, Arial, Helvetica, sans-serif"><a href="pt07_ch3205.html"><font size="3">Emerging
    Technologies on the Web</font></a></font></b></p>
    <p> </p>
    <p><font face="Verdana, Arial, Helvetica, sans-serif">Get ready to SURF!</font></p>
    <p><font face="Verdana, Arial, Helvetica, sans-serif">As you cruise around this
    site you will also find lots of hyperlinks to other sites all across the World
    Wide Web.</font></p>
</div>
<div id="Layer7" style="position:absolute; left:517px; top:198px; width:139px; height:631px; z-index:7">
    <p><font color="#999999"><b><font size="2" face="Verdana, Arial, Helvetica, sans-serif"><a href="index.html"><font color="#9999CC">HOME</font></a></font></b></font></p>
    <p><font color="#9999CC"><a href="intro.html"><b><font size="2" face="Verdana, Arial, Helvetica, sans-serif">INTRODUCTION</font></b></a></font></p>
    <p><font color="#999999"><b><font size="2" face="Verdana, Arial, Helvetica, sans-serif">PART
    I<br>
    <a href="pt01start.html">What is the Internet?</a></font></b></font></p>
    <p><font color="#999999"><b><font size="2" face="Verdana, Arial, Helvetica, sans-serif">PART
    II<br>
    <a href="part02start.html">The Internet's Underlying Structure</a></font></b></font></p>
    <p><font color="#999999"><b><font size="2" face="Verdana, Arial, Helvetica, sans-serif">PART
    III<br>
    <a href="part03start.html">Connecting to the Internet</a></font></b></font></p>
    <p><font color="#999999"><b><font size="2" face="Verdana, Arial, Helvetica, sans-serif">PART
    IV<br>
    <a href="part04start.html">Communicating on the Internet</a></font></b></font></p>
    <p><font color="#999999"><b><font size="2" face="Verdana, Arial, Helvetica, sans-serif">PART
    V<br>
    <font color="#6666CC"><a href="part05start.html">How the World Wide Web Works</a></font></font></b></font></p>
    <p><font color="#999999"><b><font size="2" face="Verdana, Arial, Helvetica, sans-serif">PART
    VI<br>
    <font color="#6666CC"><a href="part06start.html">Common Internet Tools</a></font></font></b></font></p>
    <p><font color="#999999"><b><font size="2" face="Verdana, Arial, Helvetica, sans-serif">PART
    VII<br>
    <font color="#6666CC"><a href="part07start.html">Multimedia on the Internet</a></font></font></b></font></p>
    <p><font color="#999999"><b><font size="2" face="Verdana, Arial, Helvetica, sans-serif">PART
    VIII<br>
    <font color="#6666CC"><a href="part08start.html">Intranets and Shopping on
    the Internet</a></font></font></b></font></p>
    <p><font color="#999999"><b><font size="2" face="Verdana, Arial, Helvetica, sans-serif">PART
    IX<br>
    <font color="#6666CC"><a href="part09start.html">Safeguarding the Internet</a></font></font></b></font></p>
    <p><font color="#999999"><b><font size="2" face="Verdana, Arial, Helvetica, sans-serif"><a href="index.html"><font color="#000000">Return
    to <br>
    Table of Contents</font></a></font></b></font></p>
    <p> </p>
    <p> </p>
</div>
<div id="Layer8" style="position:absolute; left:351px; top:380px; width:129px; height:132px; z-index:8"><img src="bot.gif" width="151" height="154"></div>
<div id="Layer9" style="position:absolute; left:120px; top:622px; width:77px; height:68px; z-index:9"><a href="map.html"><img src="map.gif" width="83" height="83" border="0"></a></
<div id="Layer10" style="position:absolute; left:215px; top:623px; width:65px; height:76px; z-index:10"><a href="searchHIW.html"><img src="search.gif" width="83" height="83" border
<div id="Layer11" style="position:absolute; left:312px; top:622px; width:67px; height:101px; z-index:11"><a href="helpme.html"><img src="help.gif" width="83" height="83" border="0"
</body>
</html>
```

How Dynamic HTML Works

1 Dynamic HTML (DHTML) differs from traditional HTML in that it enables web page changes on-the-fly, after they've been downloaded. In plain HTML, after a page is downloaded, it is static and can be changed only when a user takes an action of some kind. But DHTML, for example, could cause an animation of a rocket to fly across your browser window several seconds after the page has been downloaded—without you doing anything.

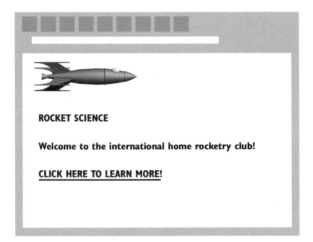

2 DHTML does its work without having to contact the server after the page downloads, so it can perform some interactive functions more quickly than other technologies that have to contact the server. The instructions for performing the commands are in the HTML commands that are in the page itself.

3 Although DHTML is often referred to as if it were a single technology, it is, in fact, a general term used for a group of technologies that can work together or by themselves to change a web page after the page has been downloaded to your computer. These technologies are the Document Object Model (DOM), Cascading Style Sheets (CSS), and client-side scripting languages, such as JavaScript.

4 The DOM defines every object and element on a web page and enables those objects to be manipulated or accessed. This includes fonts, graphics, tables, and visual elements, as well as elements you can't necessarily see, such as the browser's version number and the current date and time. Without DOM, all the elements on a page are static. So on the simplest level, DHTML could use the DOM to change the font of every letter, individually, on a web page.

5 Cascading Style Sheets are, in essence, templates that apply formatting and style information to the elements of a web page. They're called *cascading* because any single page can have more than one style sheet associated with it. Additionally, Cascading Style Sheets enable images to overlap one another. This enables animations to be created easily on a page.

6 Client-side scripting languages perform much of the work of DHTML. These languages access the DOM and manipulate its elements, and they do the same to Cascading Style Sheets. They perform the actions of DHTML. So a script, for example, could turn a word a different color when a mouse moves across it, or it could create easy-to-use collapsible navigation on every page on a website.

How XML Works

 XML solves several major problems for web developers. Without it, to deliver web pages to different devices such as computers, cell phones, and wireless Palm devices, a developer must create and maintain three separate websites, with special coding for each device—HTML for the computer, WAP for the cell phone, and what's called web clipping for the wireless Palm devices. It's an expensive, difficult, and time-consuming proposition. And even if a developer is building a site only for computers, every time the design changes, all the pages must be recoded—again, an expensive and time-consuming proposition.

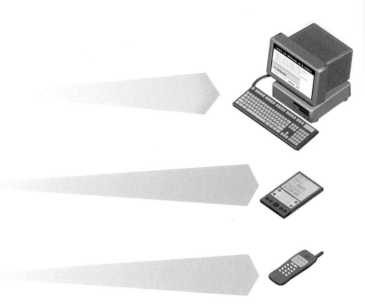

2 With XML, a developer can create the website just once. Then the site can be automatically formatted to several types of devices, such as Internet-connected computers, wireless Palm devices, and cell phones using WAP. And even if the site is being built for only computers, when there is a redesign, with XML, all the pages need not be rebuilt.

```
<Sale Flyer>
<Offer>Get It While It's Hot!</Offer>
<Promotional Copy>
You can't miss this one!
One-time offer only —
gaming systems at prices
you won't believe! </Promotional Copy>
<Product>Sony PlayStations</Product>
<Price> $159.95</Price>
Sale ends <End Date> May 15
</End Date>
</Sale Flyer>
```

3 The most important concept to understand about XML is that the language is used only to convey information about content, not about the presentation of the content. So, for example, it doesn't give instructions on what size text should be. But it uses tags to define the type of content on the page. Then it uses other techniques, as you'll see in the next steps, to display those pages. In that way, a single page can be displayed many different ways, without having to go back and alter the original page—only the designs, which are separate from the content, need to be changed.

4 When XML content is posted on a website, different designs need to be applied to that content so that it can be viewable by devices connecting to it—for example, cell phones. Extensible Style Language Transformations (XSLT) can be applied to the XML. XSLT can take XML and apply different designs to it or change it to other forms of XML—for example, it can take the XML and turn it into a WAP page that can be viewed by a cell phone and take the same XML and turn it into a HTML document with a different design.

5 When a device visits a site built with XML, there needs to be some way for the site to know what type of device it is—a computer, for example, or a cell phone. Common Gateway Interface (CGI) scripts can detect which device is contacting the site.

6 After the site knows what kind of device is visiting, it takes the XML, and, using XSLT, changes it into the proper format—for example, a WAP document that the cell phone can view with its WAP microbrowser or an HTML document for a computer.

Note
XML is the basis of one of the newest web technologies, Web Services, which allow programs and services to be delivered across the Internet using a web browser. For more information about Web Services, turn to Chapter 25. XML is also frequently used to allow applications, databases, and organizations to exchange information.

How AJAX Works

1 AJAX (Asynchronous JavaScript and XML) allows web developers to create interactive websites that function more like desktop programs than slow, static websites. Gmail and Google Maps are two examples of sites built using AJAX.

2 When someone visits an AJAX site, the browser loads the HTML page, as it would normally. The HTML page uses JavaScript for interactivity. (For details about how JavaScript works, see Chapter 34, "How Java, ActiveX and JavaScript Work.") When a visitor makes a request for more information, for example to fetch a map, the JavaScript makes the request.

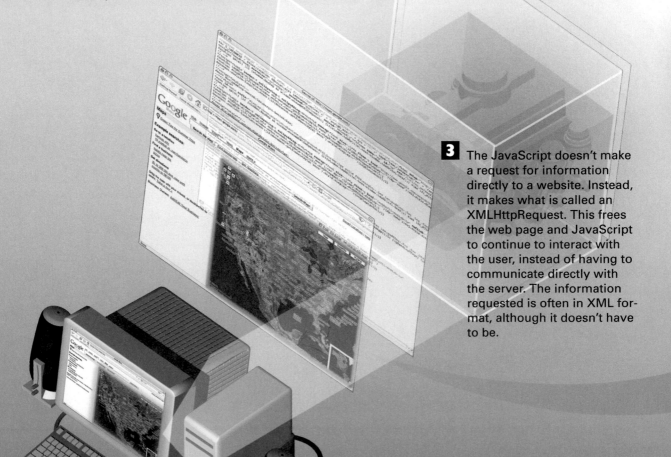

3 The JavaScript doesn't make a request for information directly to a website. Instead, it makes what is called an XMLHttpRequest. This frees the web page and JavaScript to continue to interact with the user, instead of having to communicate directly with the server. The information requested is often in XML format, although it doesn't have to be.

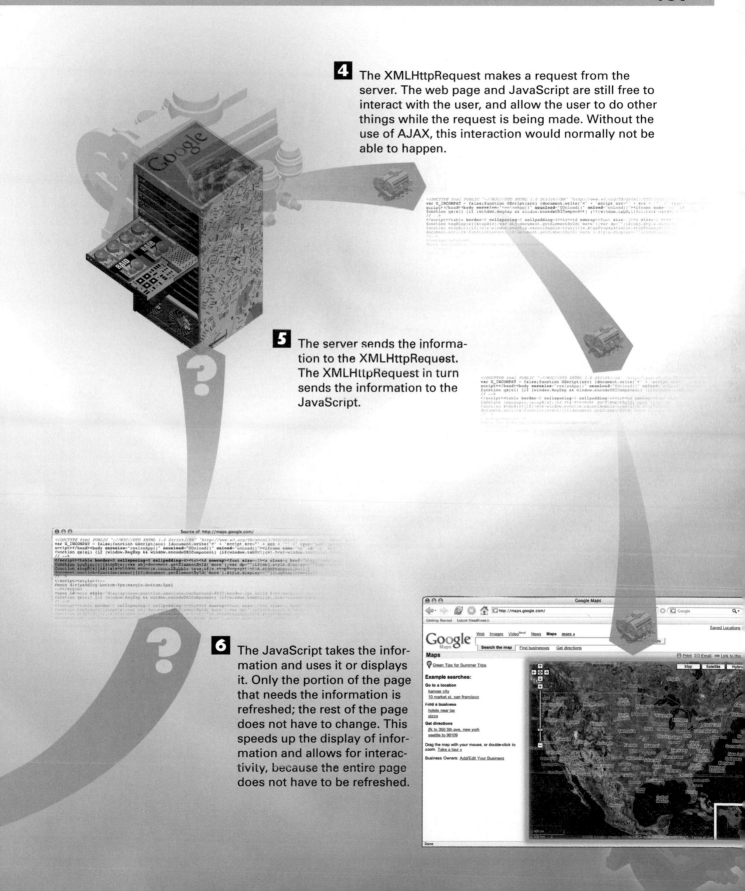

4 The XMLHttpRequest makes a request from the server. The web page and JavaScript are still free to interact with the user, and allow the user to do other things while the request is being made. Without the use of AJAX, this interaction would normally not be able to happen.

5 The server sends the information to the XMLHttpRequest. The XMLHttpRequest in turn sends the information to the JavaScript.

6 The JavaScript takes the information and uses it or displays it. Only the portion of the page that needs the information is refreshed; the rest of the page does not have to change. This speeds up the display of information and allows for interactivity, because the entire page does not have to be refreshed.

CHAPTER
20

How Hypertext Works

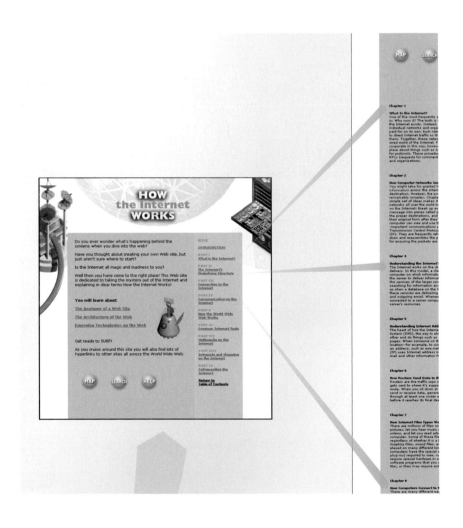

IN the late 1960s, a computer scientist named Ted Nelson introduced hypertext, a concept that lays the foundation for the World Wide Web and its connections between documents, or pages.

Nelson wanted to create a new way of exploring information. He wanted to provide the reader with a spontaneous means of accessing more and more in-depth information about something that sparked the reader's interest when reading text on the page. Rather than reading a document from beginning to end, digesting the material in a sequential order, the reader could highlight a word and receive more information on the meaning of that word, for example.

Nelson imagined that you could read the United States Constitution, come across the term "electoral college," and then open another document that explains how the electoral college works. From that document, you might open another document that lists the votes of the electoral college from its founding to the present. From there, you might choose to open a document about former president William Jefferson Clinton, then another about the former First Cat, Socks, then another about the care and feeding of felines, and so forth. Ultimately, you could find a subject that wasn't even remotely connected to the Constitution, but which you would find interesting or entertaining.

This hypertext concept was obviously on Tim Berners-Lee's mind when he began thinking about how researchers could share their work across the Internet. He envisioned a system in which a document could be linked to other documents, enabling researchers to easily find more and related information simply by following a link from one document on the network to another.

Typically, hypertext consists of a hyperlink that appears onscreen as a highlighted word, icon, or graphic. By moving a mouse cursor over the item or object and clicking it, you easily navigate to additional information. On the Web, that information can be located at any other place on the Web, be it on the same host server or one across the globe. A linked object can be various media, such as text (linking from one character to a whole document, for example), a graphical button (such as direction arrows that move from page to page), or still images (photos, icons, or a comic strip), for example. The documents and objects that are being linked to can be on the same site as the original document or in an entirely different document.

Hypertext links are embedded into a web document using Hypertext Markup Language (HTML). A text link usually appears onscreen as an underlined word or phrase and is sometimes rendered in a different color from other text, depending on how your web browser interprets the HTML codes. When you place the mouse cursor on this underlined text and click the mouse button, you initiate a request by the browser for a new web page or—if the text references an internal link to information in the same document—direct your browser to scroll to another, specific point within the same document.

Images or icons can also act as hyperlinks. When you move the mouse cursor over the icon or graphic and click the mouse button, you launch the request to retrieve the linked information.

How Hyperlinks Work

1 The "hyperlinking" begins when you first retrieve a web page from a remote web server. Target links within the page move you quickly from one part of the page to the next.

`<a href="#target">Part 1</a>`

`<a href="#target">Part 2</a>`

`<a href="#target">Part 3</a>`

2 A *relative* link is used to initiate a request by your web browser to retrieve a page located on the same web server as the page from which you are linking. Web developers use relative links when they're pointing to a page under their control because this enables them to more easily maintain their HTML coding if their server locations change.

`<a href="/oursite/relative/chapter_4.html">Chapter 4</a>`

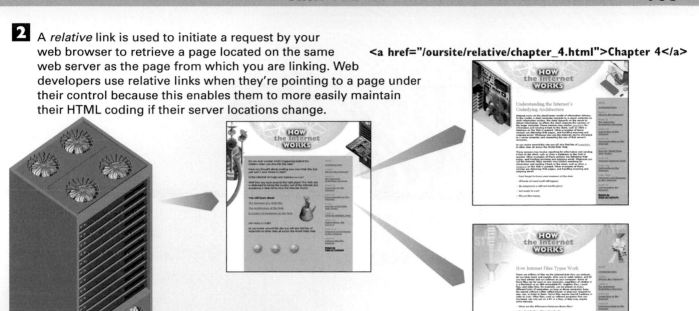

`<a href="/oursite/relative/chapter_7.html">Chapter 7</a>`

3 A hyperlink that leads to a completely different web server uses an *absolute* link. Because these links might not be under the control of the web developer who created the page, there is a chance that this will be a "dead link"—the page will have been moved without the web developer knowing about it.

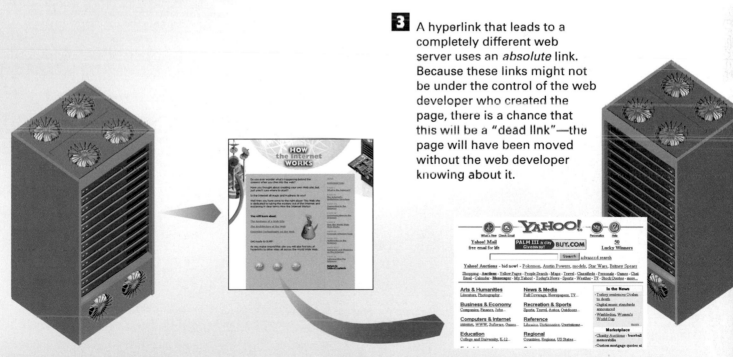

`<a href="http://www.yahoo.com"><img src="searchyahoo.gif"></a>`

CHAPTER 21

How URLs Work

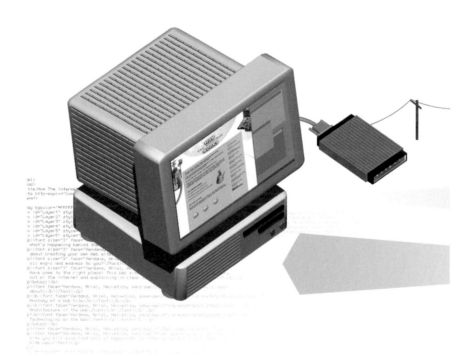

THE web pages and the hosts that make up the World Wide Web must have unique locations so that your computer can locate and retrieve the pages. The unique identifier for a host is called the Internet Protocol (IP) address, and the unique identifier for a page is called the uniform resource locator (URL). A URL functions much like a postal or email address. Just as postal and email addresses list a name and specific location, a URL, or web address, indicates where the host computer is located, the location of the website on the host, and the name of the web page and the file type of each document, among other information.

A typical URL looks like this:

http://www.whitehouse.gov/president/index.html

If you were to interpret the instructions in this URL from left to right, it would translate to: "Go to the host computer called whitehouse (a government agency), in a directory called president, and retrieve a hypertext document with the filename index.html." The URL, or address, tells the browser which document to fetch and exactly where to find it on a specific remote host computer somewhere on the Internet.

The first part of the URL indicates what type of transfer protocol will be used to retrieve the specified document. The most common request is for a hypertext document that uses Hypertext Transfer Protocol (HTTP).

The second portion of the URL refers to the specific host computer on which the document resides, which is to be contacted by the browser software. This part of the address is also called the *domain name*. See Chapter 5, "How Internet Addresses and Domains Work," for more information about domains.

The third part of the URL is the directory on the host computer that contains a specific website or multiple websites. This is always located after the first single slash in the URL and is essentially the subdirectory on the hard disk that houses the website. Subdirectories might also be indicated in this part of the address. For example, if the previous URL were changed to http://www.whitehouse.gov/history/presidents/, there would be two subdirectories—`history` and `presidents`.

In the preceding example, the filename is chapter1.html. This is always the last portion of the URL. If you see an address without a filename, it is assumed that the filename index.html contains the requested web page. Therefore, the default document a web server will deliver to the client when no other filename is listed is index.html. (Note that sometimes the last portion of the URL might not be a filename—it could be other types of information required by a web server, such as codes required to log on to the web server.)

The illustration in this chapter shows the process necessary to request and retrieve a web document. When a request for a document occurs for the first time in a web-browsing session, the host computer must first be located to find the file. After that, the specific subdirectory and document are retrieved.

How URLs Are Structured

1 The first part of the URL indicates which type of transfer protocol will be used to retrieve the specified document. The most common request is for a hypertext document that uses the HTTP protocol.

3 The third part of the URL is the directory on the host computer that contains a specific website. A host computer can house multiple website. This third segment of the address is essentially the root directory that houses the site. Subdirectories might also be indicated in this part of the address.

http://www.sample.com/samples/sample.html

2 The second portion of the URL is the specific host computer on which the document resides, which is to be contacted by the browser software. This part of the address is also called the *domain*. Domain names end in a suffix that indicates which type of organization the domain is. For example, .com indicates a commercial business, .edu indicates an officially accredited college or university, .gov indicates a government office, .mil indicates a military facility, and .org indicates a not-for-profit organization. The suffix also can indicate the country in which the host computer is located. For example, .ca is in Canada, and .au is in Australia.

4 The last segment of the URL is the filename of the specific web page you are requesting. If no filename is indicated, the browser assumes a default page, usually called index.html.

How URLs Help Retrieve Web Documents

1 The web browser installed on your local computer sends your TCP/IP software a signal that it is ready to request a document. TCP/IP makes a connection with the host TCP/IP software. After the connection is established, your browser makes a request for a document by sending its URL through the two-way connection maintained by TCP/IP to the server.

2 The HTTP server is the portion of the host computer that runs HTTP server software. TCP/IP makes and maintains the connection this way. The browser can use HTTP to send requests and receive pages through the host's web server software. This software enables the host to communicate with the client browser, in HTTP, over TCP/IP.

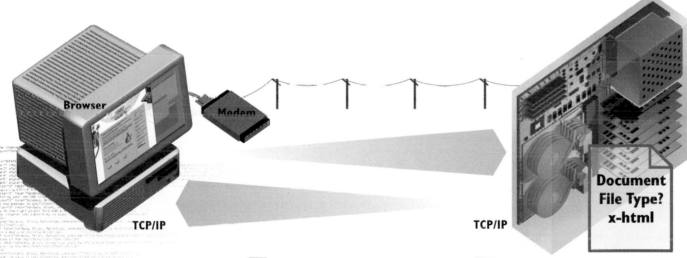

HTTP Server

Browser

Modem

TCP/IP

TCP/IP

Document File Type? x-html

5 The browser on your local computer reads the file type. If it is an HTML document, the browser examines the content, breaking it down into meaningful parts. Two general parts include text, which is displayed by the browser word for word, and HTML markup information called *tags*, which are not displayed but contain formatting information, such as normal text, bold headers, or colored hypertext. The results are displayed on your monitor.

4 If the document is found, the host checks its file type (usually either x-html or x-text) and sends this information to the client with the requested page. When the client receives the page, it first checks the file type. If the type is one it can display, it does so; otherwise, it prompts the user to see whether she wants to save it to disk or open it using a helper application. The x-html file type is by far the most common one used when transmitting web pages.

3 The server then receives the transmitted URL and responds in one of three ways. It follows the directory path given in the URL; the server finds the file on its local hard disk and opens it; or the server runs a CGI script or detects an error (such as `file not found`) and generates an error document to be sent back to the client.

CHAPTER

22

How Image Maps and Interactive Forms Work

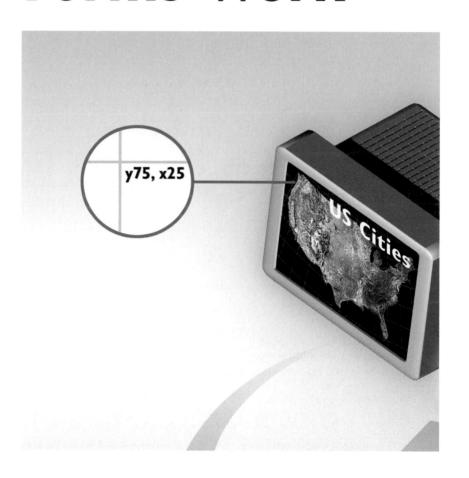

GRAPHICS called image maps and functions called interactive forms demonstrate two of the more common and helpful uses of HTML. *Image maps* are static images that have been turned into clickable images with various clickable parts. *Interactive forms* are HTML-based pages you fill out by providing information such as your name, email address, and similar information. Both image maps and interactive forms are created using Common Gateway Interface (CGI), a communications protocol by which a web server can communicate with other applications. (For more information about how CGI works, turn to Chapter 35, "How CGI Scripting Works.")

Image maps can be thought of as fancy hyperlinks. However, instead of a word, an entire icon, or an image linking to another page, an image is divided into different segments, or coordinates, that link to different HTML pages. That is, image maps link to another document through a predefined *hot* area within an image. As soon as you click your mouse on a hot spot, a CGI script and a special image map coordinates file with the suffix .map go to work. A CGI application reads the map file to match coordinates of a mouse click with a corresponding URL. For instance, imagine an electronic map of the United States in which you click Washington, D.C. In the HTML code for that page, the electronic map is surrounded by a tag and an attribute called `ISMAP`. The code looks something like this:

```
<A HREF="some.server/maps/clickable.map">
<IMG SRC="clickable.map" ISMAP>
</A>
```

The x,y coordinates of your mouse click are sent to the server. The coordinates are received by the server and then redirected to a CGI application. The CGI application scans the file for matching coordinates and then forwards the corresponding URL to the server. Lastly, if the web page resides on the same server, it delivers that web page to the client browser. If not, the server returns the URL to the client browser, which in turn sends a request to the correct server for the page. You then see the page about Washington, D.C. begin to load on your browser. Behind the scenes, the server passed your mouse click coordinates to a CGI application via the CGI. Then, the CGI application matched those coordinates to its URL in a .map file. Finally, the CGI sent the URL back to the server, which redirected the client browser to the new web page.

Forms work differently, although they also use CGI. In a form, when you fill in information on a web page, that information goes to the server for processing. Next, the server redirects the information to a CGI application that is called by the form *submit*. (CGI scripts are activated by the server in response to an HTTP request from the client.) Lastly, a CGI application might send form data to another computer program, such as a database; save it to a file; or even generate a unique HTML document in response to the user's request.

How Image Maps Work

1 In this map example, the user clicks Seattle. The x,y grid coordinate is 75, 25. In the HTML code, the browser recognizes the ISMAP image tag attribute. The mouse click activates the browser to send the x,y coordinate of the click to the server. The location of the `National.map` file is also sent to the server.

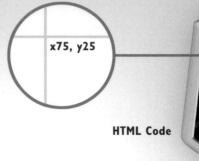

HTML Code

2 The server hands off the coordinate and map file data to a CGI application. The CGI application matches the coordinates to the URL that has been requested by the user by clicking that portion of the map. This URL is handed back to the server, and the server sends the page to the client.

**Page or
URL Response**

Request 75,25

3 The web document is either served up (if it resides on the same server) or the client browser is forwarded to the new URL.

4 The client browser either displays the returned page or (based on the returned URL) sends a request to the correct server for the page.

How Interactive Forms Work

1 In working with an interactive form, the user clicks a data-entry submit button. The data in the data fields is sent to the server with the request.

Home> Products> Windows: <

Login to Download

Login to Download	
Name	
Email	
Postal Code	

☑ Notify me of updates

Platform of product you are downloading:
WINDOWS ⬍

Are you using for:
SELECT ⬍

Do you own another product?
SELECT ⬍

Do you own a Palm OS device?
SELECT ⬍

GO!

Submit Form Data

2 When a form submission is received by the server, it activates a CGI application, a program, or a script that interacts with a web server; it then passes the resulting information to a web form. (The application could add the form data to a database or compare it to a password list of eligible users, among other tasks.) The program's output goes either to another program, such as a database, or into a unique HTML document, or both.

CHAPTER
23

How Web Host Servers Work

TO serve up pages, websites need a *host*—a computer—and server software that runs on the host. The host manages the communications protocols and houses the pages and the related software required to create a website on the Internet. The host machine often uses the Unix, Windows, Linux, or Macintosh operating systems, which have the TCP/IP protocols built in.

The server software resides on the host and serves up the pages and otherwise acts on the requests sent from the client browser software. The server software is not responsible for TCP/IP communications—the host operating system does that—but instead the server software handles the HTTP requests and communications with the host operating system.

Different types of server software (database servers, FTP servers, or network servers, for example) perform various types of services for various types of clients. Specifically, a *web server* is an HTTP server, and its function is to send information to the client software (typically a browser) using the Hypertext Transfer Protocol (HTTP).

Usually, the client browser requests that the server return an HTML document. The server receives this request and sends back a response. The top portion of the response includes transmission information, and the rest of the response is the HTML file.

A web server does more than send pages to the browser, however. It passes requests to run Common Gateway Interface (CGI) scripts to CGI applications. These scripts run external mini-programs, such as a database lookup or interactive forms processing. The server sends the script to the application via CGI and communicates the results of the script back to the browser, if appropriate. (For more information about CGI, turn to Chapter 35, "How CGI Scripting Works.") Moreover, the server software includes configuration files and utilities to secure and manage the website in a variety of ways.

How Web Server Software Works

 Client (browser) software sends its request for data to the host, where the web server software processes the request.

2 Included in the browser's request are the desired information and the file formats the browser can accept.

HTML Page to Browser

HTML with Database Results to Browser

3 If the browser asks for an HTML file, the web server retrieves the file, attaches a header to the file, and sends it to the browser.

A computer with a single IP address can host several types of servers. This means the address might require a port number to identify the correct server if it is not the IP's default server. Each port is associated with a particular server. Ports are identified by a number from 0 to 65,535, but common server types, such as FTP servers, are given the same number by convention.

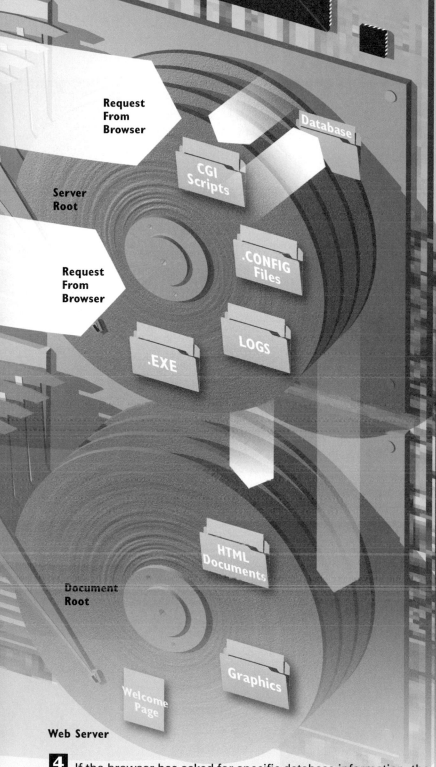

Request From Browser

Server Root

Request From Browser

Database

CGI Scripts

.CONFIG Files

LOGS

.EXE

HTML Documents

Document Root

Graphics

Welcome Page

Web Server

FTP Server Port #21

Gopher Server Port #70

Telnet Server Port #23

Usenet Server Port #119

WAIS Server Port #210

4 If the browser has asked for specific database information, the web server passes a request through CGI to the application, which performs a database lookup, for example. The CGI script returns the results to the web server, which in turn attaches a header to the data and sends it to the browser.

The host computer must have a unique IP address to send and receive information across the Internet. Because raw IP addresses are very intimidating, they are assigned a unique domain name, which is less daunting. The domain name is part of a hierarchical lookup system called the Domain Name System (DNS).

IP Address = Domain Name
83.122.231.21 books.que.com

CHAPTER
24

How Websites Work with Databases

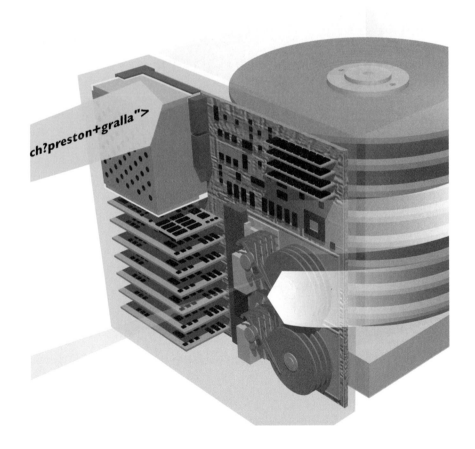

ONE of the most useful applications of the Web is its capability to link a website with a database so web surfers can search for information. In essence, the web page becomes the front-end for database applications, enabling you to select search criteria and execute even complex searches of a database that resides on the host computer.

A well-known and widely used example of this type of linking between website and databases is the popular Yahoo! website (www.yahoo.com). The Yahoo! site serves as a front-end to an extensive database of website descriptions, which can be searched according to keywords. The Welcome page includes a search dialog box in which you enter a keyword that represents the subject matter you are looking for. Clicking the Search button sends a request from the browser to the web server to bring back a list of all websites that contain your keyword.

Not only can the Web serve up data, it can also collect it. For example, many websites ask users to "register" their names, addresses, and other demographic information, which is then captured and stored in a database.

But how does this all work? You don't have to be a corporate giant—or for that matter even a capable programmer—to link your website to a database. In fact, linking a website to a database can be relatively simple. The database can take just about any form and can be as simple as a FileMaker Pro database or as complex as an Oracle SQL database. A variety of technologies bridge websites and databases, including Perl, .NET, Common Gateway Interface (CGI), and others. (For more information about CGI, turn to Chapter 35, "How CGI Scripting Works.")

On the client side of the database, you see a web page that includes a form in which you enter your search terms. When you execute the search, the web server passes your search information to a CGI script, which then searches the database. So a search on the Yahoo! site for public relations firms might look like this:

http://search.yahoo.com/bin/search?p=public+relations

When the web server receives this URL, it identifies the URL as a trigger for a CGI script (called *search* in this example) and passes it along with the search criteria ("public relations," in this example) to the miniprogram using CGI. The CGI script then sends the search to the database, receives the results of the query, and passes it on to the web server to be sent back to the client. That's a lot of handing off of requests and data, but typically even a search of a large database is very fast because the majority of Linux, Unix, and Windows-based databases—the types most often used—can perform these tasks simultaneously. All this happens behind the scenes, of course—you won't need to do any kind of database work or scripting yourself. Instead, the websites you visit have easy-to-use interfaces that take care of interacting with databases; you'll have to type only what you're looking for.

How the Web Works with Databases

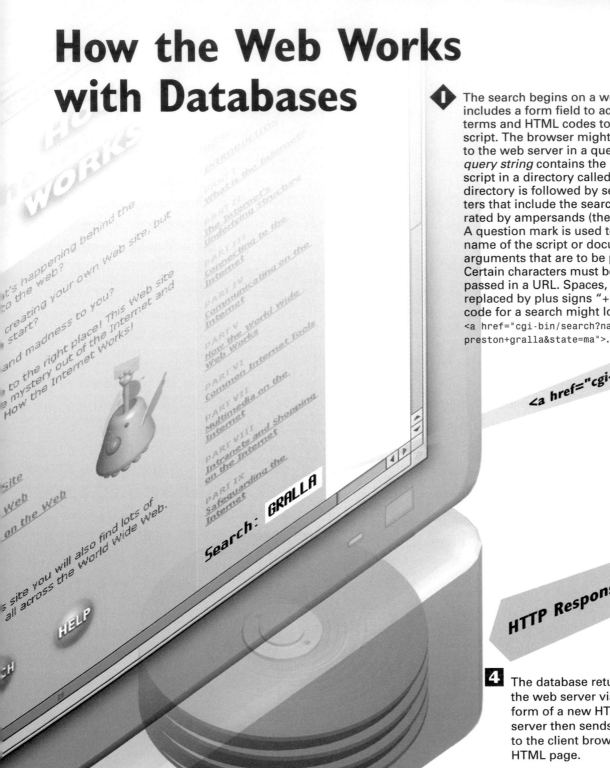

1 The search begins on a web page that includes a form field to accept search terms and HTML codes to execute a CGI script. The browser might pass the data to the web server in a query string. The *query string* contains the name of the CGI script in a directory called `cgi-bin`. This directory is followed by search parameters that include the search terms, separated by ampersands (the character "&"). A question mark is used to separate the name of the script or document from the arguments that are to be passed to it. Certain characters must be encoded when passed in a URL. Spaces, for example, are replaced by plus signs "+". So the HTML code for a search might look like this:

```
<a href="cgi-bin/search?name=
preston+gralla&state=ma">.
```

`<a href="cgi-bin/search?gralla">`

HTTP Response

**SEARCH RESULTS
Preston Gralla**

4 The database returns the data to the web server via CGI in the form of a new HTML page. The server then sends the page back to the client browser as a new HTML page.

2 When the web server receives the URL with the embedded search terms, it sends the information through the CGI program to the database. Typically, the program is stored in a unique directory that contains all the CGI scripts serviced by the web server.

Database Server

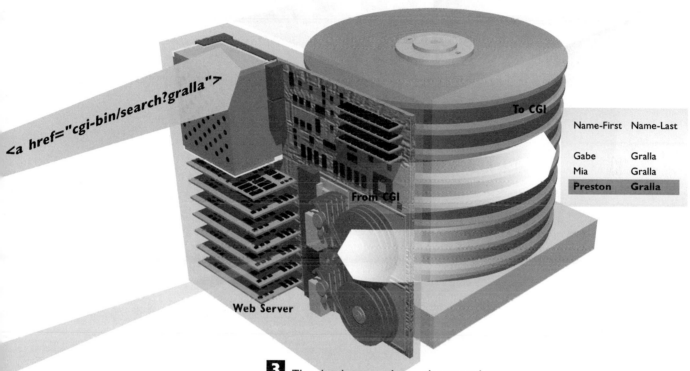

<a href="cgi-bin/search?gralla">

To CGI

From CGI

Web Server

Name-First	Name-Last
Gabe	Gralla
Mia	Gralla
Preston	Gralla

3 The database retrieves the record or records that match the search criteria. The database record might contain text and numeric data as well as references to graphics or other data types.

How .NET and Web Services Work

WEB services, and its cousin, .NET, are little known technologies that use the Internet to dramatically increase businesses' and individuals' productivity. They allow programs and services to be run remotely across the Internet, and also allow services to be delivered automatically to people's desktops. The technologies are extremely malleable and can be used for a wide variety of purposes. For example, web services can be used to automatically deliver up-to-the-minute weather and stock information to someone's computer, and they can also be used to automatically tie together the computer systems of business partners, so that they can easily exchange goods, services, and information.

The two technologies are much talked about, much hyped, and frequently misunderstood. But throw away all the hype, and they're simply modular software components wrapped inside a specific set of Internet communications protocols, which can be run across the Internet. They're quietly revolutionary technologies, because they in essence can do away with the need for an operating system to run software. Specific Internet protocols and web browsers, instead, work much like an operating system and let people run applications and use services inside their web browsers.

While the term web services is often used broadly, in fact, the only true web services are those that use a number of specific protocols and technologies. At the heart of web services is the Extensible Markup Language (XML), which is used to describe a web service, and then help find and run a specific web service. (For more information about XML, turn to Chapter 19, "How Markup Languages Work.") Simple Object Access Protocol (SOAP) is the web services communication standard. Other important technologies, explained in the following spread, include the Web Services Description Language (WSDL) and Universal Description, Discovery and Integration (UDDI). The web service itself is a piece of software written in a language such as Java, and that can be found and run over the Internet using these protocols and technologies.

Web services and .NET share a very similar architecture. Both require that applications be written and then run using XML, SOAP, WSDL, UDDI, and related technologies. The difference is in how the actual applications are written and run. Web services are typically written in Java, and can be run in any browser that has Java capabilities.

Understanding .NET and Web Services

WSDL

Stock Analyzer

contents may include: .NET code use with caution some parts indigestible

© 2005 Michael Troller Design

217.109.78.93

Service Descriptor

2 A language called the Web Services Description Language (WSDL) is used to create a description of the service. The description includes information such as the exact location of the service (where on an application server it resides) and how to run the service, as well as higher-level information, such as what business is hosting the service, the kind of service it is, keywords associated with the service, and similar information. This service descriptor is in the Extended Markup Language (XML), and includes all information necessary for someone to find and run the service.

Application

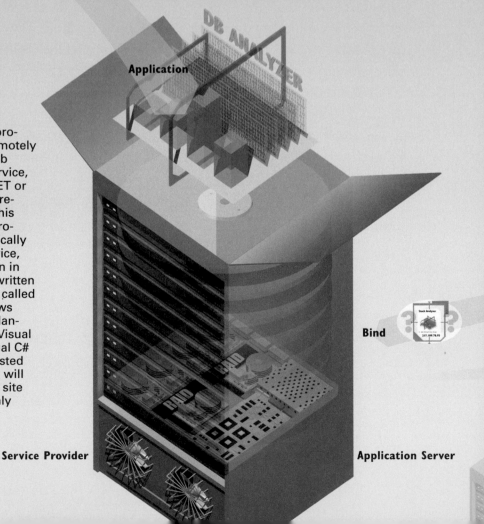

Bind

1 Web services and .NET allow programs or services to be run remotely across the Internet, using a web browser. First the program, service, or applet that will be run in .NET or as a web service needs to be created. (Throughout the rest of this illustration, we'll refer to the program, service, or applet generically as a "service.") For a web service, the service is frequently written in Java. For .NET, it is generally written using a development platform called Visual Studio .NET, which allows developers to use a variety of languages, including Microsoft's Visual Basic .NET, C++ .NET, and Visual C# .NET. After it is written, it is posted to an application server, which will deliver it when requested. The site hosting the service is commonly called a service provider.

Service Provider

Application Server

Service Registry

3 Using a communications protocol called the Simple Object Access Protocol (SOAP), the service descriptor is published to a Service Registry. The registry uses Universal Description, Discovery and Integration (UDDI), a group of specifications that lets companies publish information about themselves and their web services, and lets others search through that information in order to find a web service, bind to it, and run it.

Find a Web Service

SOAP Protocol

Service Descriptor

4 When a person or company wants to find and run a web service, they search through the Service Registry for it, using the SOAP protocol. (The person or company looking to find and run a web service is called a Service Requestor.)

Service Requestor

5 They find the Service Descriptor that matches a web service they want to run. The Service Descriptor informs the Service Requestor where to find the web service, and how to run it.

SOAP Protocol

Web Service

6 Based on that information, the Service Requestor "binds" to the web service, and runs it.

CHAPTER

26

How Grid Computing Works

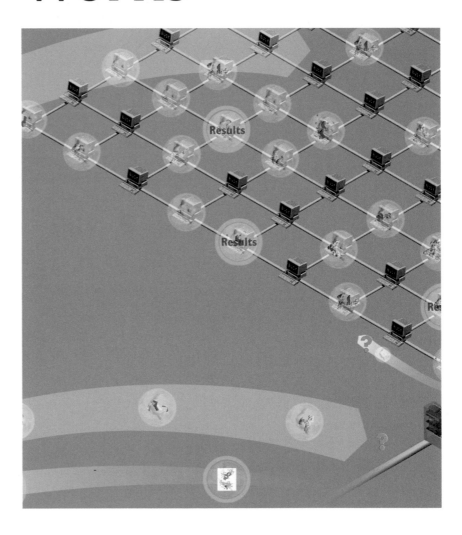

THE world's biggest supercomputer is not an individual machine with massive processing power. Instead, it's a collection of tens of thousands of normal-sized individual computers like the one sitting on your desk, whose power can be combined into one giant system.

That's the promise of grid computing. And it's not just a promise. It's already working.

The theory behind grid computing is fairly straightforward. It combines the computational power of many computers, servers, databases, and other computing resources in a network or across the Internet. A main server or servers breaks up large computational tasks, such as solving complex problems relating to biochemistry, into smaller subtasks and sends those subtasks to computers that are part of the grid. When those computers have idle time and resources, they perform the subtask, and send the results back to the server or servers, which collates all the subtasks and solves the computational problem.

There have been many grid implementations, but the largest and best-known so far is the Search for Extraterrestrial Intelligence project (SETI@home), overseen by the University of California, Berkeley. In it, four million people in 226 countries downloaded a screensaver that kicked in when their computer was idle, and analyzed radio signals for signs of extraterrestrial intelligence. SETI@home scientists claim that the combined resources of its computing grid were more powerful than all the supercomputers on the planet combined. Similar grids have been used for mapping genomes and analyzing proteins.

Similar grids, however, will be increasingly used by corporations to apply their own computing resources to large problems. In this kind of architecture, all the computers in a corporation would register themselves with the corporate grid, and when idle time was detected in computers, they could be applied to other tasks. For example, if a server is normally used only a few times a month to process a corporate payroll, it could be used for other computing tasks when it would be otherwise idle if used as part of a grid.

Companies such as IBM and Sun are increasingly using grid computing as well. For example, IBM has launched a multibillion dollar "on-demand computing" program in which businesses can outsource computing tasks to IBM, and IBM in turn uses a grid to do that processing.

To date, most grid projects use their own individual architectures. However, there is an attempt to create a set of standards that can be used when building grids and grid projects. The standards are being established under the aegis of the Globus Project, which already has a set of proposed standards out, and has released toolkits that developers can use to help build grids.

It's likely that in the long term, grid computing will become a standard part of the way that businesses and the Internet work. It will have moved from the search for extraterrestrial life to the center of corporate life.

Understanding How Grid Computing Works

1 Grid computing technology is relatively new, is a work in progress, and can be applied in many different ways. In this illustration, we show how a person or a company might use it to request that a complex computational problem be solved using the grid, or to get the combined computing resources of the grid to solve some other problem. First, the person or company sends a request to the grid with details of the problem that needs to be solved. This can be sent in a variety of ways, including over the Internet using a web form. The request can be sent to the grid using XML.

2 The request is handled by the grid's main cluster server. This server examines the request, and checks the grid's resources to see which servers currently have resources available to them to apply to the problem. It breaks up the request into discrete computational subtasks. It then sends those subtask requests over the Internet to local cluster servers.

Current task:
PPA folding sequence 819

?

Results

Results

Main cluster server

7 The main cluster server combines all the completed subtasks into a solution to the requested problem. It then compiles the completed task into a form that the requester can understand and sends the results back to the requester.

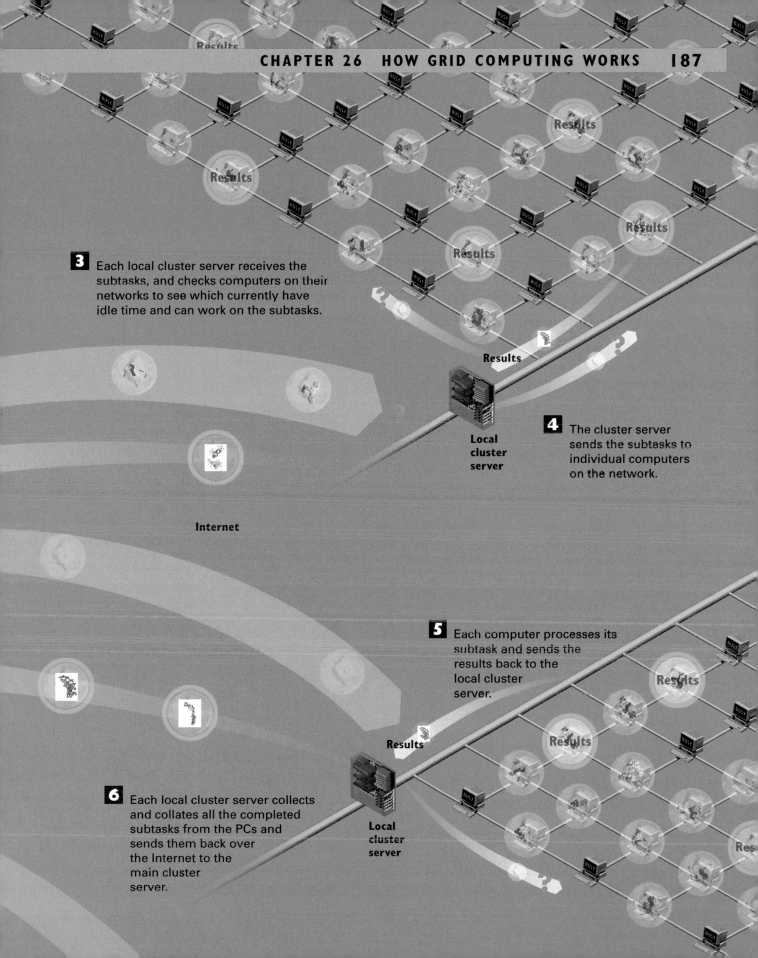

3 Each local cluster server receives the subtasks, and checks computers on their networks to see which currently have idle time and can work on the subtasks.

Results

Local cluster server

4 The cluster server sends the subtasks to individual computers on the network.

Internet

5 Each computer processes its subtask and sends the results back to the local cluster server.

Results

6 Each local cluster server collects and collates all the completed subtasks from the PCs and sends them back over the Internet to the main cluster server.

Local cluster server

P A R T

5

USING THE WORLD WIDE WEB

THE technologies that underpin the World Wide Web—such as HTML, hypertext, and so on—are remarkable things, as you've seen in Part 4, "How the World Wide Web Works." But the true point of the Web isn't its underlying technologies. Instead, it's how those technologies are put to use.

In this section of the book, you'll look in detail at some of the most interesting uses of the Web, everything from how Google works to how mapping sites work, and how so-called *wikis* work.

Chapter 27, "How Internet Searching Works," examines Internet search engines. The Internet contains such a vast amount of information that it's often impossible to find exactly what you want. Search engines look through the entire Internet—not only web pages, but other sites such as newsgroups—and find information you're looking for, based on keywords you type.

Chapter 28, "How Google Works," takes a look behind the scenes at Google, the most popular search site on the Internet, and a site that has changed the way that most people use the Internet. Before Google, finding information was, to put it mildly, a challenge. After Google's launch, it's far easier to find what you want. The chapter shows you exactly how Google searches the Internet for you. And it also takes a look at the dark side of Google as well—the vast amount of information that it can gather about you as you use the site.

Chapter 29, "How Map Sites Work," shows you how mapping sites such as MapQuest and Google Earth work. These sites are remarkable; type in a location, or two locations, and they come back in seconds with a detailed map, or map and directions between the two locations. As you'll see, much of the work is not done on the Internet itself, but rather first by companies that provide the actual mapping data to the map sites.

Chapter 30, " How Wikis and the Wikipedia Work," takes a look at one of the more recent and intriguing uses of the Internet. A wiki is a site that allows multiple people to cooperatively update information. The biggest wiki in the world, by far, is the Wikipedia, which is a free, online encyclopedia written, updated, and edited by thousands of volunteers across the globe.

CHAPTER

27

How Internet Searching Works

AN enormous amount of information is available on the Internet, but there is so little organization to the Internet that it can seem impossible to find the information or documents you want. A number of solutions have sprung up to solve the problem. Two of the most popular are indexes and search engines.

Indexes present a highly structured way to find information. They enable you to browse through information by categories, such as arts, computers, entertainment, sports, and so on. In a web browser, you click a category, and you are then presented with a series of subcategories. Under sports, for example, you'll find baseball, basketball, football, hockey, and soccer. Depending on the size of the index, several layers of subcategories might be available. When you get to the subcategory you're interested in, you are presented with a list of relevant documents. To get to those documents, you click the links to them. Yahoo! (http://www.yahoo.com/) is the largest and most popular index on the Internet. Yahoo! and other indexes also enable you to search by typing words that describe the information you're looking for. You then get a set of search results—links to documents that match your search. To get the information, you click a link.

Another popular way of finding information is to use *search engines*, also called *search tools* and sometimes called *web crawlers* or *spiders*. Search engines operate differently from indexes. They are essentially massive databases that cover wide swaths of the Internet. Search engines don't present information in a hierarchical fashion. Instead, you search through them as you would a database, by typing keywords that describe the information you want. (Many search engines now also include indexes as well as search tools, but they are primarily used for searching.)

For most people, Internet searching means only one site—Google. (For information about how Google works, see Chapter 28, "How Google Works." But, in fact there are other popular search engines as well, such as Ask.com. Although the specifics of how search sties operate differ somewhat, generally they are all composed of three parts: at least one spider, which crawls across the Internet gathering information; a database, which contains all the information the spiders gather; and a search tool, which people use to search through the database. Search engines are constantly updated to present the most up-to-date information, and they hold enormous amounts of information. Search engines extract and index information differently. Some index every word they find in a document, for example, and others index only the key 100 words in each document. Some index the size of the document; some index the title, headings, subheadings, and so on.

Additionally, each search engine returns results in a different way. Some weigh the results to show the relevance of the documents; some show the first several sentences of the document; and some show the title of the document, as well as the URL.

Each of the many Internet search engines and indexes have their own strengths and weaknesses. To cast the widest possible net when looking for information, you should search as many of them as you can. The problem is that doing so is too time-consuming. So a type of software called *meta-search* software has been developed. With this software, such as Copernic, you type a search on your own computer. The software then submits the search to many Internet search engines, indexes simultaneously, compiles the results for you, and then delivers the results to your computer. To visit any resulting site, just click the link, the same as if you were on an index or a search engine site.

How Internet Search Engines Work

1 Each search engine uses a crawler or spider with its own set of rules guiding how documents are gathered. Some follow every link on every home page they find and then, in turn, examine every link on each of those new home pages, and so on. Some spiders ignore links that lead to graphics files, sound files, and animation files. Some ignore links to certain Internet resources, such as newsgroups, and some are instructed to look primarily for the most popular home pages. It can take a spider from several seconds to many minutes to crawl each site it finds, depending on the size and complexity of the site.

Gathered:
183 documents: 327 hyperlinks
Discarded:
23 WAIS databases 4,729 graphics files

2 As the spider discovers documents and URLs, software agents are instructed to get the URLs and documents and send information about them to indexing software.

Gathered:
487 documents: 938 hyperlinks
Discarded:
69 WAIS databases 2,019 graphics files

Database

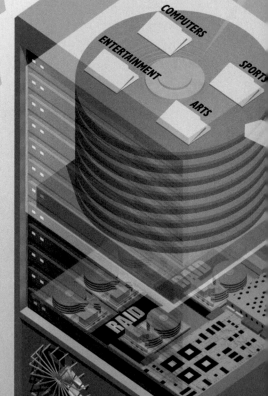

3 The indexing software receives the documents and URLs from the agent. The software extracts information from the documents and indexes it by putting the information into a database. Each search engine extracts and indexes different types of information. Some index every word in each document, for example, but others index only the key 100 words in each; some index the size of the document and the number of words in it; some index the title, headings, and subheadings; and so on. The kind of index built determines what type of searching can be done with the search engine and how the information will be displayed.

6 When you click a link to one of the documents that interests you, you're sent straight to that document. The document itself is not in the database or on the search engine site.

EMANCIPATION PROCLAMATION

Whereas on the twenty-second day of September, in the year of our Lord one thousand eight hundred and sixty-two, a proclamation was issued by the President of the United States, containing, among other things, the following, to wit:

"That on the first day of January, in the year of our Lord one thousand eight hundred and sixty-three, all persons held as slaves within any State or designated part of a State, the people whereof shall then be in rebellion against the United States, shall be then, thenceforward, and forever free; and the Executive Government of the United States, including the military and naval authority thereof, will recognize and maintain the freedom of such persons, or any of them, in any efforts they may make for their actual freedom.

Web Page

"Request: Lincoln.html"

5 The database is searched based on the criteria you've set. Results are returned in HTML pages. Each search engine returns results in a different way. Some weigh the results to show how relevant the document is to your search; some show the URL, as well as the first several sentences of the document; and some show the title of the document and the URL.

4 When you visit a search engine and want to search the Internet for information, you type words on a web page that describe the information you want to find. Depending on the search engine, more than just keywords can be used. For example, you can search by date and other criteria with some search engines.

Server

How Meta-Search Software Works

 Meta-search software is software that sits on your computer and enables you to search through many Internet search engines simultaneously and to view and use the results. When you want to search for something on the Internet, you type descriptive words or a search term into the meta-search software.

Meta-Search Software

Query	
?	Enter your search word(s) or phrase:
	Preston's Picks

Preston's Picks

http://www.hotfiles/home.html
http://www.hotfiles/index.html
http://www.hotfiles/prespick/presmain.html

Preston's Picks

http://www.hotfiles/index.html
http://www.hotfiles/prespick/presmain.html

5 The agent sends the results back to the meta-search software. After the agent sends its report back to the meta-search software, it goes to another search engine and submits a search in that engine's proper syntax and again sends the results back to the meta-search software.

Preston's Picks

http://www.hotfiles/home.html
http://www.hotfiles/index.html
http://www.hotfiles/prespick/0401/pc.html

Preston's Picks

http://www.hotfiles/prespick/0401/pc.html
http://www.hotfiles/prespick/pres0401.html
http://www.hotfiles/prespick/0401/pc.html

6 The meta-search software takes all the results from all the search engines and examines them for duplicate results. If it finds duplicate results, it deletes them. It then displays the results of the search, ranking each *hit* by the likelihood that it contains the information you requested. It figures out the ranking by examining the title of the site found, the header information in the site, and the words on the site.

Results

		Title	Address	Rank	Hit Count	Date Found
🖅	☐	ZDNet Software Library - Top Rated Home & ...	http://www.hotfiles.com/home.html	8	2	5/8/98 4:16:10
		write(''); Home & Education options Make the grade in math. You need not be a believer to appreciate Bible's poetry and parables.				
🖅	☐	ZDNet Software Library - Top Rated Shareware	http://www.hotfiles.com/index.html	2	3	5/8/98 4:16:10
		.leftnav2 { color: #FFFF00; } .leftnav { color: white; } = 3.0) {btype=1;} else if (browser_name == Microsoft Internet Explorer && browser_version = 3.0) {btype=1;} // popup window //InterURL = url; if (btype==1) { var ApplyWindow = window. Our collection of top-rated b...				
🖅	■	ZDNet Software Library - Preston's Picks	http://www.hotfiles.com/prespick/presmain.html	1	5	5/8/98 4:16:10
		Preston Gralla, ZDNet's "shareware guru," is executive editor of software for ZDNet. Each month, Preston selects his favorite new shareware programs from the ZDNet Software Library, giving you a chance to download the very best we have to offer.				
🖅	☐	Preston's Picks for April	http://www.hotfiles.com/prespick/0498/pc.html	5	1	5/8/98 4:16:10
		It also lets you create playlists of your files, so that you can in essence put together your own multimedia album. .. - Chris Wilson Fakalofa, Kia ora, Preston, ... - Sione My sympathies to owners of Win.				
🖅	☐	Preston's Picks for April	http://www.hotfiles.com/prespick/.../pres0498.html	6	2	5/8/98 4:16:10
		var cleargif_date=(new Date()). .. - Preston Gralla Clyde: We use cookies for our ... - Preston Gralla Just wanted to say THANKS for ... - Larry D. Stauffer Hey Clyde, you should have thr.				
🖅	☐	ZDNet Software Library - Preston's Picks for ...	http://www.hotfiles.com/prespick/pres1097.html	6	1	5/8/98 4:16:10
		ZDNet Software Library - Preston's Picks for October Join for FREE! Editors' Picks / Preston's Picks Downloads Internet Explorer 4.... 10/06/97				

2 The meta-search software sends many "agents" out onto the Internet simultaneously—depending on the speed of your connection, usually from 4 to 8, but it can be as many as 32 or more different agents. Each agent contacts one or more search engines or indexes, such as Yahoo!, Lycos, or Excite.

3 The agents are intelligent enough to know how each search engine functions—for example, whether a particular engine allows for Boolean searches (searching by using AND, OR, and other variables). The agents also know the exact syntax each engine requires. The agents put the search terms in the proper syntax required at each specific search engine and submit the search—they don't have to fill out forms, as users normally do at search engines.

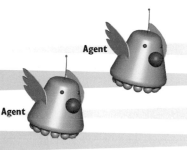

Agent

av.yahoo.com/query?p=preston%27s+pickshc=0&hs=0

http://www.hotfiles/home.html
http://www.hotfiles/index.html
http://www.hotfiles/prespick/presmain.html

Agent

www.altavista.com/cgi-bin/query?pg=q&what=web&kl=ZZ&q=preston%27s+picks

http://www.hotfiles/index.html
http://www.hotfiles/prespick/presmain.html

4 The search engines report the results of the search to each agent. The results typically include the URL of each site that matches the search, and often a summary of information found on the site, the date the site was last updated, and other data.

Agent

www.lycos.com/cgi-bin/pursuit?matchmode=and&cat=lycosquery=preston%27s+picks

http://www.hotfiles/home.html
http://www.hotfiles/index.html
http://www.hotfiles/prespick/0401/pc.html

Agent

search.excite.com/searxh.gw?search=preston%27s+picks

http://www.hotfiles/prespick/0401/pc.html
http://www.hotfiles/prespick/pres0401.html
http://www.hotfiles/prespick/0401/pc.html

Yahoo!

Alta-Vista

Lycos

Excite

Web Page

7 You browse through the results in the meta-search software. When you see a page you're interested in, you double-click it. You then are sent to that site.

CHAPTER

28

How Google Works

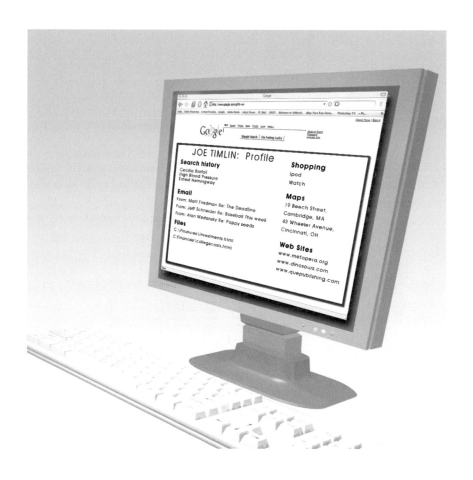

TO many people, Google *is* the Internet. The first thing they do when they go online is fire up their browser, head to Google, and start searching.

It's easy to forget that things weren't always this way. The company was founded in 1998 and became the largest search engine on the Internet in 2000, so in the grand scheme of things, the site is a relatively new phenomenon.

There were plenty of search engines around before Google burst on the scene, some of them still in existence, and some of them all but forgotten? Internet old-timers may remember when Alta Vista was the king of the search engines among those who prized fast, accurate searches.

It took Google only two years from launch to becoming the most popular search site on the Internet. What happened? Why did Google become so popular?

This is one instance of where better technology trumped marketing. Google became more popular because it was far better than any other search site, and word quickly spread by word of mouth.

So what was Google's "secret sauce"? It certainly wasn't the interface. Google's page is about as simple as it comes—in essence, just a search box.

The secret to Google's speed and accuracy are the algorithms it uses when it searches. It uses many factors to determine which are the most relevant pages that match your search, including how popular the page is, where the search term is found within the page, and similar rules. Google's breakthrough was that it doesn't stop at only considering the page's popularity. It also looks at the quality of pages that link to that page. So if there are many well-regarded popular pages that link to a site, that site will be considered more important than a site that has less-important, less-popular pages linking to it.

Google started as a search engine, but it's become much more than that. It's practically its own universe. It has sites for helping you buy things online (Froogle), a mapping site (Google Maps), an email service (Gmail), and much more. New services are introduced practically every month.

If you do a lot of searches on Google, and use many Google services, Google can quickly know a good deal about you. One search term by itself might not mean much. But how about 10? Twenty? Five hundred? By the time you enter 500 searches, and click on thousands of results, the site could very easily put together a pretty comprehensive profile about you. Do you search frequently for information about high-blood pressure? Do you click on sites that criticize the president? What kind of entertainment do you search for? In a very short time, your searches can build up a fairly definitive profile about you.

All this is not to say that Google uses this information for nefarious purposes, or even that they necessarily gather this information. Google doesn't keep track of all your searches, unless you specifically tell it to do that. So why do it? Because it lets you re-visit that list, and makes it easy to keep going back to searches you've already done, or even search within those searches.

To date, Google doesn't necessarily track everything that it could about you. And it doesn't create personal profiles about you, to sell to the highest bidder. But there are those who worry it might in the future.

How Google *Searches* the Internet

1 When you search using Google, you're actually searching through an index of web pages. To gather the raw material for the index, Google's web-crawling robot, called Googlebot, sends a requests to a web server for a web page. It then downloads the page. Googlebot runs on many computers simultaneously, and constantly requests and receives web pages, making thousands of requests per second. In fact, Googlebot makes requests more slowly than its full capability, because if it operated full-throttle, it would overwhelm many web servers, and the servers would not be able to deliver pages quickly enough to users.

Crawling the Web

Indexable text

Googlebot

Web page

Web server

THE INTERNET

2 When Googlebot downloads the page, it finds all the links on it, and adds them to a queue, where each of those links will also be crawled and gathered. For each of those new pages it crawls, it gathers links, and crawls them as well, and continues gathering pages in this manner. This technique, called *deep crawling*, lets Googlebot find every page on every site it encounters, and also lets it find new sites to crawl.

3 To make sure that Google's index is as up to date as possible, Googlebot needs to crawl the same pages continually. Sites that frequently change, such as news sites, need to be crawled constantly throughout the day, while sites that rarely change may only need to be crawled once a month. Googlebot performs calculations on pages it crawls, determining how often they change, and based on that, decides how often to crawl that site. Pages that frequently change and so must be visited frequently are called *fresh crawls*.

LINK QUEUE

4 Googlebot extracts the full text of every page it visits and sends that information to the indexer.

CRAWL SCHEDULE	
PAGE	FREQUENCY
Amazon Home	10 min.
CNN	5 min
History of Aardvarks	Monthly
New York Time Page 1	Daily

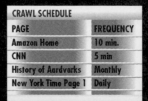

The Indexer

5 The indexer receives the text, and stores it in its database. The index is sorted alphabetically by search term. Each index entry contains the list of pages on which the term appears. The indexer doesn't index commonly used words, called *stop words*, such as *the, on, is, or, of,* and *why,* and doesn't store single digits, single letters, and some punctuation marks.

INDEXER

Aardvark

RESULTS

Performing the Search

6 When you visit Google, the page you see is delivered to you by a normal web server. When you type in your query, it's sent back to the web server. The web server then takes the query and forwards it to Google's index servers.

7 Google's index servers receive your request and match it to the most relevant documents. The method Google uses to match queries to documents is Google's "secret sauce," the key to its ability to return the most relevant results. Google uses hundreds of factors to decide which documents are most relevant, including how popular the page is (called Google's PageRank), where the search term is found within the page, and if you use multiple search terms, how close those terms are to one another in the page. It doesn't stop at examining the sheer popularity of a page. If a page is linked to from popular pages, that page will have a higher rank than if it is linked to from unpopular pages.

8 When the index servers determine the results of the search, they send the query to Google's doc servers. They retrieve the stored documents, which include site names and links, and snippets that summarize each page.

9 The doc servers send the results back to the web server, which in turn sends the results to the person doing the search. The user browses through the results and can click a link to get to any page.

Web masters who don't want their sites to be searchable via Google can instruct Google not to index their sites. To do it, they create a text file called robots.txt containing only these two lines and put it in the root directory:

```
User-agent: *
Disallow /
```

That tells all search engines, not just Googlebot, to stay away. They can also tell Googlebot or other search engines to not search their site by putting this HTML tag into the <head> section of the HTML for their web page:

```
<META name="ROBOTS" content="NOINDEX, NOFOLLOW" />
```

What Google Knows About You

1 This illustration shows many of the kinds of information that Google can find out about you. Note that Google does not sell this information to other sites, and does not use it to create personal profiles about you. But it gives you a sense of what the largest and most successful search engine in the world knows about you as use it.

2 If you turn on a Google feature called Search History, Google will keep track of every single search you perform when using the search engine, and keep that record on its servers, so it will know the history of your Internet travels, and your interests.

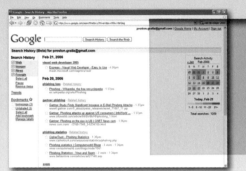

3 If you use Gmail, all your incoming and outgoing mail is stored on Gmail servers. In addition, Google computers examine all incoming mail, and analyze its text, to help it decide what ads to embed in the mail.

4 If you install Google Desktop, a piece of software that searches your PC in the same way Google searches the Web, Google could theoretically know all the contents of your hard disk.

JOE TIMLIN:

Search history
Cecilia Bartoli
High Blood Pressure
Ernest Hemingway

Email
From: Matt Friedman Re: The Dee
From: Jeff Schneider Re: Baseball
From: Alan Medansky Re: Poppy s

Files
C:\Finances\investments.html
C:Finances\collegecosts.html

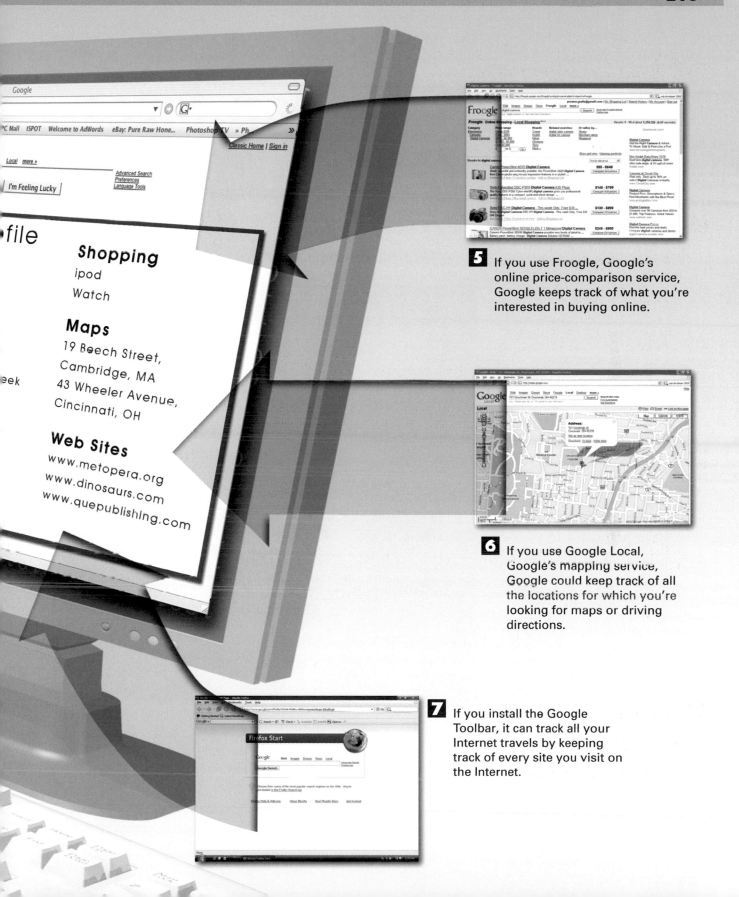

5 If you use Froogle, Google's online price-comparison service, Google keeps track of what you're interested in buying online.

6 If you use Google Local, Google's mapping service, Google could keep track of all the locations for which you're looking for maps or driving directions.

7 If you install the Google Toolbar, it can track all your Internet travels by keeping track of every site you visit on the Internet.

CHAPTER
29

How Map Sites Work

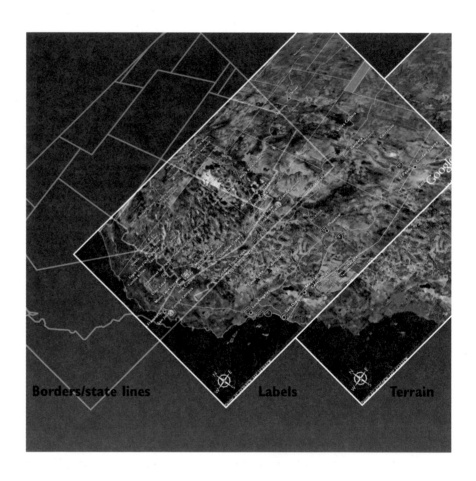

Borders/state lines   Labels   Terrain

NEED to find driving directions from Cincinnati to Seattle? Looking for Afghani restaurants in Cambridge, Massachusetts? Want to get a detailed a map of Lubbock, Texas?

All that, and more, are available on mapping sites on the Internet. There are a number of mapping websites you can visit, but the two most popular are MapQuest and Google Maps. MapQuest is the older and more established of the two, and the more targeted as well. It serves up maps and directions, but not much else. Google Maps, on the other hand, lets you also find local information on the maps you're looking at, such as nearby restaurants, museums, and more.

Although mapping sites look quite different from one another, and have different interfaces, if you take a look under the hood, they all operate relatively similarly.

Mapping sites, as a general rule, do not actually create the underlying mapping information themselves. Instead, they get that information from a commercial provider of mapping information. These providers typically sell mapping information not only to map sites, but to private businesses that need mapping information as well.

The providers regularly update the maps they sell to mapping sites in several different ways. Commonly, they hire people to actually drive the streets, and then update their maps to reflect any new construction, changes in streets and landmarks, and so on.

Map providers give more than just raw mapping information to map sites like MapQuest and Google Maps. They also provide a database that calculates the best driving directions from one point to another. The directions are based on a variety of complex algorithms, but generally they try to find the directions that take the least amount of time to drive, rather than the shortest distance between two points.

Map sites may make use of the same basic mapping databases, or similar databases, but the features they offer to visitors—and the interface they use to deliver those features—are quite different.

MapQuest, for example, uses a simple, basic HTML interface, and concentrates on directions and maps. Google Maps, on the other hand, uses a far more interactive interface that allows visitors to more easily zoom in and zoom out, switch to a satellite view, and navigate through maps by dragging with a mouse. Google Maps does this by using a technique called AJAX. (For more details about AJAX, see the illustration "How AJAX Works" in Chapter 19, "How Markup Languages Work.")

Google also offers a tool more sophisticated than mere maps, Google Earth. Google Earth lets you "fly" to any location on earth in a virtual tour, using high-resolution photos and animations.

How Map Sites Work

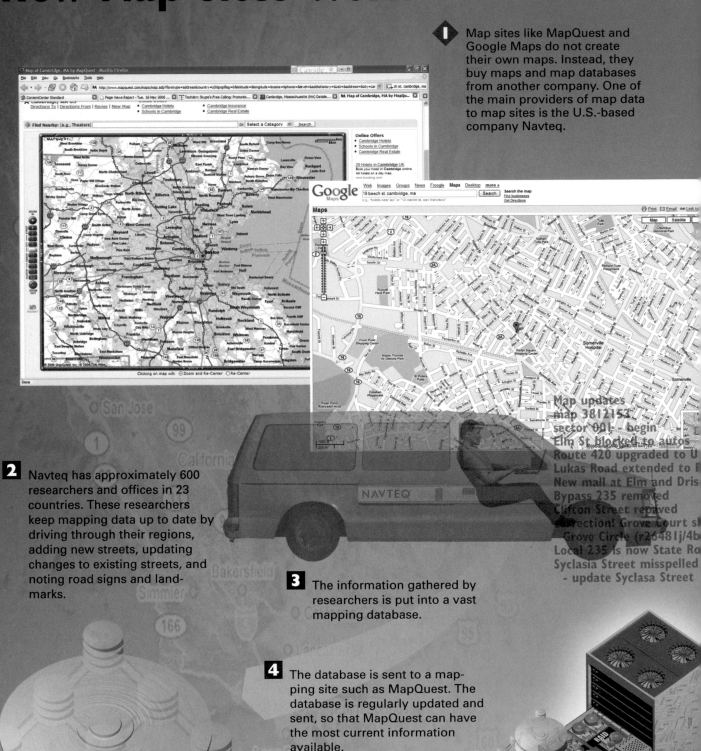

1 Map sites like MapQuest and Google Maps do not create their own maps. Instead, they buy maps and map databases from another company. One of the main providers of map data to map sites is the U.S.-based company Navteq.

2 Navteq has approximately 600 researchers and offices in 23 countries. These researchers keep mapping data up to date by driving through their regions, adding new streets, updating changes to existing streets, and noting road signs and land-marks.

3 The information gathered by researchers is put into a vast mapping database.

4 The database is sent to a mapping site such as MapQuest. The database is regularly updated and sent, so that MapQuest can have the most current information available.

5 When you type in a request for driving directions on MapQuest, your request goes to a Geocoding server. This server's job is to determine what exact maps need to be displayed. It takes the addresses that you type in, and determines their exact longitude and latitude coordinates.

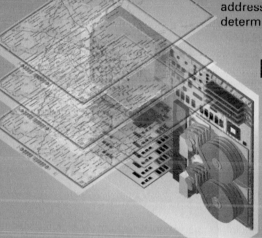

Directions from "A" to "B"?

Driving directions?

6 It sends those coordinates to a mapping server, and requests the map that matches the set of beginning and ending coordinates. The mapping server fetches the map information, and sends it to a routing server. The routing server examines the starting and ending addresses. It uses a complex set of algorithms to determine the fastest route.

7 The algorithms consider many factors. They consider the length of each segment, and the expected average speed to travel that segment. Each segment also has a "costing," which calculates how likely a driver is likely to be slowed down. "Costing" counts things such as turns, stoplights, and speed zones. It assigns a "costing" number from 1 to 5 for each road segment. A 1 is least likely to have delays (an interstate highway, for example), and a 5 is most likely to have delays (a local road, for example.)

Route B is usually fastest. Here is the map and step-by-step driving directions.

Route A   Route B   Route C

8 Based on its algorithms, it calculates the driving directions. The directions and accompanying map are delivered to the person requesting them—all in a matter of seconds.

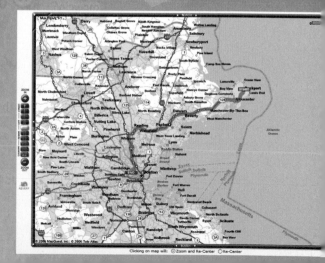

How Google Earth Works

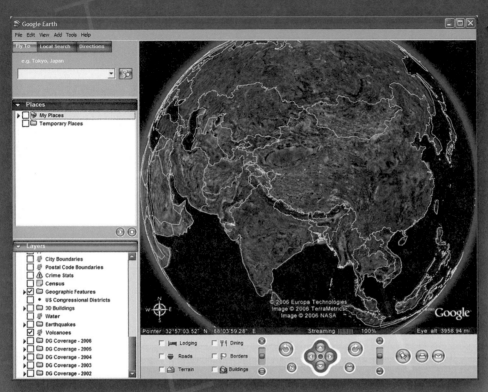

1 Google Earth was initially created by a company called Keyhole, and was called Earth Viewer. Google bought the company and its software, and renamed the software Google Earth. Keyhole continues to produce the software. It gets photos used in Google Earth in many different ways, such as via airplane and satellite. In some instances, it has gotten photos using hot air balloons and kites.

2 One way Google Earth gets photos is via aerial surveys. A gyroscopic-stabilized camera is placed in an airplane that flies at between 15,000 feet and 30,000 feet. The exact height at which it flies depends on the resolution of the images. The plan files a specific route over the area to be mapped, and takes a series of overlapping photographs. The overlap is used so that enough detail can be provided to remove any distortions that are caused by variations in the shape of the Earth's surface.

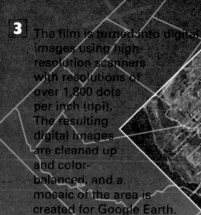

3 The film is turned into digital images using high-resolution scanners with resolutions of over 1,800 dots per inch (dpi). The resulting digital images are cleaned up and color-balanced, and a mosaic of the area is created for Google Earth.

4 On top of the photographs, Google adds layers of information, such as parks, country borders, road names, schools, museums, and other information. It gathers this information from many sources, including government agencies and commercial data providers.

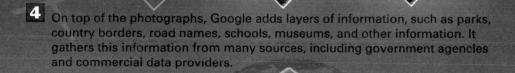

5 To use Google Earth, you need to first download and install the Google Earth software.

6 When you run Google Earth, the photographs and maps are not on your local computer. Instead, they come from Google's servers, which have many terabytes of mapping data and photographs.

30

How Wikis and the Wikipedia Work

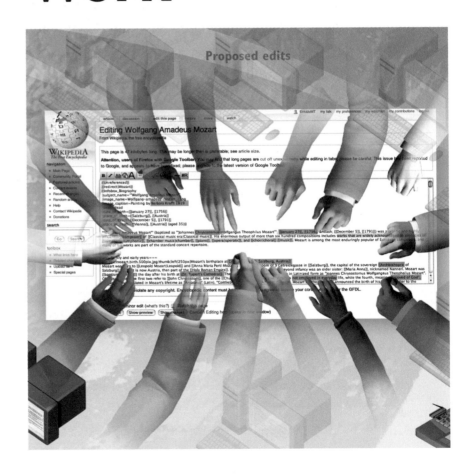

IF you had to get to the core of the Internet's primary purpose, it would come down to this: the ability to find information and share information with others.

There's no better place to see that mission in action than in *wikis*, and especially the well-known *Wikipedia*. A wiki is a website that lets groups of people work together to create and edit bits of information, and then lets anyone who visits the wiki view that information.

That may sound abstract, so let's take the best-known example of a wiki, the Wikipedia at www.wikipedia.org. The Wikipedia, as its name implies, is an huge online encyclopedia that anyone can use and edit. As of this writing, versions of the Wikipedia are available in ten languages—with the English version alone having more than one million entries and constantly growing.

Anyone can create or edit an entry in the Wikipedia; it depends on a kind of vast communal intelligence to be sure that no errors are made or introduced into it. Volunteers constantly check it for errors and many people with special interests monitor entries to be sure that the Wikipedia stays accurate.

How accurate is it? Surprisingly so, at least measured against traditional encyclopedias. In March 2006, the well-respected science magazine *Nature* performed an in-depth analysis of a wide range of scientific articles from the Wikipedia and the *Encyclopedia Britannica*, and found that they were about equally accurate. The study found that in the 42 entries it tested, "the difference in accuracy was not particularly great: the average science entry in Wikipedia contained around four inaccuracies; Britannica, about three."

That's not to say that the Wikipedia is not prone to abuse, because it is. There have been some well-publicized problems with the site. For example, one article falsely suggested that a one-time assistant to Senator Robert Kennedy may have been involved the senator's assassination. Additionally, podcasting pioneer Adam Curry was accused of editing the podcasting entry to remove references to the work of his competitors. There have been other instances as well. Because of this, some high school and college teachers warn their students not to rely solely on the Wikipedia, and some even ban its use outright.

The Wikipedia is the best-known wiki in the world, but it's far from the only wiki. For example, there is the Wikispecies (http://species.wikipedia.org/wiki/Main_Page), a wiki about the species of life on earth; the Wikiquote (http://en.wikiquote.org/wiki/Main_Page), a wiki of quotes; and the Wiktionary (http://en.wiktionary.org/wiki/Main_Page), a wiki dictionary.

Wikis are making their way into the corporate world as well. Companies have set up internal wikis for providing technical help and support, to help collaborate on work, and for many other purposes as well. Expect that in the future, wikis will be used even more as well.

How the Wikipedia Works

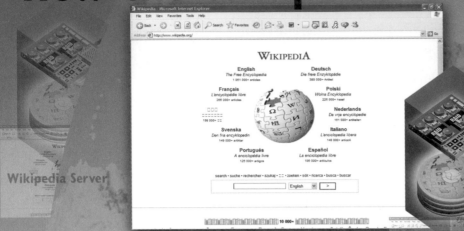

1 The Wikipedia is so popular and visited so frequently that it needs to be hosted on literally hundreds of servers all over the world, including in the United States, France, Amsterdam, and Korea.

2 The Wikipedia, like other wikis, is a communal effort, and is written and edited by multiple people. Anyone who wants to edit or add to an entry in the Wikipedia can click the edit this page link at the top of the entry.

3 A form appears that enables the person to make the change. The changes are immediately made live, without anyone checking them.

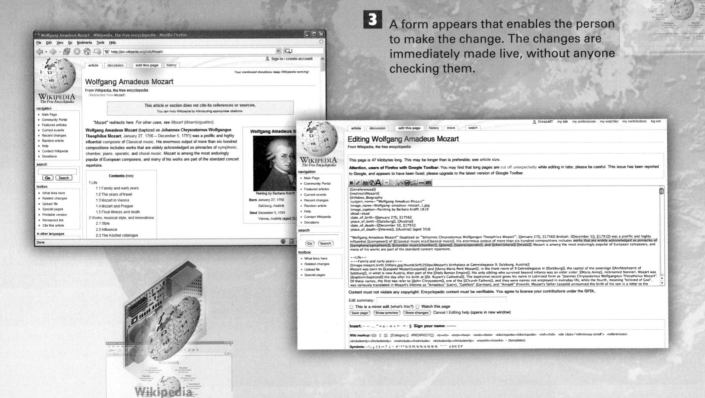

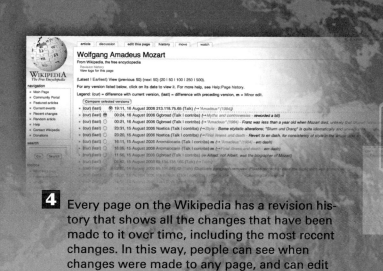

4 Every page on the Wikipedia has a revision history that shows all the changes that have been made to it over time, including the most recent changes. In this way, people can see when changes were made to any page, and can edit them in case they believe errors were introduced.

5 People with an interest in a topic can be automatically alerted whenever a page is changed. They can then check the page to see whether any errors were introduced. When someone wants to be alerted when a page is changed, that page is added to their watchlist.

Proposed edits

Proposed edits

Proposed edits

posed edits

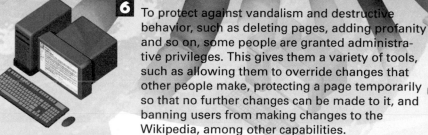

6 To protect against vandalism and destructive behavior, such as deleting pages, adding profanity and so on, some people are granted administrative privileges. This gives them a variety of tools, such as allowing them to override changes that other people make, protecting a page temporarily so that no further changes can be made to it, and banning users from making changes to the Wikipedia, among other capabilities.

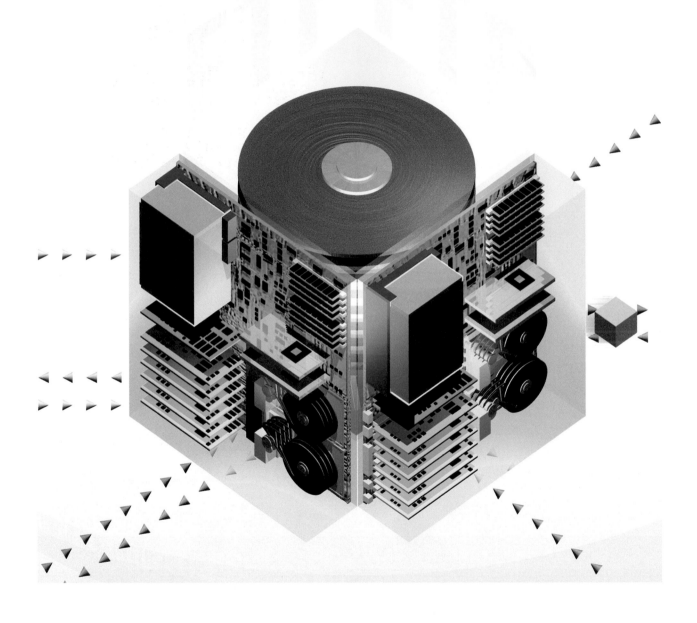

P A R T

USING COMMON INTERNET TOOLS

AN enormous amount of information and entertainment is available on the Internet, but how do you access it? Although using the Internet gets easier every day, it's still not quite as simple as turning on your television or reading your daily newspaper.

The solution is to use a variety of Internet tools. These tools enable you to tap into the colossal resources of the Internet. Some of these resources, such as the World Wide Web, are quite well known. Others, such as FTP (file transfer protocol) are used quite often—and sometimes people use them without even knowing it. Still others, such as Telnet, are not nearly as popular, although they are still useful. Many of these Internet tools predate the Web, but they are still useful today.

For many people, the term *Internet* really means the World Wide Web, but as this section of the book shows, a world exists well beyond the Web. (Turn to Part 4, "How the World Wide Web Works," for information about the Web—the fastest growing and most visible part of the Internet.) And this section of the book also shows you some of the advanced underlying technologies that make the Internet and the World Wide Web a richer, more interactive, more entertaining, and more productive medium. Many of these technologies have changed the very nature of the Internet and have turned it into a truly interactive medium. The technologies also enable web publishers and Internet developers to more effectively present information to people.

This section looks at how the most common and useful Internet tools work.

Chapter 31, "How Telnet Works," covers one of the older Internet technologies, and one that is still in widespread use—Telnet. Telnet enables you to take over the resources of a distant computer while sitting at your own computer. What you type on your keyboard is sent across the Internet to the distant computer, the commands are carried out by the distant computer, and the results of your commands are sent to your own computer screen. It appears as if you're sitting at the distant computer's keyboard. Telnet is used in many ways, notably by libraries making their catalogs available over the Internet. When you log in to a distant computer using Telnet, you often use a menuing system.

Chapter 32, "How FTP Works," covers one of the most popular uses of the Internet—downloading files. Generally, files are downloaded from the Internet using FTP, the Internet protocol. Not only will you look at how FTP works, but you'll also look at how files are compressed and decompressed on the Internet. A compressed file takes less time to be sent over the Internet to your computer. You might not know it, but many times when you're on a website and download a file, you're actually using FTP.

Chapter 33, "How Agents Work," looks at agents on the Internet. *Agents* are programs that do your bidding across the Internet automatically, without you doing anything. They can find the latest news and download it to your computer; they can find you the best deal on the CD you want to buy; they can perform important web maintenance tasks; and more. They are becoming so complex that systems are being developed to enable agents to interact with one another so they can perform jobs cooperatively.

Chapter 34, "How Java, ActiveX, and JavaScript Work," examines three other types of technologies that are transforming the Internet—Java, JavaScript, and ActiveX. These technologies add multimedia and interactivity, but more importantly, they begin to treat the Internet as if it were an extension of your computer. In essence, they enable your computer and the Internet to interact as if they were one large computer system. This enables things such as news tickers, interactive games you can play with others, multimedia presentations combining animations, sounds, music, graphics, and much more.

Java, a computer language developed by Sun Microsystems, enables applications to be run from the Internet. The programs run inside your web browser. One benefit of Java applications is that they can be run on any computer, such as a PC, Macintosh, or Unix workstation.

ActiveX, a competing technology from Microsoft, can also essentially turn the Internet into an extension of your computer. Similar to Java applets, ActiveX controls are downloaded to your computer and run there. They can do anything a normal application can do and can also interact with the Web, the Internet, and other computers connected to the Internet. To run them, a browser that supports ActiveX, such as Internet Explorer, is necessary.

JavaScript, which despite its name is not really related to Java, is simpler than Java and ActiveX and can be written by people who don't have substantial programming experience. JavaScript is commonly used to create interactive forms, site navigation, and similar features.

Finally, Chapter 35, "How CGI Scripting Works," examines CGI (Common Gateway Interface) scripting. This might appear as one of the more mundane Internet technologies, but without it, very little web interactivity would take place. CGI is a standard way in which the Web interacts with outside resources—most commonly, databases. You've probably run CGI scripts many times without knowing it. If you've filled out a form on a web page to register to use a site and then later received an email notification with a password for you to use, you've probably run a CGI script. CGI enables programmers to write code that can access information servers (such as web servers) on the Internet and then send the information to users.

CHAPTER 31

How Telnet Works

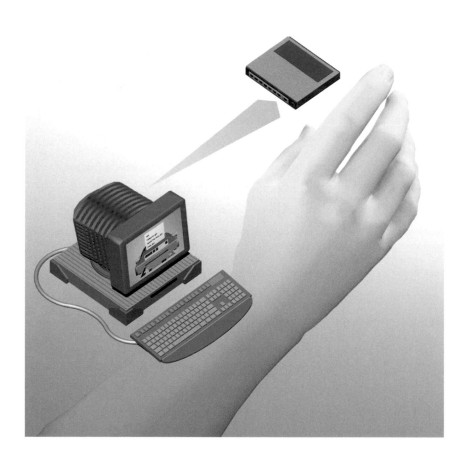

ONE of the more remarkable features of the Internet is the way it lets you use the resources of a distant computer somewhere else in the world. From your own home or office, you can log on to another computer, issue commands just as if you were at that computer's keyboard, and then gain access to all the computer's resources. You do this with an Internet resource called Telnet. Telnet follows a *client/server model*, which means that you run a piece of software on your own PC (the client) to use the resources of a distant server computer. This distant computer is called the *host*.

The host allows many clients to access its resources at the same time; it isn't devoted to a single user. To use Telnet and the host's resources, you must know the address of the Internet host whose resources you want to access.

When you use Telnet, before you can take over the resources of a host computer you typically have to log on to the host. Often, you can use the name "guest" to log on. Some systems require that you also give information about yourself, such as your name and address. And some might require that you choose a username and a password that you will use the next time you log in.

You can access many hosts on the Internet by using Telnet. They are all different computers, so many of them don't work or look alike. For example, some might be Unix-based systems, some might be Windows-based computers, and some might be Macintoshes, as well as a variety of other computers, and they all work and look different from one another. As a way to make things easier, many hosts use a menuing system that gives you access to their resources.

Telnet gives you a way to use those menuing systems by using something called *terminal emulation*. It lets you use your computer to emulate the type of keyboard and computer that each of the different computer systems expect. Different computers often require different kinds of terminal emulation, but one common kind is called VT-100 emulation, so if you use Telnet software and tell it to use VT-100 emulation, that's a safe emulation to use.

Telnet clients are available for all the major operating systems, including Unix, Linux, Macintosh, and all versions of Windows. If you use Unix or the Windows DOS command prompt, you'll typically use a Telnet client by simply typing the word **Telnet** followed by the Internet address of the computer you want to access. For example, if you wanted to gain access to a computer run by the federal government that gives access to the Library of Congress, you'd type **Telnet locis.loc.gov**. A Windows- or Macintosh-based Telnet client is easier to use than a DOS- or Unix-based Telnet client because the former remembers hostnames for you. With clients, you can often keep an address book of hostnames so you can easily revisit them.

Telnet is one of the oldest uses of the Internet, and is not nearly as common today as it was at one time. It is more often used by system administrators to log on to and control systems than it is used by everyday Internet users. Still, it continues to serve its purpose, and has not yet gone away.

Understanding Telnet

I To use Telnet, you need to know the Internet address of the host whose resources you want to use; your Telnet client contacts the host, using its Internet address.

locsis.loc.gov

Router

2 When you contact the host, the distant computer and your computer negotiate how they will communicate with each other. They decide which terminal emulation will be used. Terminal emulation determines how your keyboard will transmit information to the distant computer and how information will be displayed on your screen. It determines, for example, things such as how certain keys like the backspace key will work. VT-100 is the most common type of terminal emulation.

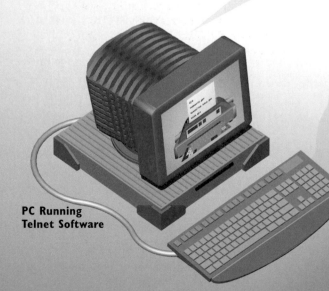

**PC Running
Telnet Software**

3 When a client and a server communicate, they use the Telnet protocol. The Telnet protocol assumes that each end of the connection—the client and the server—is a network virtual terminal (NVT). Each NVT has a virtual "printer" and a virtual "keyboard." The keyboard sends data from one NVT to the other. When you type text on your keyboard, you're using the NVT keyboard. The printer is not really a printer at all— it receives and displays the data on the computer screen. When a distant Telnet connection sends you data and you display it on your screen, it is the printer that displays the information.

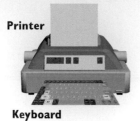

Network Virtual Terminal

Printer

Keyboard

Network Virtual Terminal

Printer

Keyboard

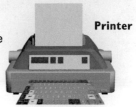

4 Typed text in a Telnet session accumulates in a buffer on your computer. When a complete line of data is ready for transmission, or when you give a command to transmit data (such as pressing the Enter key), the data is sent across the Internet from your NVT keyboard. Along with the data is the host's IP address, which ensures the packet is sent to the proper location.

To: fedworld.gov

from: 137.42.9.68

5 Your IP address is also sent, so that information can be routed back to you. Additionally, specific Telnet commands are sent that the other NVT uses to decide what to do with the data or how to respond to the data. For example, when data is sent from one NVT to another, and certain information must be sent back to the originating NVT for a process to proceed, the Telnet Go Ahead (GA) command is sent.

6 The Telnet host receives the data you've sent. It processes the data and returns to your screen (your NVT printer) the results of using the data or running the command on a distant computer. So, for example, if you type a series of keys with the letters `dir` and press Enter, the distant computer carries out the `dir` command. That computer also returns to your screen the `dir` command and sends the results of running that command on the distant computer.

DIR
fedworld.gov
spacelink.nasa.gov
nasa.gov

DIR

7 Because packets must go through many Internet routers in each direction between your computer and the host, a delay might occur between the time you send a command and the time you see the results on your own computer screen.

32

How FTP Works

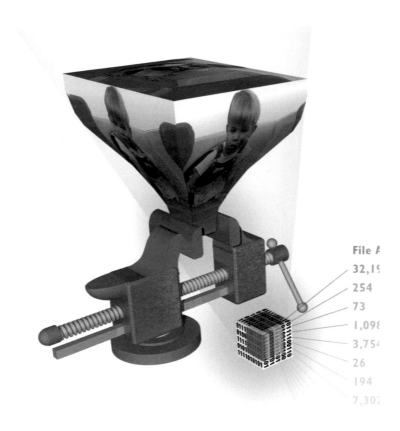

File A

32,19

254

73

1,098

3,754

26

194

7,302

ONE of the most popular uses of the Internet is to download files—that is, transfer files from a computer on the Internet to your computer. These files can be of many types: programs that you can run on your own computer; graphics you can view; sounds and music you can listen to; or text files that you can read. Many tens of thousands of files are downloaded every day over the Internet. Most of those files are downloaded using the Internet's File Transfer Protocol, commonly referred to as FTP. You can also use FTP to upload files from your computer to another computer on the Internet.

FTP, like many Internet resources, works on a client/server model. You run FTP client software on your computer to connect to an FTP server on the Internet. On the FTP server, a program called an FTP daemon (pronounced "demon") allows you to download and upload files.

To log on to an FTP site and download files, you must type in an account number (or username) and a password before the daemon will allow you to enter. Some sites allow anyone to enter and download files, but an account number (or username) and password must still be entered. Often, to get in, you use anonymous as your username and your email address as your password. Because of this, these sites are often referred to as *anonymous FTP sites*. Some FTP sites are private and allow only certain people with the proper account number and password to enter.

FTP is fairly simple to use. When you log on to an FTP site, you can browse through the available files by changing directories and seeing a listing of all the files available in each directory. When you see a file you want to download, use your client software to instruct the FTP server to send you the file.

As the World Wide Web gains popularity, downloading software is becoming even easier. You can use your web browser and click links to files. Behind the scenes, FTP is often still downloading the files. FTP remains the most popular way to download files from the Web and the Internet. The HTTP protocol of the Web can be used for downloading files from the Web, but it's not as efficient as FTP, so it isn't used as frequently.

One problem with downloading files over the Internet is that some files are so large that it can take a tremendous amount of time to download them, even when you use a high-speed, broadband connection. As a way to speed up file transfers and save space on the FTP server, files are commonly compressed, or shrunk in size using special compression software. Many different methods are used to compress files. Depending on the file type, files are usually compressed from 10–50%. After downloading the files, you'll need to run the compression software on your own computer to decompress the files so you can use them.

How an FTP Session Works

❶ FTP, like many other Internet resources, runs on a client/server model. To use it you'll need client software on your computer. To begin an FTP session, run the FTP client software and contact the FTP server from which you want to download files. You can get FTP client software in hundreds of places on the Internet. FTP programs are also included on Windows-based computers, but typically offer less functionality than these FTP clients.

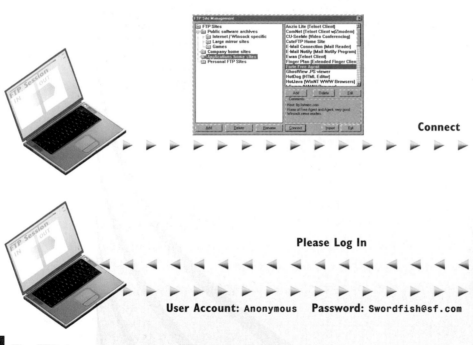

Connect

Please Log In

User Account: Anonymous **Password:** Swordfish@sf.com

FTP Server

Command Link

❷ The FTP daemon runs on the FTP server. This daemon handles all FTP transactions. When an FTP client contacts a server, the daemon will ask for an account number (or username) and password. Many FTP sites let anyone log on to them to download files and software. This is called anonymous FTP. With anonymous FTP, you often use anonymous for your account name and your email address for your password. Note that some FTP clients will automatically log on to the FTP server for you when you connect so you won't be asked to log on.

❸ When you log on to the FTP server, a connection called a *command link* is opened up between your computer and the server. Your computer uses this link for sending commands to the server, and the server uses this link for sending messages and information back to your computer.

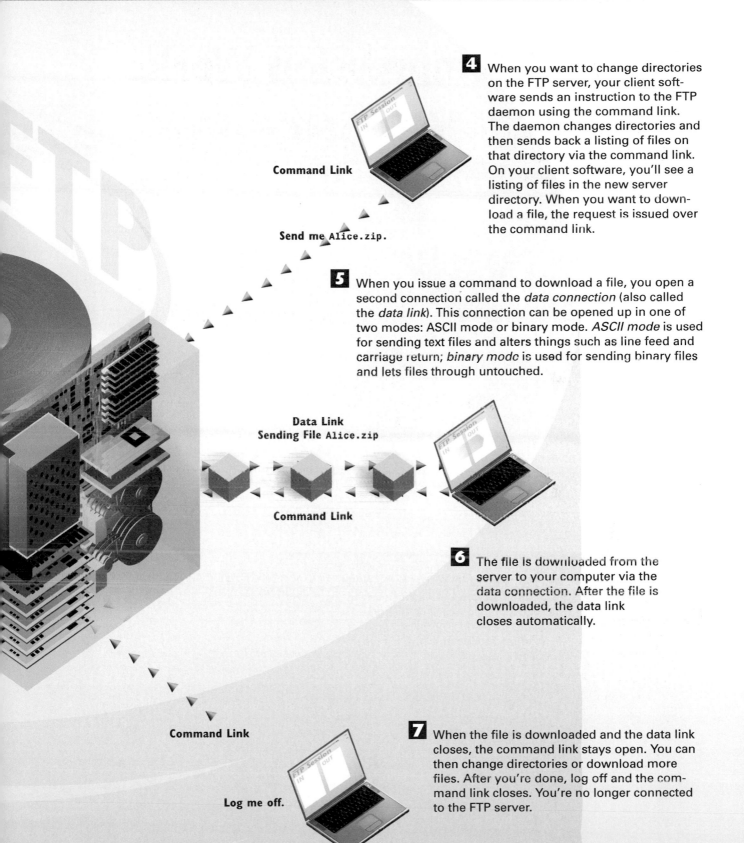

4 When you want to change directories on the FTP server, your client software sends an instruction to the FTP daemon using the command link. The daemon changes directories and then sends back a listing of files on that directory via the command link. On your client software, you'll see a listing of files in the new server directory. When you want to download a file, the request is issued over the command link.

Command Link

Send me Alice.zip.

5 When you issue a command to download a file, you open a second connection called the *data connection* (also called the *data link*). This connection can be opened up in one of two modes: ASCII mode or binary mode. *ASCII mode* is used for sending text files and alters things such as line feed and carriage return; *binary mode* is used for sending binary files and lets files through untouched.

Data Link
Sending File Alice.zip

Command Link

6 The file is downloaded from the server to your computer via the data connection. After the file is downloaded, the data link closes automatically.

Command Link

Log me off.

7 When the file is downloaded and the data link closes, the command link stays open. You can then change directories or download more files. After you're done, log off and the command link closes. You're no longer connected to the FTP server.

How File Compression Works

1 Compression programs use *algorithms*—complex mathematical formulas—to shrink files. In the first step in the process, the algorithm examines the file to be compressed and looks for repeating patterns of data.

Uncompressed File

$[a_2b^3 \sim q_4] \div c^4 \sim cosineb - I^4$

Compression Software

Compressed File

2 When the algorithm finds patterns of data that repeat, it replaces the patterns with smaller *tokens*. In a file that has many repeating patterns, many tokens are used to replace data so the compressed file is much smaller than the original file.

File Analysis

32,196	token A
254	token B
73	token C
1,098	token D
3,754	token E
26	token F
194	token G
7,302	token H
2,714	token I
12	token J
377	token K

3 A *header* can also be added to the file as it is compressed. This header contains information about the file, such as the filename, the file size, and the compression method used. This information is used to help reconstruct the file when it is uncompressed.

7 File *extensions*, the letters that appear after the period at the end of a filename, tell you whether and how a file is compressed.

Usually Windows

File.pak

File.zip

File.lzh

File.arj

File.pak

File.zoo

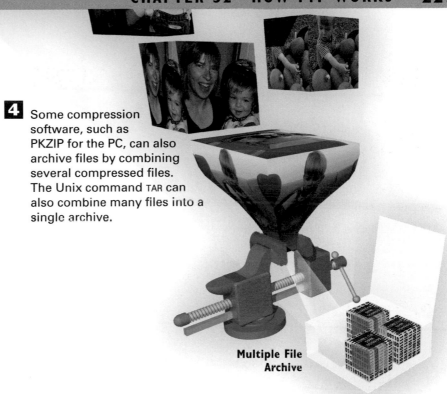

4 Some compression software, such as PKZIP for the PC, can also archive files by combining several compressed files. The Unix command TAR can also combine many files into a single archive.

Multiple File Archive

5 When you want to use a compressed file you find on the Internet, transfer it over the Internet to your computer.

Example.zip

6 To use the file, you'll need decompression software on your computer. The decompression software looks into the file's header and examines the tokens in the file. The decompression software uses a decompression algorithm to reconstruct the original file, which you can then use on your computer.

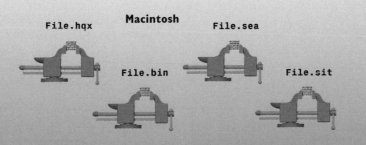

Macintosh

File.hqx

File.bin

File.sea

File.sit

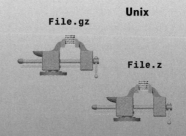

Unix

File.gz

File.z

CHAPTER 33

How Agents Work

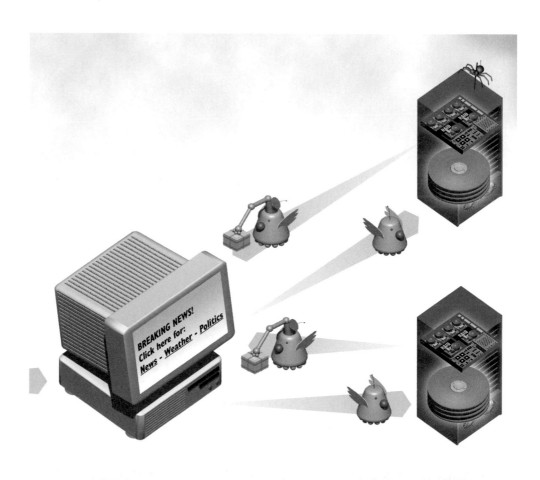

BREAKING NEWS!
Click here for:
News - Weather - Politics

THE Internet has grown so quickly and its resources are so vast that we need help navigating around it. Special software called *agents* can help us access the Net's resources.

Although there are a lot of technical definitions for agents, put simply, agents are programs that do your bidding automatically. Many of them run over the Internet or on individual computers every day. Agents can find the latest news for you and download it to your computer; they can automatically monitor Internet traffic and report on its total usage; they can find you the best deal on the CD you want to buy; they can perform important web maintenance tasks; and they can do far more. They are becoming so complex that systems are being developed to allow agents to interact with one another so they can perform jobs cooperatively.

On the Internet, agents are commonly called *spiders*, *robots* (often shortened to "bots"), and *knowbots*, among other terms. Those used for searching automatically create indexes of almost every resource on the Web and then allow people to search through those indexes to find things more quickly. Common search tools such as Google and AltaVista use spiders in this way. This specialized use of spiders is discussed in Chapter 27, "How Internet Searching Works."

All these agents are software programs that are invisible to the user. You just determine the task you want done, and behind the scenes the agent automatically goes off and performs that task. A variety of programming languages can be used to write agent programs.

Agents might well alter the way we all use the Internet in the future. Not only do they respond to our requests, but they also "learn" from our requests the types of tasks and information that interest us. They then go off on their own and perform those tasks and get that information, even before we make these additional requests. As we use these types of agents more, they'll become even smarter and more efficient.

Robots and agents can cause problems for some websites. For example, they can overload web servers by swamping them with too many requests in too short a time. That means users who try to get access to those web pages will be denied access, or access will be exceedingly slow.

Another problem has to do with the way websites make money. Many websites sell ads to support themselves and charge advertisers based on the number of pages that have been viewed. If many of those pages "viewed" are in fact never seen by people and are instead accessed only by a computer via a robot, both advertisers and the website suffer.

Several ways exist to solve these problems and limit robot access. One way includes creating a file called `Robots.txt` that describes the areas that are off limits to robots, which the robots would automatically read, adhere to, and not visit. Another is to use a technology that automatically detects whether a robot or a human has visited a page and forgo charging advertisers whenever robots visit.

Agents on the Internet

I A simple Internet agent is one that gathers news from a variety of sources while you're not using your computer or while you are using your computer for another task. News agents can work in several ways. In the simplest example, you fill out a form saying which type of news you're interested in and on what schedule you want your news delivered. Based on that information, at preset intervals, the news agent dials into news sites around the Internet and downloads news stories to your computer, where you can read them as HTML pages.

2 Shopping agents let you search the entire Internet for the best bargains. On the Web, you fill out a form detailing the product you want to buy. When you submit the form, the shopping agent launches programs that search through a variety of shopping sites and databases on the Internet. The agent looks into the databases of those sites and finds the best prices. It then sends back to you the links to the sites so you can visit the sites with the best prices and order from there.

Protected
Web Server

Unprotected
Web Server

4 When robots and spiders do their work on a remote Internet site from where they were launched, they can put an extra load on the site's system resources—for example, by swamping the server with too many requests in too short a time. Because of this, some system administrators are interested in ways of excluding robots in certain circumstances, such as not allowing robots into certain web directories. A variety of ways have been devised to limit robot access, including creating a file called Robots.txt that describes the areas off limits to robots, which the robots would read, adhere to, and not visit. But there is nothing that guarantees the robots must adhere to this rule. It's up to the good faith of the person writing the robot to adhere to it.

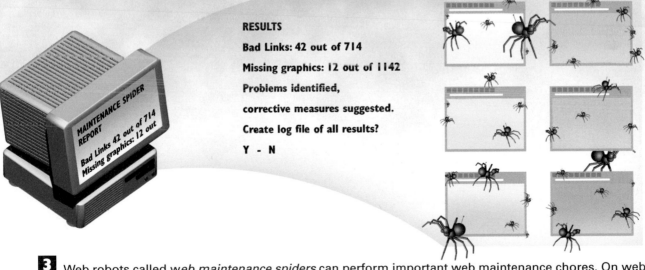

RESULTS

Bad Links: 42 out of 714

Missing graphics: 12 out of 1142

Problems identified,

corrective measures suggested.

Create log file of all results?

Y - N

MAINTENANCE SPIDER
REPORT
Bad Links 42 out of 714
Missing graphics: 12 out

3 Web robots called *web maintenance spiders* can perform important web maintenance chores. On websites, particularly large ones, very often HTML pages can include links that become outdated. In other words, the object being linked to has been taken off the Internet. Whenever a user clicks the link, an error message is sent. A web maintenance spider can look at every link on every HTML page on a website and trace each link to see whether the linked object still exists. It then generates a report of dead links. Based on that report, the system administrator can rewrite the HTML code, getting rid of the bad links.

CHAPTER

34

How Java, ActiveX, and JavaScript Work

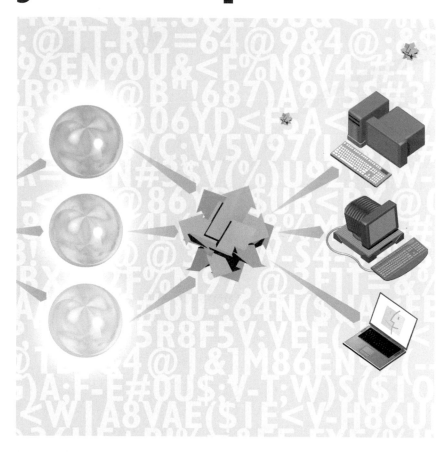

THE Internet is no longer a place that you visit with your computer and merely look at documents or gather information—increasingly, it is an extension of your computer. You can now run programs that reside on the Internet rather than on your own computer, and tools have been developed that enable your computer and the Internet to interact as if they were one large computer system. This allows for all kinds of things never before possible: news tickers that flash breaking news; interactive games; multimedia presentations combining animation, sound, and music; and much more.

Three important programming tools associated with web technology are Java, ActiveX, and JavaScript. *Java*, a computer language developed by Sun Microsystems, enables applications to be run from the Internet—the same as word processing and spreadsheet programs are run on your computer. It is similar to the C++ computer programming language and is object-oriented, which means programs can be created by using many preexisting components instead of by a programmer writing the entire program from scratch. Although most Java programs are run from the Internet, they don't have to be and can be run just like any other type of program.

Java programs run inside your web browser if you have a Java-enabled browser, such as Netscape. When Java programs are run inside a browser, they are called *applets*. You don't need to do anything to run a Java applet. When you visit a website that has a Java applet on it, the applet is downloaded automatically from a web server and then run automatically in your browser. Java applets can be run on any computer, such as a PC, a Macintosh, or a Unix workstation.

ActiveX, a technology from Microsoft, enables Internet programmers to create programs—commonly referred to as ActiveX *controls* or *components*—that can essentially turn the Internet into an extension of your computer. Similar to Java applets, these controls are downloaded to your computer and run there. They can do anything a normal application can do, in addition to interacting with the Web, the Internet, and other computers connected to the Internet. To run these controls, a browser that supports ActiveX, such as Internet Explorer, is necessary.

One benefit of ActiveX controls is that they are written as components, which means they can be put together, much like building blocks, to build larger and more complex applications. Another benefit is that, because you have already downloaded a component, you won't ever need to download it again. So, when you visit a page with a complex ActiveX application on it, you might need to download only a small portion of it because you might already have the other components on your computer.

JavaScript is a scripting language that is less complex and therefore much easier to learn than Java and ActiveX. People without substantial programming experience can write scripts with JavaScript. It's also an interpreted language, which means that its commands are executed by the browser in the order in which the browser reads them. It's commonly used for things such as creating drop-down boxes, navigational aids, and interactive forms, although it can be used for creating more complex applications, as well.

How Java Works

Java is a compiled language, which means that after a Java program is written, the program must be run through a compiler to turn the program into a language a computer can read. Java differs from other compiled languages, however. In other compiled languages, computer-specific compilers create distinct executable binary code for all the different computers on which the program can run. In Java, by contrast, a single compiled version of the program—called Java *bytecode*—is created by a compiler. Interpreters on different computers, such as a PC, Macintosh, or SPARC workstation, understand the Java bytecode and run the program. In this way, a Java program can be created once and then used on many types of computers. Java programs designed to run inside a web browser on the World Wide Web are called applets. Java-enabled browsers contain Java bytecode interpreters.

Conventional Program

1100100
0001001
1101000
1101110
0000100

PC Compiler

SPARC Compiler

Macintosh Compiler

PC Executable File

SPARC Executable File

Macintosh Executable File

Java Program

1100100
0001001
1101000
1101110
0000100

Java PC Compiler

Java SPARC Compiler

Java Macintosh Compiler

Java Bytecode for All Computers

PC with Java Interpreter

SPARC with Java Interpreter

Macintosh with Java Interpreter

3 When you visit a home page with a Java applet on it, the applet downloads to your computer. To run the Java applet, you need a web browser that has a bytecode interpreter that can run Java applets. Many browsers, such as Netscape Navigator, have these interpreters built into them.

2 After a Java program is compiled into bytecodes, it is put on a web server.

6 The Java applet is run; because it allows for animations and interactivity, it opens many other kinds of multimedia possibilities.

5 After the bytecodes have been verified, they are put into a restricted area in your computer's memory and run. By putting the applet into this special area of your computer, further care is taken that no virus can harm your computer.

4 Because Java applets are programs that run on your computer, theoretically they could carry a virus just like any other computer program could. To help ensure that no viruses infect your computer, when a Java applet is downloaded to your computer, the applet first goes through a process of verification—a process that ensures that the bytecodes can be run safely.

Download Java Applet News Ticker

Restricted for Java Applets

NEWSFLASH! Nanotechnology breakthrough at Stanford;

RAM

News Ticker Java Applet Verified: OK

How ActiveX Works

1 First, a programmer creates an ActiveX control. A variety of programming tools can be used to create controls, such as Visual Basic or the C programming language. A control can be as complex as a program that checks your computer for viruses and then eradicates them, or as simple as showing a website in an outline view. After the control is created, it is posted on a web server, and information about the control is coded into the web page through use of the HTML <object> tag.

Web Server

ActiveX Control

Programmer

"Yes"

2 When you visit a web page that contains an ActiveX control, your browser sees the HTML <object> tag. This tells your browser that an ActiveX control is present. The tag contains a variety of information required to run the control. It can tell the browser where the control is located on the server, for example, and which type of file it is. It can point to the control (which has an .ocx extension); to an installation file (which has an .inf extension); to a compressed file (which has a .cab extension); or to other kinds of files.

```
<OBJECT ID="ourMenu"
WIDTH=0, HEIGHT=0
CLASS ID="CLSID:9BC24D87-
E21A-10DF-B7D2-180089E9610A
CODEBASE="http://www.que.com/
ActiveX/QueControls.CAB#
Version=1, 0, 8, 0">
```

3 Some ActiveX controls need more than a single control to work. In that event, the HTML page contains multiple references to ActiveX controls needed to run the control on that page. The controls can be located on the same server, on a different server on the same website, or on another site and server on the Internet.

Active X Control

Web Server

4 Using the information in the `<object>` tag, the browser starts to download the ActiveX controls. If you have set your browser to a certain level of security, you get a message asking whether you want to download the control. To ensure even more security, ActiveX controls can be digitally *signed* by a digital certificate authority, such as VeriSign. This signing assures you that the control you want to run was written by the person to whom it is attributed. If a problem occurs with the control, you will be able to contact that person.

ActiveX Control

Web Browser

WELCOME

Do you want to download control XYZ?

ActiveX Control

5 If you have low security set on your browser, or if you give the okay to download the control, the control and its related ActiveX controls are downloaded to your computer. Some of the controls already might be on your system, so you won't need to download them. After the control is downloaded, the file is decompressed (if it was compressed), information about it is put into the Windows Registry, and it is installed on your computer. The control then runs. An ActiveX control can do anything any other program can do. It can interact with your computer and with any Internet resource, such as the Web, FTP, Telnet, or virtually any other Internet resource. It can also directly use the Internet's TCP/IP protocols so that it need not ride on top of another Internet resource.

How JavaScript Works

1 JavaScript is an *object-oriented* language, which means that it works by manipulating objects on a web page, such as windows, buttons, images, and documents. It groups these objects into hierarchies, which enables programmers to manipulate them more easily. It's also an *interpreted* language, which means that its commands are executed by the browser in the order in which the browser reads them.

```
Window
    Document
        Elements
        Button
        Check Box
        File Upload
        Password
        Radio
```

2 JavaScript commands are put directly into the HTML file that creates a web page. Depending on the script being run, the commands can be put into several places in the file. Often, the commands are put near the top of the file. Special codes set off the commands, alerting the browser that they're JavaScript commands. If the commands are put before the HTML `<body>` tag at the top of the file, the script can start executing while the HTML page is still loading.

```
<HTML>
<READ>
<SCRIPT LANGUAGE=
"javascript">
<!--Hide Script from
older browsers
document.write
```

```
window.open
then
document.write
then
window.status=
"these are the times
that try men's souls"
then
```

3 The heart of the way JavaScript works is to take actions on objects. These actions are called *methods*. Using this basic concept, JavaScript can be used for a wide variety of sophisticated, interactive features, but we'll look at a simple script that opens a new browser window to a specified size, puts a specific web page in it, and names the window. In the basic syntax of JavaScript, first the object is named, and then a period appears, followed by the action taken on the object—the method. So, the command to open a new window in JavaScript is window.open. In this instance, window is the object, and open is the method. This command opens a new browser window.

window.open

JavaScript

HTML PAGE

HTML HTML HTML HTML HTML HTML HTML
HTML HTML HTML HTML HTML HTML HTML
HTML HTML HTML HTML HTML HTML HTML
HTML HTML HTML HTML HTML HTML HTML
HTML HTML HTML HTML HTML HTML HTML
HTML HTML HTML HTML HTML HTML HTML
HTML HTML HTML HTML HTML HTML HTML

How JavaScript Works

```
window.open ("http://
www.howitworks.com/
jscript.html",
 "How_JavaScript_Works",
"height=1750,
width=150")
```

4 You can add further instructions to the `window.open` command. You do this by adding parameters after the command. You put all the parameters inside one set of parentheses, put each individual parameter inside quotation marks, and then separate the parameters by commas. So, the command `window.open("http://www.howitworks.com/jscript.html","How_JavaScript_Works","height=650,width=150")` opens a new browser window 650 pixels high and 150 pixels wide with the `http://www.howitworks.com/jscript.html` in it. The title, "How JavaScript Works," in the command gives the window a name so it can be manipulated by name after it has been created.

Blank Window

CHAPTER
35

How CGI
Scripting Works

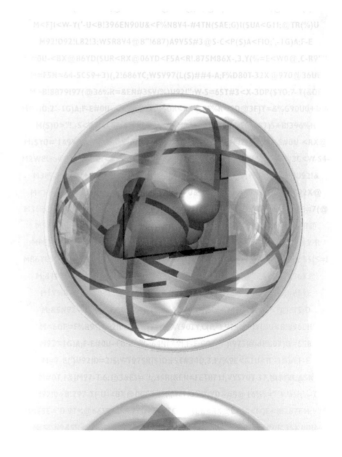

IF you browse the Web for very long, you are sure to come across the term *CGI*, or *Common Gateway Interface*. CGI refers to the communications protocol by which a web server can communicate with other applications. For example, a CGI application, sometimes called a *script*, is often used to enable Web users to access databases or to get information from forms people fill out. CGI can also be used to create agents that do things such as check a website to see whether it has any broken links. (By the way, don't confuse CGI as used on the Internet with the term Computer Graphics Imaging, also called CGI. Computer Graphics Imaging is a technology used to create special effects in movies.)

Essentially, CGI is a standard way in which the Web interacts with outside resources. Often, that outside resource is a database. You've probably run CGI scripts many times without knowing it. For example, if you've filled out a form on a web page to register to use a site and then later received an email notification with a password for you to use, you've probably run a CGI script. In that case, the CGI script probably took the information you filled in on the form and performed several actions on it, including putting the information in a database, automatically creating a password, and then sending you mail.

CGI and CGI applications are often confused. *CGI applications* receive data from the server and return the data via the Common Gateway Interface. CGI applications are written in a variety of programming languages, including Perl, PHP, and ASP, although they can be written in C, C++, Pascal, AppleScript, or others as well. CGI itself is a standardized means of communicating between a CGI application and the HTTP server. It's the "doorway" of sorts through which the web server sends requests and the CGI application collects and returns data.

In the example of providing information on a web page designed to accept user input, CGI performs many tasks. First, you submit unique information—such as a name or email address—to the server for processing. Next, the server redirects the information to a CGI application that is called by the form "submit." CGI scripts are activated by the server in response to an HTTP request from the client. Lastly, a CGI application might send form data to another computer program, such as a database; save it to a file; or even generate a unique HTML document in response to the user's request. This is known as an *interactive form*.

In the illustration that accompanies this chapter, we'll look at a CGI program that enables someone to search a movie database for information.

Understanding CGI Scripting

1 People who connect to the website don't need to know programming to access CGI programs. Instead, a programmer writes a CGI program. A number of languages can be used for CGI, such as C or C++, FORTRAN, Visual Basic, and AppleScript. An application written in a programming language such as C must be passed through a program called a *compiler* before it can be run. The compiler turns the application into a language CGI can understand. Other languages, called *scripting languages*, do not need to be compiled first. CGI scripts tend to be easier to debug, modify, and maintain than compiled programs so they are used more frequently. Perl is probably the most popular language used for writing CGI scripts.

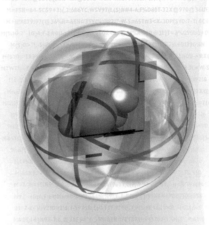

Search Database Program

Compiler Program

Complied Search Database Program

On the Town Information

2 After the program is written and compiled, or the script is written, the program is put into a special directory on the web server, such as /cgi-bin, where all the CGI programs are stored and maintained. The person in charge of the web server determines which directory should hold CGI programs. If someone writes a program and doesn't put it in the proper directory, it won't run. This is a security feature. If there were many different directories people could use to store and run CGI programs, keeping track of them all would be difficult, and someone from the outside could create and post a program that could be dangerous to the software that's already there.

/cgi-bin

Web Server

6 The CGI program receives the data from the database and formats it in a way that will be understandable to the user. For example, the program might take the information and put it into HTML format so the user can read it using her web browser. The CGI program sends the results in HTML format to the user, who displays it in a web browser. The user can then access that HTML page. She can click links to visit other pages, print pages, and view graphics and multimedia files.

5 The CGI program contacts a database and requests the information the user is looking for. The database sends the information to the CGI program. The information can be in a variety of formats, such as text, graphics, sound and video files, and URLs.

Database

**Get:
On the Town**

4 When you visit the website and click the URL, the CGI program is launched. If the CGI program allows you to search a database, for example, it sends a form in HTML format. You then fill out the form detailing what you want to find. When you finish the form and click Send, the data from the form is sent to the CGI program.

3 After the CGI program is posted to a special directory, a link to it is embedded in a URL on a web page.

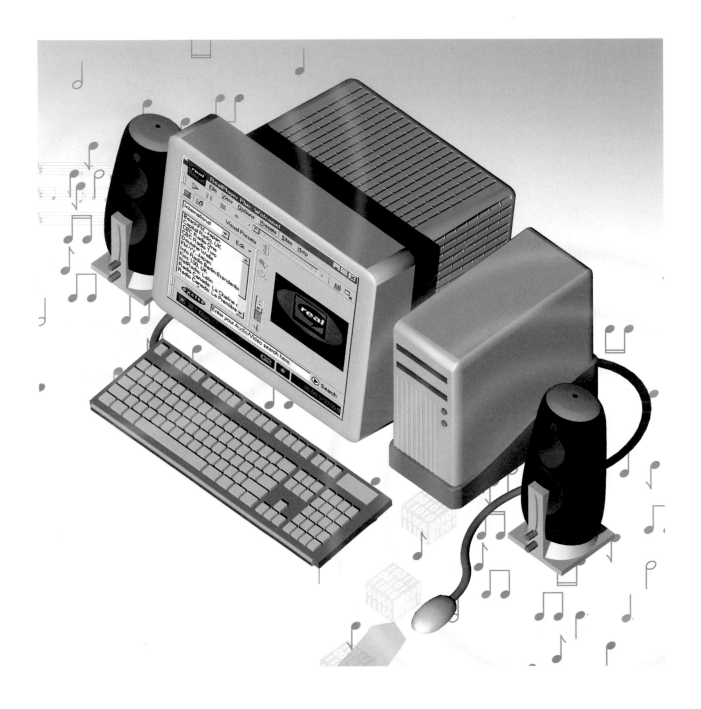

P A R T

7

ENJOYING ENTERTAINMENT AND MULTIMEDIA ON THE INTERNET

POSSIBLY the most dramatic and remarkable part of the Internet is the multimedia content and entertainment you can find there. You can listen to music, sound clips, and live radio stations from your computer. You can share your favorite music files with others all over the world. You can watch video clips of the news and other events. And you can even have live videoconferencing with people from all over the world.

You can do all that with the Internet's audio and video capabilities. You won't need expensive hardware and software to do it—free or inexpensive software will do the trick, along with a sound card and speakers that ship with most computers, or that are available separately.

The Internet's multimedia capabilities go beyond mere playing of audio and video clips and listening to Internet radio stations. You can participate in virtual worlds and join in virtual chat sessions in which you build your own online persona, called an *avatar*, which communicates with other avatars. The Internet enables the creation of remarkable online multimedia content, combining animation, sound, and programming via technologies such as streaming audio and video, Flash, and multicast IP.

This section of the book discusses how major aspects of multimedia and entertainment on the Internet work. Chapter 36, "How Music and Audio Work on the Internet," covers audio and music. You'll see how audio files are sent to your computer and played. You'll look at how streaming audio works in detail. Streaming audio enables you to play sounds and music on your computer while the audio file is being transferred to your computer, so you don't have to wait for the file to download.

Chapter 36 also looks at the use of the most popular music format on the Internet—MP3. MP3 files are near–CD-quality sound files, yet are small enough that they easily can be downloaded. This chapter also shows how Internet radio broadcasting works. Increasingly, radio stations broadcast live over the Internet so you can listen in using special software or just your browser. Many of these stations are Internet-only stations that broadcast only online, although many real-life radio stations around the world also broadcast over the Internet.

Chapter 37, "How iPods, iTunes, and Podcasting Work," examines the hardware and software that more than any other, has changed the way people buy and listen to music. It peers into the innards of the iPod, and shows you how that popular portable music player works. It also shows how the companion iTunes software works its magic. Finally, it explains how podcasting works—radio-like shows that can be subscribed to and downloaded to your PC, iPod, or other portable music player.

Chapter 38, "How Music Sharing and File Sharing Work," looks at one of the most controversial uses of the Internet—the way music files can be shared with others. It shows you the inner workings of file-sharing software that enables anyone to download their favorite music from other music lovers and make their music available to others as well. It also allows you to share other kinds of files, such as movies. The chapter also delves into the use of BitTorrent, the newest file-sharing software, which even the movie studios have begun to embrace.

Chapter 39, "How Multicast IP and the MBone Work," looks at multicast IP and the MBone. Multicast IP enables videos to be broadcast to many thousands of people simultaneously, without clogging up the Internet's backbone. The MBone is a high-speed Internet backbone used for transmitting multicast IP video across the Internet.

Chapter 40, "How Virtual Reality Is Created by VRML," examines virtual reality. Virtual reality enables the creation of virtual worlds—3D creations on the Web through which you can walk, fly, or interact with your surroundings. As the bandwidth of the Internet increases, these virtual worlds are increasingly popular.

Finally, Chapter 41, "How Animation on the Web Works," looks at some of the most popular types of animation technologies, from the very simple to the very sophisticated. You'll learn how client pull and server push technologies enable the easy creation of simple animations. You'll also look at Shockwave, an extremely sophisticated way in which animation, audio, and other types of interactive technologies can be used to create powerful multimedia presentations on the Web. You'll even learn about the newest and most powerful kind of web animation—Flash—which goes several steps beyond the capabilities of Shockwave.

CHAPTER

36

How Music and Audio Work on the Internet

SOUNDS, voices, and music are an everyday part of the Internet. Through the Internet, you can listen to radio stations, interviews, music, sound clips, and much more.

You can listen to all this music and sound by downloading audio files—files that have been digitized so that a computer can play them. You'll find many music files and sound clips in a variety of sound formats online. Each of these formats has a different extension associated with it, such as .wav, .mp3, or .au. To play these files, you first have to download them and also download audio-player software to play them on your computer. Every new computer sold has this software already built in, such as Windows Media Player, iTunes, RealPlayer, or Musicmatch Jukebox.

You can also listen to music from the Internet without first downloading the music files to your PC. You do this via what is called *streaming audio*. With streaming audio you don't have to wait until the entire audio file is downloaded to play it. Instead, you listen to the audio while it downloads to your computer. A variety of technologies allow for streaming audio. For all of them, you'll need to have the proper audio player for each specific kind of streaming audio. This chapter looks at one of the most popular audio streaming technologies, called RealPlayer. Other kinds of streaming technologies exist, such as that used by the Windows Media Player. However, all streaming technologies work similarly.

One problem with streaming audio is that the sound quality generally isn't as good as a music CD, although the quality is being improved all the time. However, MP3, a popular kind of audio file type, offers CD-quality audio. Furthermore, the MP3 files themselves aren't that large—usually less than 4MB or 5MB per song. With other kinds of computer music technology, these songs can take up 20MB and more. Technologies have been developed that enable MP3 files to be streamed so that you can listen to them as they download to your computer. This technology gives you the best of both worlds—high-quality sound without having to wait for the whole file to download.

One of the more intriguing new audio uses of the Internet is the capability to listen to radio stations from all across the world. An increasing number of radio stations stream their live broadcasts over the Internet, and you can listen right from your browser or use software such as RealPlayer or the Windows Media Player. Entirely new radio stations have sprung up that broadcast only over the Internet.

How RealPlayer Streaming Audio Works

1 When you use your web browser and click a link to a RealPlayer sound clip on a home page, the link doesn't lead directly to a sound file. Instead, your web browser contacts the web server, which then sends a file called a *RealPlayer metafile* back to your browser. This metafile is a small text file that has the true location—the URL—of the RealPlayer sound file you want to play. The metafile also has instructions telling your web browser to launch the RealPlayer sound player, which is required to play the clip.

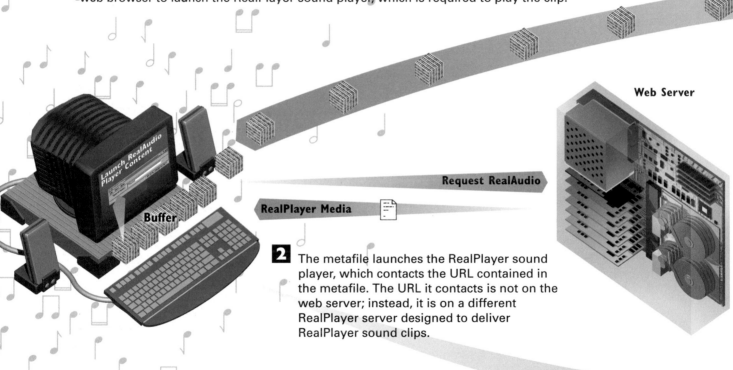

Web Server

Request RealAudio

RealPlayer Media

Buffer

2 The metafile launches the RealPlayer sound player, which contacts the URL contained in the metafile. The URL it contacts is not on the web server; instead, it is on a different RealPlayer server designed to deliver RealPlayer sound clips.

5 The packets are sent to a buffer on the receiving computer. When the packets exceed the capacity of the buffer, they are sent to the RealPlayer player, which then plays the sound file. RealPlayer allows you to jump ahead or back in a sound or music clip. When you move to a different place in the clip, the RealPlayer player contacts the server and tells it to start sending the file from that new place in the clip.

4 The RealPlayer clip is compressed and encoded. The sound file is too large and takes too long to send and play if it is not compressed. The clip is sent in IP packets using UDP (User Datagram Protocol) instead of the Internet's normal TCP (Transmission Control Protocol). Unlike TCP, UDP doesn't keep re-sending packets if they are misplaced or other problems occur. If packets had to keep being re-sent, the sound player on the receiving end would constantly be interrupted with packets and could not play the clip.

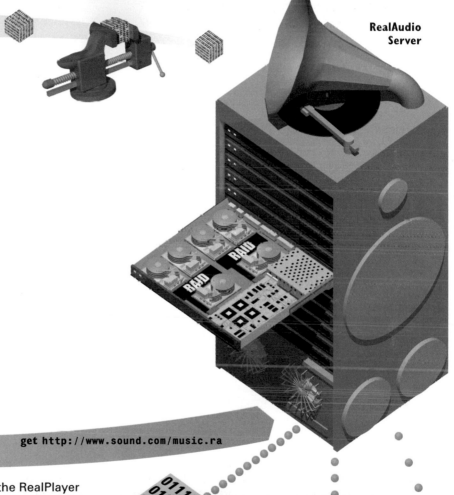

RealAudio Server

This damaged packet will be discarded.

get http://www.sound.com/music.ra

3 The RealPlayer server and the RealPlayer sound player "talk" to one another so that the server knows at what speed the user is connected to the Internet. If the connection is a low-speed connection, a smaller RealPlayer file is sent that contains less data. This file is of lesser quality than a file sent via a high-speed connection. If a high-speed connection is used, a larger, higher-quality sound file is sent. This provides for better sound quality.

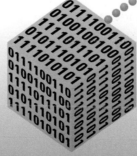

Cable/DSL

56Kbps

28.8Kbps

How MP3 Music Files Work

1 One of the most popular ways to distribute music on the Internet is through the use of MP3 music files. The files use special algorithms that shrink the size of the files while retaining CD-like quality. Before MP3 files can be posted, however, the music has to be recorded. The music is recorded no differently than any other kind of music and is then put on a CD.

2 The music from the CD has to be converted to the MP3 format so that it can be posted on the Internet. A typical way to convert the music is to use a *ripper*—a piece of software that takes the music from the CD and converts it to MP3 format. The software uses special algorithms that shrink the size of the file dramatically so that a typical song is under 3MB and still maintains high quality. (In earlier kinds of PC music formats, those files would be 20MB and more.) This mix of small size and high quality is what sets the MP3 standard apart from other Internet music formats.

MP3 Ripper

Get MP3 File

MP3 File

MP3 Player

7 The MP3 files can also be transferred from a computer to a *portable MP3 player*—a small audio device that can play music in the MP3 format. The MP3 files are stored on a memory card in the device and can be erased or overwritten with new MP3 files.

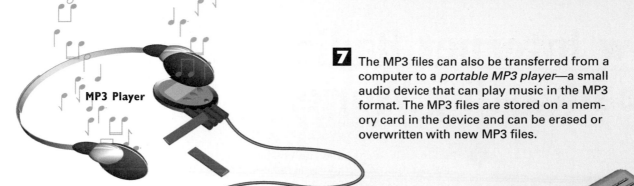

6 One issue with MP3 files is that they can be considered a violation of an artist's copyright—for example, if the file was created and posted without the artist's permission. In some instances, an MP3 player won't play an MP3 file if someone who didn't get the artist's permission ripped the file from a CD. In other instances, the file will play, but may contain copyright information about the MP3 file. However, in many instances, the file can be played and does not include copyright information.

4 When someone wants to download the MP3 file, he visits the website or FTP download site and downloads the file to his computer.

Get MP3 File

5 After the file is downloaded, it can be played with a special piece of software called an MP3 player. Some software and Internet servers can *stream* the MP3 file—play it while it's being downloaded. In most cases, however, the file is first downloaded and then played.

3 After the file has been converted to an MP3 format, it's posted to a site on the Internet where people can download it.

Web Server

How Internet Radio Broadcasting Works

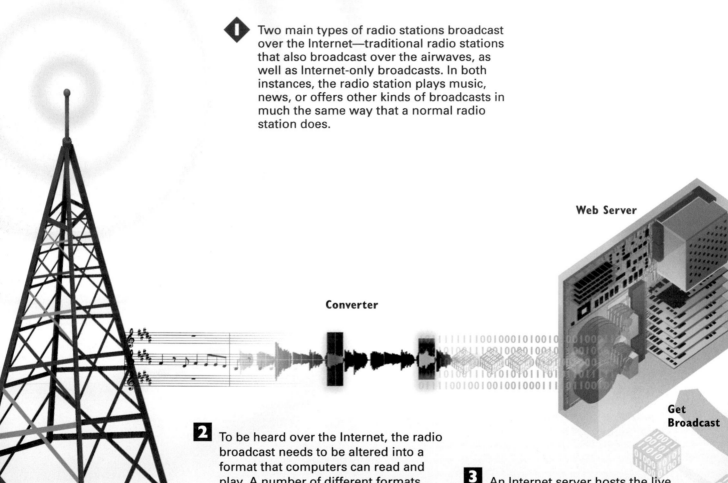

1 Two main types of radio stations broadcast over the Internet—traditional radio stations that also broadcast over the airwaves, as well as Internet-only broadcasts. In both instances, the radio station plays music, news, or offers other kinds of broadcasts in much the same way that a normal radio station does.

Web Server

Converter

Get Broadcast

2 To be heard over the Internet, the radio broadcast needs to be altered into a format that computers can read and play. A number of different formats exist—most notably RealPlayer and Windows Media Player. Software turns the normal broadcast into one or both of those formats. (To get RealPlayer, go to www.realnetworks.com. For Windows Media Player, go to www.microsoft.com. Other software also lets you listen to Internet radio, such as Musicmatch from www.musicmatch.com.)

3 An Internet server hosts the live broadcast in the RealPlayer or Windows Media Player formats.

6 The client software now plays the broadcast live on the person's computer. The broadcast can be controlled like a radio broadcast—the sound can be lowered or raised, and, depending on the software used, the quality of the sound can be altered. Generally, the higher the speed of the connection between the PC and the web server, the higher the audio quality of the broadcast.

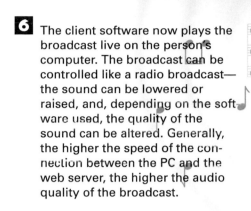

5 When the link is clicked, the client software contacts the server. The server sends the broadcast to the PC in a steady stream.

4 When someone wants to listen to a radio broadcast, he launches his client software radio player, such as RealPlayer. If he has Internet Explorer 5.0 or higher, he can also launch a radio toolbar that sits near the top of the browser window. From this toolbar, he can choose radio stations to listen to. To listen to a radio station, someone clicks a link in the player or in the browser. He can also visit a radio station site and click a link on the site.

CHAPTER

37

How iPods, iTunes, and Podcasting Work

WAS there digital music before the iPod? Contrary to what many people might think, the answer is yes. Well before the iPod became a technological and cultural sensation, millions of people were listening to digital music on their computers. And not just on their computers—they were listening to music on their portable music devices, called MP3 players.

Although the iPod certainly wasn't the first device for playing digital music, it changed the way people listened to and purchased music, and became a part of the cultural landscape. Before the iPod, the people who primarily listened to digital music on their computers and MP3 players were experienced computer users. After the iPod, even grandmothers with little computer experience could be seen plugging the familiar ear buds into their ears.

The iPod was introduced in 2001 and became an overnight sensation. Its popularity grew even more over time, as the confluence of legal, business, and technological innovation grew it into the phenomenon it has become today.

On the legal front, the music industry began cracking down on people who shared music files with each other using software such as Kazaa and similar programs. High-profile prosecutions began to make people fearful of downloading music. At the same time, the music industry took the creators of Kazaa and similar programs to court, successfully shutting down a number of them.

What does this have to do with the iPod? Plenty. Apple recognized that there was a massive pent-up demand for digital music, but no easy, legal way for people to buy that music. Music publishers didn't sell many of their songs online, and could not agree on a single way to sell music. People had no easy way to find and buy music they liked.

Apple saw a business opening and launched its iTunes Music Store. The iTunes Music Store is directly integrated into iTunes software for listening to music, "ripping" music from CDs, and "burning" music onto CDs. iTunes also integrated directly to the iPod, so that music downloaded into iTunes could be automatically copied to the iPod.

The introduction of the iTunes Music Store changed forever the way people buy and listen to music. Singles were made available for under a dollar and sales exceeded the expectations of the music industry. It became the biggest music site on the Internet; people finally had a legal way to buy and listen to digital music.

The iPod changed the way we buy and listen to music, but the changes it wrought didn't stop there. It also changed the way people listen to radio as well, via a technique called *podcasting*. With podcasting, anyone can create their own radio program, and then people can subscribe to that program so it downloads automatically to their iPods on whatever schedule they choose.

At first, podcasters were do-it-yourselfers, but soon the commercial world caught on as well. Today, there are many thousands of podcasts available, from people creating them in their living rooms to high-quality broadcasts from traditional radio stations.

How iPods Work

1 When you load music into your iPod from your computer, it's stored on iPod's hard disk in MP3 or Advanced Audio Code (AAC) format. Both formats compress the original music so the files don't take up too much space. Stored along with each file is metadata that contains information about it, such as the artist name, album name, music category, and so on. This allows you to easily categorize and find music you want to play. The number of songs you can store on an iPod varies according to the hard disk size and how much each song has been compressed. With typical compression using the AAC format, you can store about 10,000 songs on a conventional iPod's 40GB hard disk.

2 You select the song you want to play by clicking the Play button. You can also create a playlist (a series of songs) to be played so you don't have to choose each song individually.

3 The iPod retrieves the file or the playlist from the hard disk and copies it to a memory chip. It is technically possible for a music device such as the iPod to play music directly from the hard disk, but it places the file instead in memory because if it played the file from a hard disk, the song might skip if the device were jostled in some way. Because the memory chip contains no moving parts, the music won't skip if the device is jostled. The hard drive turns off while the music is playing, and only turns back on again when the music has completely played.

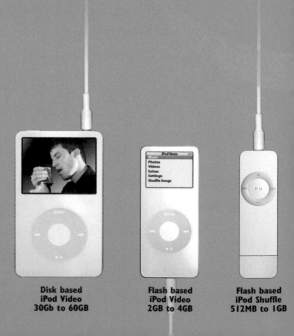

Disk based iPod Video 30Gb to 60GB

Flash based iPod Video 2GB to 4GB

Flash based iPod Shuffle 512MB to 1GB

4 A microprocessor takes the file from the memory chip and decompresses it so the file can be played.

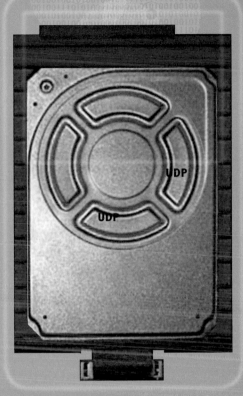

5 A digital-to-analog converter converts the file from a digital format to an analog signal, changing the 0s and 1s of a digital file into the sound waves that human beings can hear.

6 An amplifier increases the strength of the analog signal and sends the signal to the audio port.

7 Headphones or speakers plugged into the audio port allow you to listen to the music.

How iTunes Works

1 iTunes isn't file-sharing software like BitTorrent or like Kazaa was. Instead, it's software owned by Apple that lets you buy or listen to music on your PC or Mac, and transfer the music to your iPod.

2 At its most basic level, iTunes is a music player that can play a wide variety of digital music, can also rip music from a CD to a computer, and can create CDs out of digital music on your PC.

3 iTunes also allows you to buy music from the iTunes Music Store. Apple makes arrangements with music publishers to sell the music, and splits the proceeds with them.

Record Companies:
We'll give you access to our vast catalog of music, videos, and other media.

Apple:
We'll split the profits with you and put DRM in the files to protect your intellectual property.

4 When you buy music from iTunes, it downloads to your computer where you can listen to it.

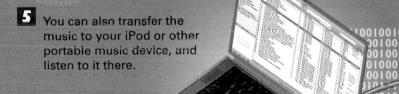

5 You can also transfer the music to your iPod or other portable music device, and listen to it there.

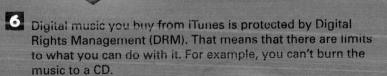

6 Digital music you buy from iTunes is protected by Digital Rights Management (DRM). That means that there are limits to what you can do with it. For example, you can't burn the music to a CD.

How Podcasting Works

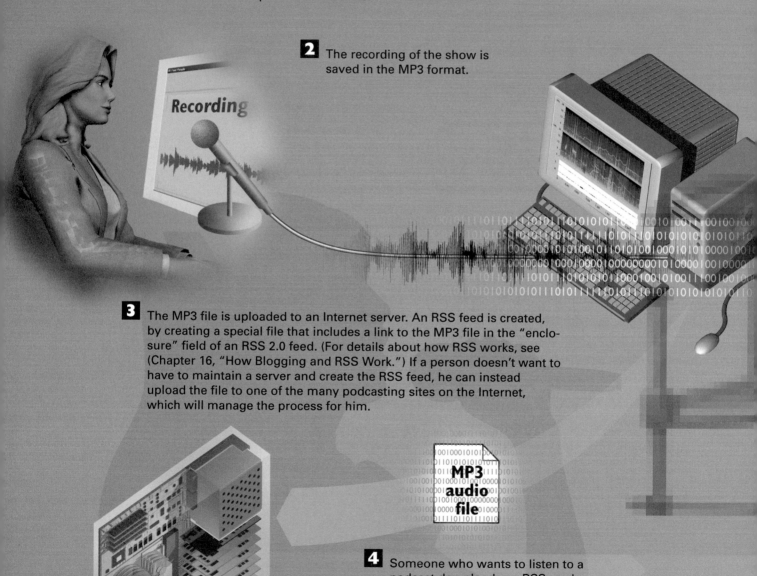

1 Podcasts can be created by anyone, and can be as simple as a person talking into a microphone on his PC, or as sophisticated as a high-quality news or music show. First, the podcast is recorded. An individual can record it with a microphone attached to his computer, or the show can be recorded in a professional studio.

2 The recording of the show is saved in the MP3 format.

3 The MP3 file is uploaded to an Internet server. An RSS feed is created, by creating a special file that includes a link to the MP3 file in the "enclosure" field of an RSS 2.0 feed. (For details about how RSS works, see (Chapter 16, "How Blogging and RSS Work.") If a person doesn't want to have to maintain a server and create the RSS feed, he can instead upload the file to one of the many podcasting sites on the Internet, which will manage the process for him.

4 Someone who wants to listen to a podcast downloads an RSS reader, iTunes, or other software capable of subscribing to podcasts.

5 The person pastes the URL of the podcast into the reader, or else clicks a link on the page allowing him to subscribe to the podcast. Some software, such as iTunes, also includes built-in directories and search tools to find and listen to podcasts.

6 The software downloads the podcast, allowing the person to listen to it.

7 iTunes and other software will also automatically copy the podcast to an iPod or other MP3 player when the iPod or MP3 player is connected to a computer via a docking cradle or USB port.

Comedy

Daily Show

Music - Opera (Bartoli)

Political Commentary

```
<?xml version="1.0" encoding="UTF-8"?>
<rss xmlns:itunes="http://www.itunes.com/dtds/podcast-1.0.dtd" version="2.0">
 <item>
<title>The World of Cecilia Bartoli</title>
<itunes:author>Preston Gralla</itunes:author>
<itunes:subtitle>A short feature about the world's greatest mezzosoprano</itunes:subtitle>
<itunes:summary>Cecilia Bartoli is more than just the world's greatest mezzosoprano.
She has also uncovered musical treasures long lost to history. Learn more about this
remarkable singer and musicologist</itunes:summary>
```

Music - Opera (Bartoli)

MP3 audio file

CHAPTER

38

How Music Sharing and File Sharing Work

EVERY once in a while a new feature or application takes the Internet by storm and not only changes the way many people use the Internet, but, at times, even changes the world beyond the Internet's borders.

Several years ago that's what music-sharing software did. Not only did it change the way that many people used the Internet, but it also threatened the multibillion dollar music industry. Music-sharing software forever changed the way people thought of and listened to music.

It did all this by putting into effect a very simple idea—let people share their music with each other over the Internet. Despite all the hype, technology, and lawsuits, that's what it all comes down to.

People can make digital copies of their CDs by using a piece of *ripping* software that turns CD tracks into digital files that can be played on a computer—most commonly files in the .mp3 music format. Music-sharing and file sharing software aren't rippers. Instead, they let people find music and other files in digital format by searching through the music collections of thousands of other people. When someone finds a song he wants, he can download it to his computer from another person. Then he can listen to that song on his computer by transferring it to an MP3 player and listening to it there, or burning it onto a CD and listening to the song in a CD player.

The music industry cried "Foul!" and brought the original file-sharing software, Napster, to court on copyright violations. The court cases dragged on for a while, but ultimately Napster lost and was put out of business. It may resurface as a legal, for-pay music-sharing service at some point.

But despite the lawsuits, the genie is out of the bottle. Other software and file-sharing networks enable people to do the same thing.

This kind of technology, which enables people to share files directly with one another, is called *peer-to-peer*. Peer-to-peer has gone far beyond allowing people to share music—people can share any kind of file from spreadsheets to movies. The BitTorrent peer-to-peer network, for example, is often used to share movies and entire CDs.

A whole new kind of application has sprung up in Napster's wake: business peer-to-peer software. The most notable example is Microsoft-owned Groove software that enables people in corporations to create their own private workspace where they can share files, messages, and software. Multibillion dollar corporations have already signed on and are using the software.

In addition, businesses also use BitTorrent as a way to more efficiently distribute software. So ironically, a technology that started as guerilla music-sharing software might find fruition as a corporate mainstay.

How Peer-to-Peer Software Shares Files and Music

1 This illustration shows how Kazaa worked. Kazaa was once the most popular file-sharing software, but has been put out of business by lawsuits. But other file-sharing software works in similar ways, so this illustration shows how they work as well. To use Kazaa, download and install it on your computer. After you install the software, it connects to a Kazaa server, which sends to your PC a list of "supernodes" on the Kazaa network. These supernodes function as localized search sites for the Kazaa file-sharing network. They are ordinary PCs that the network notices have high-speed connections and powerful processors. So, depending on your PC's speed and Internet connection, it could be designated a supernode at some point.

2 Your PC contacts a nearby supernode and sends information to it about all the music on your computer, the location on your computer of that music, your IP address, and your Kazaa ID.

3 The supernode puts this information into its database.

4 When you want to search for music, type in the artist and song title you're looking for in Kazaa. The Kazaa client contacts the nearest supernode. The supernode looks in its database and finds the artist and song title for which you're looking. It also queries other supernodes and asks them for the artist and song title as well. The supernode then compiles a list of every copy of every artist and song and shows you on whose computer you can find each.

5 You choose the song you want to download and from whose computer you want to download. You bypass the supernodes and download the song directly from the person's computer.

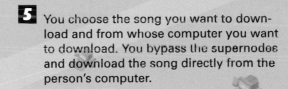

How BitTorrent Works

1 BitTorrent has become the preferred way to download movies and CDs, and it works slightly different than other file-sharing software. It downloads bits and pieces of the requested file from multiple computers, and then assembles them into one file after it receives all the pieces. To use BitTorrent, you first need to download and install a client piece of software. BitTorrent clients are free, and available from many places on the Internet, including at www.bittorrent.com.

2 When someone wants to download a CD, movie, or similar content, they visit a site that specializes in BitTorrent downloads. They click on the link of what they want to download.

torrent info:
cker servers: 293

torrent file #:
65-92874-1934-19378

ailable seeds:
4123.084324
4237.039374
16.1034

3 The site downloads a small *torrent* file to the person's computer. The torrent file is essentially a "pointer" file that has in it information and instructions about where and how the CD or movie can be downloaded. Among the information is the address of a *tracker server*, as well as the filename, size, and the checksum of every block in the music or video file they will download, which helps ensure they're downloading the real music or video.

torrent piece#
91444 of 92357

torrent piece#
9021 of 92357

torrent piece#
573 of 92357

torrent piece#
251 of 92357

torrent piece#
742 of 92357

torrent piece#
239 of 92357

torrent piece#
35001 of 92357

torrent piece#
17 of 92357

torrent piece#
73821 of 92357

torrent piece#
237 of 92357

torrent piece#
231 of 92357

6 While the client is downloading the file, it may
also be uploading pieces
of the same file, or pieces
of other files, to other
people using BitTorrent
clients.

torrent piece#
32185 of 92357

torrent piece#
8126 of 92357

torrent piece#
10375 of 92357

5 The client downloads different pieces
of the file from different computers
in the swarm simultaneously.
Downloading from many computers
simultaneously significantly speeds
up the download process. When all
the pieces of the file are complete,
they are assembled into the complete file, which can be used like any
other file.

torrent piece#
73 of 92357

torrent piece#
29374 of 92357

torrent piece#
44035 of 92357

torrent piece#
13817 of 92357

torrent piece#
54117 of 92357

torrent piece#
84266 of 92357

Note
Download speeds in BitTorrent
depend on how much that client
has been used to upload files to
other computers. So, a computer
that leaves BitTorrent running frequently, and has uploaded files to
many other computers, will be
given privileges to download faster
than a computer that has rarely
uploaded files to other computers.

torrent piece#
107 of 92357

4 The BitTorrent client communicates with the tracker
server identified in the torrent file. The tracker server
sends along address information of all the computers
that have the complete file the person wants to download or portions of the file the person wants to download. Each of these computers are called *seed
computers*. The entire group of seed computers with all
or part of the file to be downloaded are called the
swarm.

CHAPTER

39

How Multicast IP and the MBone Work

TODAY'S Internet is made up not just of text, but of sound, video, animation, 3D objects, and more. Web pages are interactive, and video-based shows are commonly broadcast. Already, in fact, video-based shows and movies are being broadcast.

This can cause serious congestion on the wires and networks that make up the Internet. That's only one problem with video broadcasting over the Internet. There is another problem as well—there's no practical way for broadcasts to be sent over the Internet because the files clog it up. Suppose, for example, that someone wants to broadcast a telecast of a concert. The size of the file containing that broadcast might be 50 megabytes (MB). Now imagine that 10,000 people want to watch the concert. That 50MB file needs to be sent individually to each of those 10,000 people. As you can imagine, that single broadcast could easily clog entire sections of the Internet, which would prevent the broadcast from being delivered.

One answer is the Multicast Backbone, or the MBone. The *MBone* is a high-capacity Internet backbone for transmitting broadcasts using the IP multicast protocol. The MBone enables broadcasts to start out as a single transmission instead of, for example, 10,000 transmissions. Inside that single transmission are the addresses of all the people who want to see the broadcast. As the file is sent across the Internet, it eventually makes copies of itself when necessary and delivers the broadcast to the networks and individuals who want to see it.

Suppose that 100 people want to see a broadcast of a 50MB file. Fifty people who want to see it are connected to the Internet via the WorldNet Internet service provider, 25 people are on a corporate network at zd.com, and another 25 use the Internet Access Company Internet service provider. When the broadcast goes out, it goes out as one single file, not 100 separate files. The file then splits into three parts: One part goes to WorldNet, one part goes to zd.com, and one part goes to the Internet Access Company. After the file is on each of those separate networks, it is delivered to the people inside the networks who want to see it. The key here, however, is that instead of 100 files of 50MB traveling across the Internet—5 gigabytes (GB) of data—only three 50MB files travel, or 150MB of data. As you can see, the MBone can cut down tremendously the amount of traffic traveling across the Internet.

How Multicast IP Travels Along the MBone

Video Camera

1 The *MBone* (Multicast Backbone) is a high-speed Internet backbone capable of sending live video and audio broadcasts. It's a network of host computers that communicate with one another using a technique called IP (Internet Protocol) Multicast. An MBone multicast begins when a video signal is digitized and compressed so that it can be sent over the Internet. Without compression, the signal would be too large and take too long to deliver.

2 The compressed, digitized signal is sent in packets using the IP multicast protocol instead of the Internet's normal TCP protocol. The multicast protocol enables the signal to be sent to a number of sites on the Internet simultaneously. Normally, the Internet is *unicast*, which means that each signal can be sent only to a single, specific location.

IP Multicast Protocol   **MBone**

3 A major advantage of the multicast protocol is that when the video packets are sent—for example, from Europe to the United States—they are sent only one time even though they might be sent to many destinations. Normally, TCP would have to send separate video packets for each destination. The multicast protocol solves the problem by putting information about the many Internet destinations into one packet. Later in the transmission, the video signals will be delivered to each of the destinations.

TCP Packet

IP Multicast Protocol

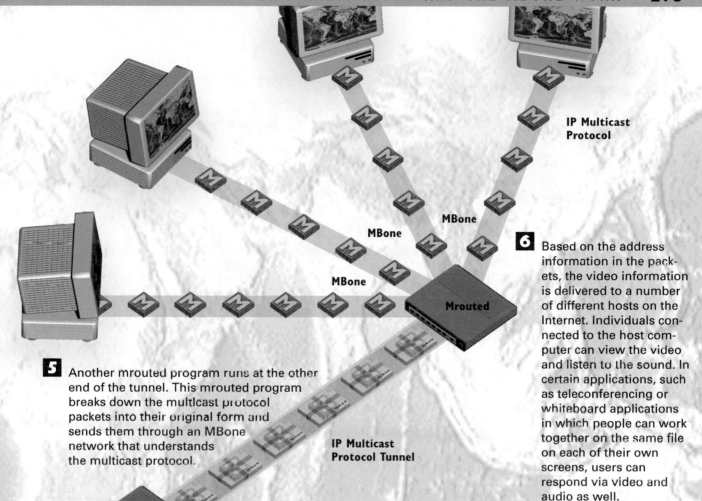

IP Multicast Protocol

MBone

MBone

MBone

Mrouted

6 Based on the address information in the packets, the video information is delivered to a number of different hosts on the Internet. Individuals connected to the host computer can view the video and listen to the sound. In certain applications, such as teleconferencing or whiteboard applications in which people can work together on the same file on each of their own screens, users can respond via video and audio as well.

5 Another mrouted program runs at the other end of the tunnel. This mrouted program breaks down the multicast protocol packets into their original form and sends them through an MBone network that understands the multicast protocol.

IP Multicast Protocol Tunnel

Mrouted

4 The MBone understands the multicast protocol, but most networks and routers on the Internet do not. However, the MBone network often requires that data travel along normal Internet routes. To solve the problem, the MBone data travels in tunnels through existing Internet networks and routers. At one end of the tunnel is a Unix workstation that runs software called *mrouted (multicast routing demon)*. This software encapsulates the multicast protocol packets inside normal TCP packets. To the Internet, the data now looks like normal TCP packets, and the data can be properly routed.

CHAPTER

40

How Virtual Reality Is Created by VRML

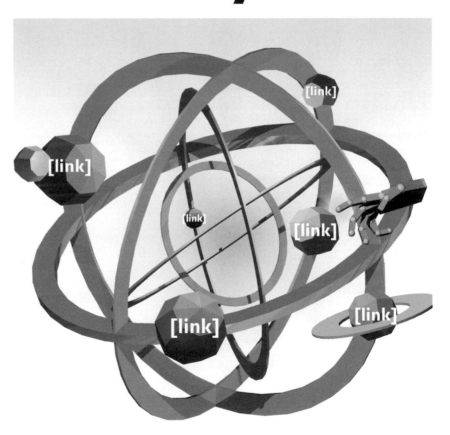

IMAGINE the Internet as a place where you could walk through three-dimensional worlds, pick up objects, examine them, and go to other Internet locations by flying or walking through doors. Picture home pages that are more than flat, two-dimensional surfaces that you can only read. What if you could be inside them, just like you can walk through a city or a building?

That's the promise of virtual reality (VR) on the Internet. In fact, it's more than just a promise—VR is already here. You'll find many virtual worlds you can explore on the Internet. You can walk through a giant computer, explore bizarre art galleries, visit outer space, go to the sites of what seem like ancient ruins, explore inside the human brain, and much more.

Virtual worlds are created using a computer language called Virtual Reality Modeling Language (VRML). This language instructs computers on how to build 3D geometric objects. Programmers and artists use the language to build complex worlds from these geometric objects. A VRML world is created by an ASCII text file containing VRML language commands—and for greater realism, graphics files can be added to this world as well. Because the virtual world is only an ASCII file, with perhaps a few graphics files, it can be downloaded quickly to your computer from the Internet, although some worlds with many graphics in them can be large.

When a virtual world is created, it is posted on an Internet server. When you want to visit that world, you either type in its URL or click a link to it, just as you do to visit any other location on the World Wide Web. To display the virtual world, you need a program capable of displaying the world—either a separate virtual reality browser, or more likely, a plug-in player that configures itself to your normal web browser.

The VRML file describing the virtual world downloads to your computer. This can take a few minutes, or well over half an hour, depending on the size of the world and your connection speed. After the file is on your computer, your CPU computes the geometry of the world, based on the VRML commands in the file. Again, depending on the size of the world and the speed of your CPU, this can take only a minute or two, or up to 10 minutes or more. After the world is computed, you can walk through it, fly through it, examine objects, and spin them. You can also visit other virtual worlds or places on the Internet by interacting with the world.

VR on the Internet is being used for far more than just creating virtual worlds people can walk through. For example, it has been used to create views of the brain and of molecules. It has been used by astronomers to show the rotation of molecular gas in a galaxy undergoing active star formation. Finally, as with everything else related to the Internet, VR will be eventually used for things that today none of us can imagine.

Despite all its appeal, one major problem with VR worlds is that they can be very large. Because of that, they can be very slow to load and interact with due to the current limited bandwidth of the Internet. As bandwidth increases, those problems might eventually go away.

How Virtual Reality Is Created by VRML

1 When someone wants to create a virtual world, she uses the Virtual Reality Modeling Language (VRML). VRML lets people create 3D worlds not by drawing them, but instead by using the VRML computer language to describe the geometry of a scene. VRML files are much smaller than graphics files. VRML files are simply text files containing instructions for drawing the VRML world. VRML files end in a .wrl extension. After the world is created, it is posted on a web server.

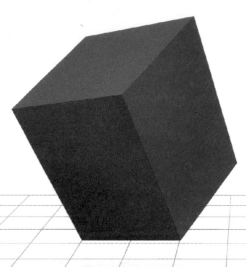

```
#VRML V1.Ø ascii
Separator {
    DirectionalLight {
        direction Ø Ø -1  # Light shining from viewer into scene
    }
    PerspectiveCamera {
        position    -8.6 2.1 5.6
        orientation -Ø.1352 -Ø.9831 -Ø.1233  1.1417
        focalDistance     1Ø.84
    }
    Separator {   # The red sphere
        Material {
            diffuseColor 1 Ø Ø   # Red
        }
        Translation { translation 3 Ø 1 }
        Sphere { radius 2.3 }
    }
    Separator {   # The blue cube
        Material {
            diffuseColor Ø Ø 1  # Blue
        }
        Transform {
            translation -2.4 .2 1
            rotation Ø 1 1  .9
        }
        Cube {}
    }
}
```

Web Server

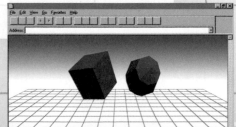

2 Here is an example of a VRML file describing a scene that has a red sphere and a blue cube in it, lit by a directional light.

[link]

[link]

[link]

[link]

[link]

6 For greater realism and detail, graphics files can be "painted" on virtual reality objects—for example, to show paintings in an art gallery. When these graphics files are painted on objects, they must be downloaded along with the .wrl file as .gif or .jpeg files. When the browser displays the virtual world, it shows those graphics files on top of VR objects so they look like part of the scene.

5 Objects in the virtual world can be links to sites on the Web, to other virtual worlds, and to animations. So, for example, if you walk through a door, you might be sent to a home page on the Internet or to another virtual world. If you're sent to another virtual world, that virtual world must be downloaded from a web server to your computer so your browser can compute the new world and you can interact with it.

4 As the file downloads, the VR plug-in is launched. It doesn't run separately from your web browser. Instead, it takes over your web browser while you're in the virtual world. After the file is downloaded, your VR plug-in creates the virtual world by taking the VRML commands in the file and having your computer compute the geometry of the scene. After the computation is done, the scene appears on your screen. The VRML file contains three-dimensional information that enables you to "walk" or "fly" through the scene using your browser. Depending on the complexity of the scene, your computer might have to do computations as you move through the scene.

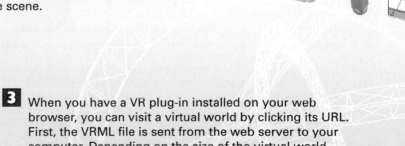

Web Browser

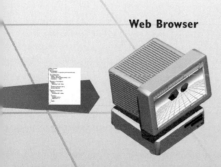

3 When you have a VR plug-in installed on your web browser, you can visit a virtual world by clicking its URL. First, the VRML file is sent from the web server to your computer. Depending on the size of the virtual world and your connection speed, the file can take from a few minutes to a half-hour or more to download to your computer.

CHAPTER

41

How Animation on the Web Works

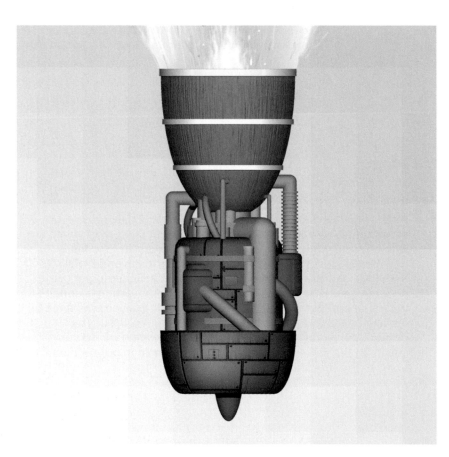

ANIMATION on the Web works no differently than animation anywhere else. Just like in a flip book, animation is a series of still images displayed in succession to create an illusion of fluid motion. The faster the frames advance, the more fluid the animation becomes. Unfortunately, the Web can be a very slow place, and an animation that should run quickly often crawls across the screen unless special technology is used.

A number of different ways exist for creating web animations, including client pull, server push, animated GIFs, and the Shockwave and Flash multimedia plug-ins. In *client pull*, an HTML page gives the browser instructions to request and load another document automatically, similar to a slideshow. Web pages are displayed one after the other with a specified time delay in between. This feature is useful for step-by-step instructions. But client pull is slowed by the need to load a whole page rather than a single cell of animation, which prevents the illusion of fluid animation.

Client pull requests are embedded within the HTTP response header of a web page that the server sends back to the client. The <META> tag inserts meta-information into a response header. *Meta-information* helps parse a web page, but the browser does not display it. A *response header* is the beginning of each HTTP response that a server sends back to a client with the requested web page.

Server push is a complement to client pull, although server push is the more complex of the two. Server push requires a *Common Gateway Interface (CGI)* script that tells the server when to automatically serve a new document or image. (For information about CGI, turn to Chapter 35, "How CGI Scripting Works.")

It also requires client browser capability of recognizing the MIME-type, `multipart/x-mixed-replace`. This MIME-type enables multiple documents to be sent within one message. To understand how server push works, imagine an email message with text, hypertext, a digital movie, and sound. You can see how multiple "documents" (media types) can be sent within a single message. The multipart message is simply a series of images that displays one image right after the other. The server sends, or *pushes*, each image. In this way, a small animation can be embedded among the text and images of an otherwise static web page.

Animated GIFs are a series of graphical GIF images that roll up into a single image—much like a flip book seems to animate a series of drawings as you thumb through the pages. The animated GIFs load into a browser just like any GIF file does; however, they load in a series to give the illusion of motion. Animated GIFs have the benefit of speed because images are cached on the client PC and loaded from memory rather than from the Internet. They represent an easy solution to adding motion to web pages.

More complex multimedia animation has become possible using Macromedia's Shockwave and Flash plugs-in. Shockwave plays multimedia files created with Macromedia's popular Director and Authorware programs, whereas Flash uses its own special tools. You must first download and install the Shockwave and Flash plug-ins before you can view any web pages that have Shockwave or Flash animations.

How Client Pull and Server Push Animation Work

Client Pull

Client pull is executed by the Refresh command. A refresh command is written into an HTML document using the <META> tag. The contents of the <META> tag are added to the header's meta-information that the server sends along with the HTTP response. During a client pull sequence, the browser reads this header information that instructs it to use your PC's internal clock to keep track of the time elapsed between pages retrieved. When the time has elapsed, the browser requests and displays the next page.

1 Each page in a client pull sequence can be located anywhere on the Web. The URL following the Refresh command might lead the browser to any active server. Page E is located on a different server than pages A–D, but is still requested automatically after five seconds.

2 If the next document to load also has a Refresh command in the header, the browser simply repeats the process. In this case, it retrieves and displays page C after 10 seconds.

3 Whoever writes the HTML source code can specify how long it will be until the request for the next page is made. Page C refreshes after only 2 seconds, and page D follows.

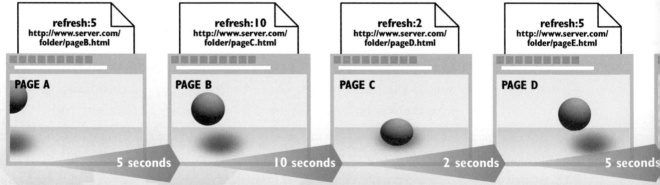

refresh:5
http://www.server.com/
folder/pageB.html

refresh:10
http://www.server.com/
folder/pageC.html

refresh:2
http://www.server.com/
folder/pageD.html

refresh:5
http://www.server.com/
folder/pageE.html

PAGE A

PAGE B

PAGE C

PAGE D

5 seconds   10 seconds   2 seconds   5 seconds

4 The Refresh command does two things. First, it indicates the time before the next page request is sent or the same page reloads. For example, page A in the illustration refreshes after 5 seconds. Secondly, if the URL follows the number of seconds, a request for that page is sent automatically after 5 seconds. After the browser parses a document's meta-information and recognizes the Refresh command in the header, it knows to send a request for the page indicated by the URL following the command.

Note
A client pull sequence might continue for as many or as few pages as the site designer wants. The last page will simply not have a Refresh command in the header. A user can stop the process manually by clicking the browser's Stop button.

Server Push

Server push is more complicated than client pull, but it enables inline animation that does not require an entire web page to load each animation frame.

1 The HTML source code for a server push animation is deceptively simple. The <IMG> (image) tag references the animation just like a static picture or icon.

2 When the browser recognizes the <IMG> tag, it makes a single request to the server for a file. But rather than retrieving an image file, the HTML reference tag <IMG SCR-URL> gives directions to a CGI script that runs the animation.

HTML PAGE
<H1>Page Heading
Chapter 1</H1>
<IMG SRC="http://
www.some.server/
animation.cgi>
<P>
Start body text here...

4 The CGI script takes advantage of the multipart/x-mixed-replace MIME type. This enables the CGI script to send, or push, a series of still images from the server to the client as if it were transferring a single file. In this illustration, the animation has four frames, and each frame is a separate file. Each new frame that arrives at the client replaces the old one, which gives the illusion of fluid movement.

3 When the request arrives at the server, the CGI script is opened and executed. (Recall that a programmer must write a CGI script—similar to authoring other kinds of software.)

Frame 1   Frame 2   Frame 3   Frame 4

refre
://www.
•lder/pa

Note
The server and client make one connection that is open for as long as the CGI script runs. You can manually end a server push animation by clicking the browser's Stop button.

CGI SCRIPT
multipart/x-replace
file: frame 1
-boundary-
file: frame 2
-boundary-
file: frame 3
-boundary-
file: frame 4
etc.

1

2

3

4

Frames of animation

How Shockwave Works

I The first step in a Shockwave animation happens in a multimedia-authoring program such as Director or Authorware. An animation designer must gather the raw materials, such as still images, music, and sound effects, necessary for a short and compelling animation.

2 The authoring program then helps arrange the elements frame by frame along a time line. It also enables the designer to match a sound effect with a particular action in the animation.

Director Software from Macromedia

3 When this step is done, the complete animation is saved as a Director or an Authorware movie file.

4 Next, the movie file must be converted and compressed into a small file that can be quickly downloaded to a user's PC.

Compresses File for Internet Delivery

Converts Director File to Shockwave File

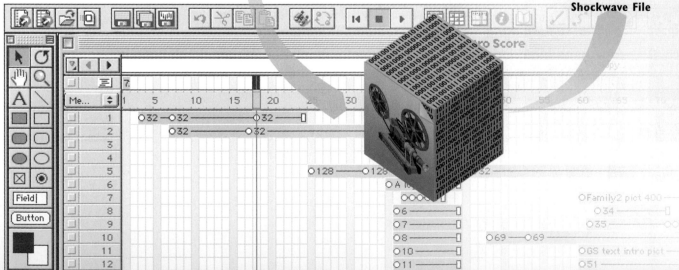

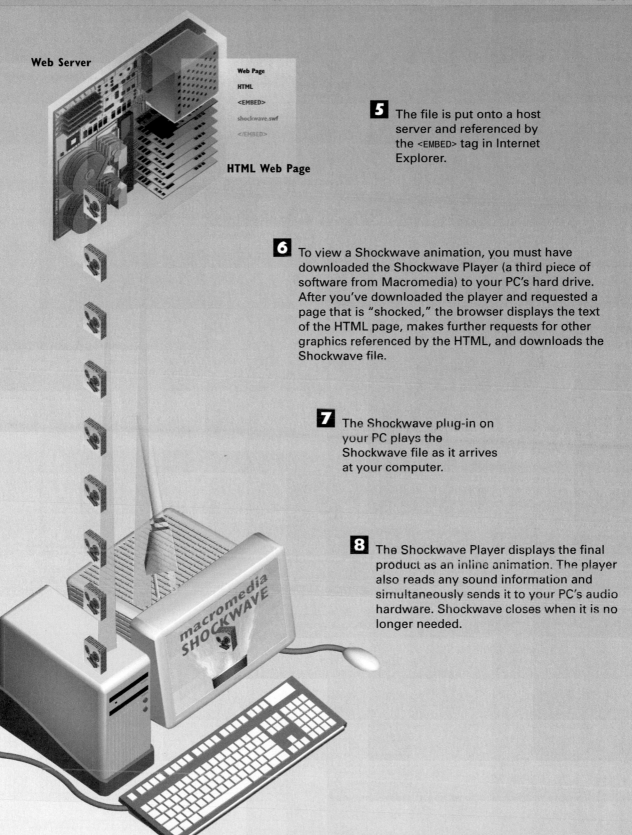

Web Server

Web Page

HTML

<EMBED>

shockwave.swf

</EMBED>

HTML Web Page

5 The file is put onto a host server and referenced by the <EMBED> tag in Internet Explorer.

6 To view a Shockwave animation, you must have downloaded the Shockwave Player (a third piece of software from Macromedia) to your PC's hard drive. After you've downloaded the player and requested a page that is "shocked," the browser displays the text of the HTML page, makes further requests for other graphics referenced by the HTML, and downloads the Shockwave file.

7 The Shockwave plug-in on your PC plays the Shockwave file as it arrives at your computer.

8 The Shockwave Player displays the final product as an inline animation. The player also reads any sound information and simultaneously sends it to your PC's audio hardware. Shockwave closes when it is no longer needed.

macromedia SHOCKWAVE

How Flash Works

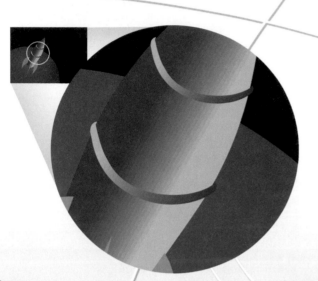

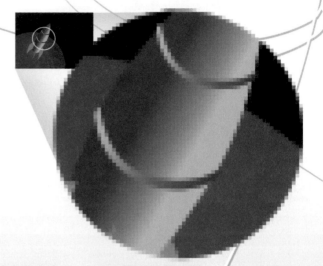

1 Flash is an animation program that enables designers to add animation, sound, and interactivity to web pages. Flash uses vector graphics instead of bit-mapped graphics. *Vector graphics* are mathematical descriptions of a shape, while a *bit-mapped* image is an actual pixel-by-pixel representation of the image. Not only are vector graphics smaller and more suitable to the Web because of reduced download time than bit-mapped images, but, unlike bit-mapped graphics, they can also be zoomed in on without any degradation in quality.

Sound FX: 4, 3, 2, 1, 0   Sound FX: BLAST OFF!   Sound FX: zoooooom

2 To create a Flash movie, a designer uses traditional animation techniques. He draws a picture in a frame, draws another picture slightly different than the first, then a third slightly different from the second, and so on.

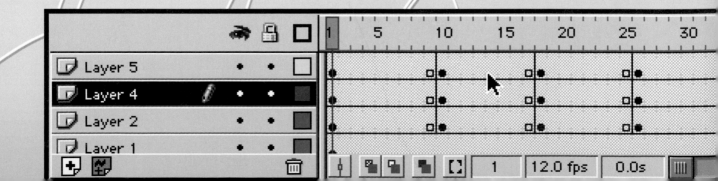

3 These pictures are all placed on a Flash timeline and are displayed one after another—appearing to move. The animator has control over the speed at which the frames replace one another, or *frame rate*.

4 The timeline is used not just for images, but for sounds as well. To play sounds at specific times, the animator drops the sound into the timeline. The Flash movie can also include links to web pages, JavaScript commands, and other kinds of interactivity. Again, all these are dropped into a timeline.

5 When a designer finishes making a movie, it is compiled into a file with an .swf format and posted on a website. Anyone who views it needs a Flash player, which is available for free and is bundled into many versions of browsers.

6 When someone visits a site with an HTML reference to the .swf file, the Flash movie begins to play. If the person doesn't have the Flash player, he is prompted to download it for free from the Macromedia site. The movie begins to play. A big benefit of Flash is that it *streams content*, which means that the movie can begin playing while the rest of the movie downloads in the background. This means that Flash movies can start playing very quickly even if they are very long ones.

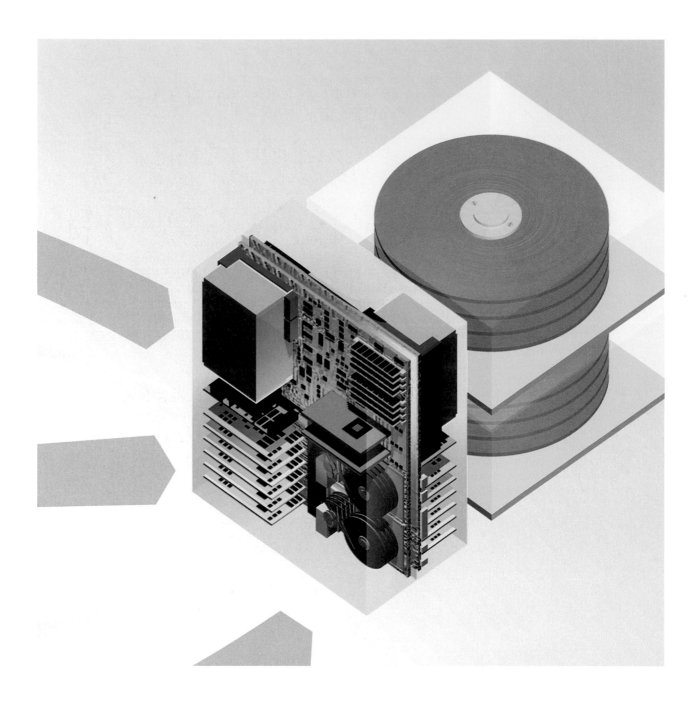

P A R T

SHOPPING AND DOING BUSINESS ON THE INTERNET

THE Internet has its roots in the military and in academia, but it has become intimately tied to the way we live and work, and it will become more so with each passing year. At work, for entertainment, to get information, and to shop—the Internet has become a vital part of our daily lives.

The Internet's dramatic growth has been fueled in large part by business and consumers. It has become one of the primary places in which businesses operate, and where billions of dollars in goods and services are bought and sold every year.

Thousands of businesses use the Internet to market and sell their products, and many people buy things from home and from their places of business through the Internet instead of at retail stores. You can use the Internet to browse through catalogs and make purchases online; to buy and sell stock, mortgages, and insurance; and even to participate in online auctions. Companies are figuring out ways not only to sell online, but also to hook those online transactions into their internal computer and billing systems.

This part of the book looks at the various ways the Internet is used for business and shopping online. It covers how the Internet is being used by businesses as their primary corporate networks and how business and commerce are being conducted on the Internet every day.

Chapter 42, "How Intranets Work," covers intranets. Intranets are private networks set up by companies for their employees, using Internet technology. They're used for many purposes, including email, group brainstorming, group scheduling, and access to corporate databases and documents, among others.

Although intranets use TCP/IP networks and technologies, the network and its resources are used only by the businesses and are not available to people outside the company. Intranets are separated from the Internet by firewalls that don't allow unauthorized access to the intranet. People who work in the company can access the intranet and use its resources, but intruders are kept out by the firewalls.

This chapter also looks at one of the most important parts of an intranet—workgroup software. This type of software ties together everyone in a corporation and enables them to work together better. Among other things, it enables people to share files and information; to cooperate more easily on projects; and in general, to work together in ways never before possible. It allows people to go beyond simply communicating and enables them to work together on shared documents.

This chapter examines a variety of workgroup software. It covers messaging software that enables people to publicly participate in group discussions. It also looks at whiteboard software, which enables people to see what is on other people's computers and work together on documents. Several people could look at a spreadsheet together, for example, and one person could mark up the spreadsheet while everyone else sees what is being done.

The chapter also explains how Virtual Private Networks (VPNs) work. VPNs allow people to securely access corporate networks remotely, from home or when they are traveling, and can be big corporate productivity boosters.

Chapter 43, "Shopping on the Internet," covers what has become one of the most popular parts of the Internet—shopping online. Today, shopping on the Internet accounts for billions of dollars a year in revenue, and every year many more billions are spent. In fact, you can't turn on your television set or open a newspaper or magazine without being confronted by advertising for a variety of online shopping sites. Although many of the original shopping sites have gone out of business, they've been replaced by the very businesses they expected to supplant—existing retailers. So, today you'll find stores such as the Gap and Wal-Mart—so called brick-and-mortar stores, or bricks-and-clicks—with big online shopping sites.

This chapter shows you what's going on behind the scenes when you shop online. It shows you how online shopping carts work—a technology that lets you gather together goods you're thinking of buying into a virtual shopping cart and then go through a checkout with them and pay by credit card. Finally, this chapter covers one of the most popular ways to shop online—buying at online auctions. Every day, millions of people buy and sell millions of items through auction sites, particularly the popular eBay. You'll see, in this chapter, how technology enables eBay to work.

CHAPTER

42

How Intranets Work

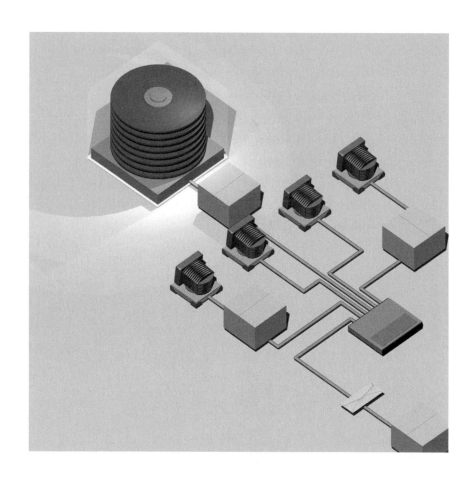

BUSINESSES increasingly use Internet technology to create private corporate networks called *intranets*. These intranets are used for a wide variety of purposes, such as email, group brainstorming, group scheduling, access to corporate databases and documents, videoconferencing, and the buying and selling of goods and services.

Intranets use TCP/IP networks and technologies as well as Internet resources such as the World Wide Web, email, Telnet, and FTP. However, the network and its resources are used privately by businesses and are not available to people outside the company. An intranet is separated from the rest of the Internet by a *firewall*—a hardware and software combination that prohibits unauthorized access to the intranet. People who work in the company can access the Internet and use its resources, but firewalls keep out intruders. Turn to Chapter 44, "How Firewalls Work," to learn more about firewalls.

Intranets use a combination of off-the-shelf software, such as web browsers, and customized software, such as database querying tools. Because intranets are based on Internet standard protocols, it will always be possible to quickly update them with the latest in network technologies.

In the long term, companies will make the most use of intranets in *workgroup applications*—software that enables people to work cooperatively with their computers. Many kinds of workgroup software exist. These programs enable people to participate in discussions and videoconferencing across the country and across the world, share databases, track documents, and much more.

The key to workgroup software is that it enables people to go beyond simply communicating and lets them work together on shared documents.

One of the most basic pieces of workgroup software is *messaging software*—programs that enable people to publicly participate in group discussions.

What makes intranet messaging software especially useful is the way it integrates with other Internet and intranet technologies. For example, some discussion software allows the use of Hypertext Markup Language (HTML) embedded inside messages. This means that from within a discussion, someone could embed a link to a web page or other intranet resource.

A more sophisticated workgroup application is *desktop videoconferencing*. This application requires that everyone involved have computer-linked video cameras as well as hardware and software that enable computers to send and receive voice and sound. While sitting at computers, people can see and speak to one another.

A related technology is called whiteboard software. *Whiteboard software* lets people see what is on someone else's computer on an intranet while sitting at their own computers. This means people on the same intranet—whether they're on opposite sides of the country from one another—can easily comment on one another's work.

Increasingly popular among businesses are Virtual Private Networks (VPNs), which let employees connect securely to the company intranet no matter where they are—at home, on the road, or anywhere else. They use a kind of "tunneling" technology to let people use the public Internet to connect to the company intranet, while keeping all communications secure and encrypted.

Using an Intranet Within a Company

1 An intranet is separated from the rest of the Internet by a *firewall*—a hardware/software combination that protects the corporate intranet from snooping eyes and malicious attacks. The firewall enables corporate employees to use the Internet and also enables certain parts of the intranet—such as areas designed for electronic commerce—to be accessed by outsiders.

Corporate Database

Mail Server

2 A key component of an intranet is an internal email system. The email system works just like Internet email. It can use normal Internet email clients, but it is designed to route traffic within an organization, so the email need not travel outside the intranet. Internal routers and mail servers send the mail to other corporate employees via the intranet. Email from the intranet that travels to and from the Internet must go through the firewall.

3 Corporate databases with important information can be made available over the intranet via web-based HTML documents and search tools. Typically, searching those databases will require the creation of CGI scripts or Java programs. These databases will be available only to corporate employees, and like the rest of the intranet, the firewall protects them.

Router

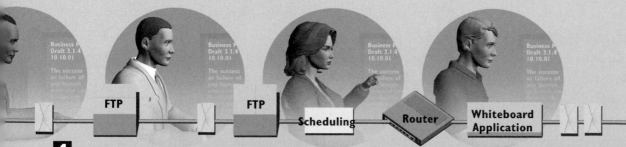

FTP **FTP** **Scheduling** **Router** **Whiteboard Application**

4 An intranet enables people to collaborate on their work electronically using groupware. *Groupware* enables people to have online brainstorming sessions, schedule group meetings, work on documents and plans together, create common databases, and perform other kinds of cooperative work.

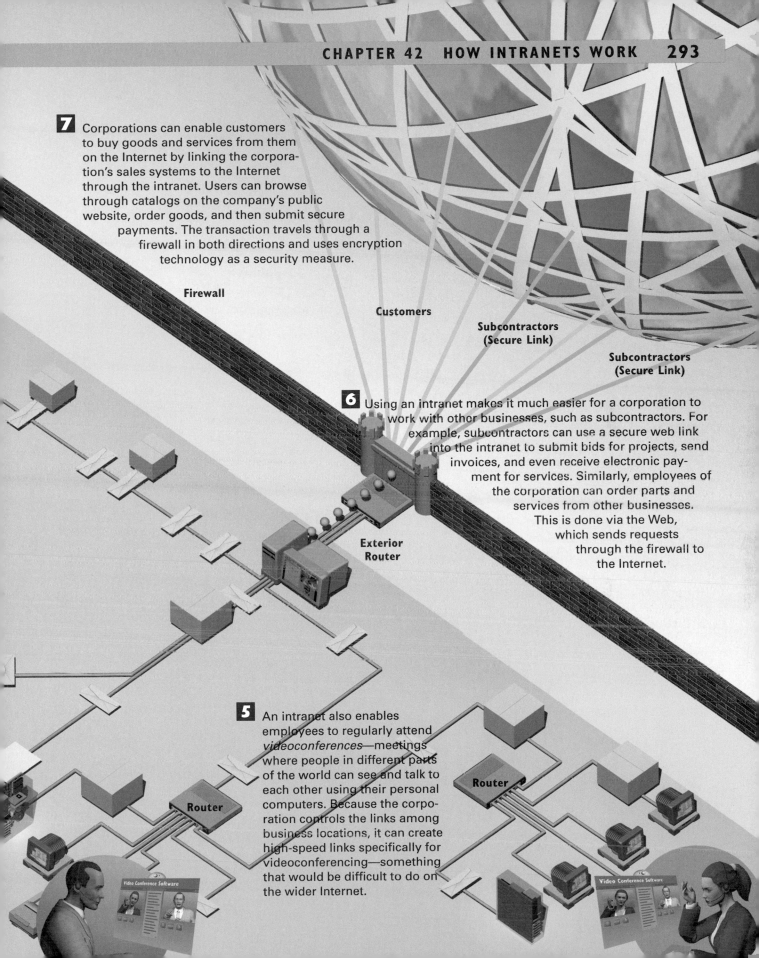

7 Corporations can enable customers to buy goods and services from them on the Internet by linking the corporation's sales systems to the Internet through the intranet. Users can browse through catalogs on the company's public website, order goods, and then submit secure payments. The transaction travels through a firewall in both directions and uses encryption technology as a security measure.

Firewall

Customers

Subcontractors (Secure Link)

Subcontractors (Secure Link)

6 Using an intranet makes it much easier for a corporation to work with other businesses, such as subcontractors. For example, subcontractors can use a secure web link into the intranet to submit bids for projects, send invoices, and even receive electronic payment for services. Similarly, employees of the corporation can order parts and services from other businesses. This is done via the Web, which sends requests through the firewall to the Internet.

Exterior Router

5 An intranet also enables employees to regularly attend *videoconferences*—meetings where people in different parts of the world can see and talk to each other using their personal computers. Because the corporation controls the links among business locations, it can create high-speed links specifically for videoconferencing—something that would be difficult to do on the wider Internet.

Router

Router

Video Conference Software

Video Conference Software

How Virtual Private Networks (VPNs) Work

1 In this example, we're showing a remote PC sending a file to someone inside a corporate network, using a VPN to tunnel through the Internet. In order to connect to the VPN, client software must be running on the PC on one end of the tunnel. The client first encrypts each of the document's packets.

VPN Client Software

Michael's Private Key

2 After the packets are encrypted, each of them is encapsulated inside a normal IP packet. The IP packets have a destination address of the PC or router at the other end of the tunnel. This ensures that as the packets travel across the Internet, the true destination IP addresses can't be read by snoopers. Only the tunnel IP address will be read.

To: 197.1.3.4

3 The packets travel across the Internet as they do normally. Routers looking at the packets see only the IP headers with the address of the VPN tunnel, not the headers inside the encapsulated packets.

Router

To: 197.1.3.4

To: 197.1.3.4   To: 197.1.3.4   To: 197.1.3.4   To: 197

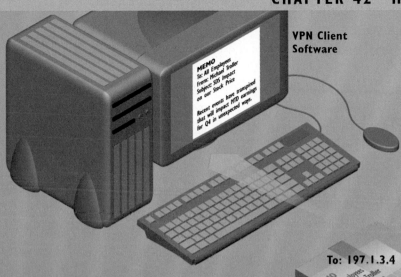

**VPN Client
Software**

6 Based on the information in the
IP header, it delivers the packets
to the destination PC.

To: 197.1.3.4

5 Next, it decrypts the
packet, including the
IP header information.

**Michael's
Public Key**

Firewall

4 At the receiving end of the
VPN tunnel, a PC or router
receives the packets. It strips
off the outside IP packet.

197.1.3.4

The Internet

Router

To: 197.1.3.4

To: 197.1.3.4

To: 197.1.3.4

To: 197.1.3.4

To: 197.1.3.4

CHAPTER

43

Shopping on the Internet

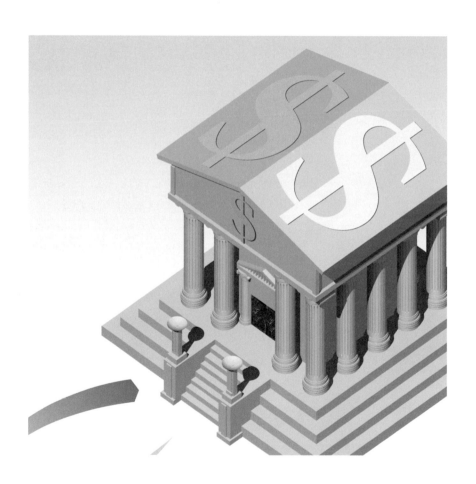

BILLIONS of dollars are spent every year shopping on the Internet—and if think tanks and market research firms are to be believed, that's only the beginning. The Internet will eventually revolutionize shopping in the same way it's revolutionized working, getting information, and communicating.

Online shopping is made possible through the use of *encryption techniques*—the ability to scramble information as it's sent through the Internet so that no one can read it except the intended recipient. Encryption is used to scramble credit card information—the primary way that people pay when buying online. (For more information about encryption, and to see how encryption works, turn to Chapter 50, "Cryptography, Privacy, and Digital Certificates." To see how encryption can keep email private, turn to Chapter 11, "How Email Works.")

Most of what you see when you visit a shopping site on the Internet is contained in databases on web servers. These databases have information about the products for sale at the site—and they're also used to automatically generate the HTML pages that make up the shopping site. So, for example, when a new product becomes available, information about that product is put into a database, and CGI scripts and a web server then work with the database to create a new item on a web page describing the product. You, in turn, can look at that product and decide whether you want to buy it.

Databases and cookies are also used when you use *virtual shopping carts*—portions of a website where you place items you're considering buying. Before buying, you can take items out of the cart or put new items in. *Cookies* track everything you put into and take out of the cart, and then *databases* work with the cookies, CGI scripts, and web servers to complete the transaction when you want to buy something.

Web databases are also used to complete the shopping transaction when you buy. When you decide you want to buy something from a site, you fill out a form, send in your credit card information, and that information is sent to a web database. The database, in turn, checks the validity of your credit card. If it's valid, the database sends a confirmation to you and then sends off an order to a warehouse or other distribution method that ships the product to you. Databases can't do all this by themselves—they work in concert with CGI scripts, web servers, and cookies.

This chapter looks at how online buying and virtual shopping carts work. Finally, you'll see how one of the most popular kinds of buying sites works—*online auctions*.

How Online Buying Works

1 Most shopping sites are built on top of databases, so when customers visit a website and browse or search for a product, they're actually searching through a database that is searched from the Web.

Database Server

Product Listing

- VCRs
- Digital Cameras
- Video Cameras
- CD Players
- Printers
- Monitors

Entering Secure Area

2 When customers see a product they want to buy, they'll usually pay by credit card. Before filling out a form with their credit card information, they're usually sent to a secure section of the website where encryption will be used to scramble the data.

Encrypted Credit Card

Order Form

123-456-789-012

6 The site confirms the order, and using CGI scripts, the web page refreshes and displays a page that the customer can print out to confirm the order. Many sites also follow up by sending an email message to the customer.

Thank you for your order.

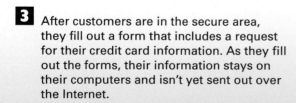

3 After customers are in the secure area, they fill out a form that includes a request for their credit card information. As they fill out the forms, their information stays on their computers and isn't yet sent out over the Internet.

5 The transaction server receives the encrypted information and decrypts it. It then checks with the credit card company to ensure whether the card is valid and can be used, in a similar way to how retail stores check whether your card is valid, except that it's done over the Internet.

Transaction Server

Ok to accept?

OK

4 After the form is filled out, the customer clicks a Submit button, or something similar, to send the information from the customer's computer to the site's secure transaction server. As the information is sent out over the Internet, it's encrypted so that it's nearly impossible to read, except by the site itself.

Ok to ship the goods.

7 The transaction server sends an order to the warehouse or other designated area that fills the order, and the order is completed as any other order is, by shipping via mail or express mail service.

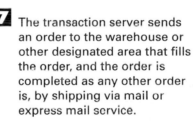

How Online Shopping Carts Work

2 When the person completes the registration form, it's sent to the web database. The database creates a record for that person and sends the person a *cookie*— a small piece of data that sits on the person's hard disk and can be used to identify that person.

Cookie

4 The web server in turn writes a new piece of data to the cookie, which identifies the item that the person wants to put in his shopping cart. More than one item can be put in the shopping cart in this way.

Change Cookie

Ready

5 When the person is ready to check out his items, he goes to a web page containing his shopping cart. When he goes to the page, the cookie tells the web server what items to display on the page.

I Usually, before a shopping cart can be used, a person must register with the site by filling out information such as name, address, and other personal information. Sometimes a credit card number is required as well.

Database Server

Register Me

3 When the shopper thinks he wants to buy something, he clicks it, which puts the item in his shopping cart. When he clicks an item, that information is sent to the web server.

Buy This

Buy item/ Delete Item

Check Out

6 When someone decides to buy the items in the shopping cart, he sends in credit card information. When the items are bought, the server updates information about those items in the cookie. Later, when the person visits his shopping cart, it is empty because the information about his purchases was deleted from the cookie, or else the cookie was designed so that it would expire after a certain amount of time.

How eBay Sells Everything
DENVER, CO

SACRAMENTO, CA   SANTA CLARA 1, CA   SANTA CLARA 2, CA

1 When you go to the eBay site, you are automatically routed to one of four eBay data centers. eBay operates four data centers to ensure the site will always be up and running—if one data center goes down, three others are still available. Two data centers are located in Santa Clara, California; one is in Sacramento, California; and one is located in Denver, Colorado. The data centers are mirrors of one another, so no matter which data center you connect to, you get the same information, auctions, and functions. The centers are connected to one another via a high-speed *Synchronous Optical Network (SONET)*.

2 Inside each data center, the eBay site is hosted on web servers running the Windows Advanced Server 2003 and Windows 2000 Server operating systems. So when you visit the website, you're connecting to one of those servers.

5 The database sends the results of the search back to the search servers, which in turn send the results to the web servers. The web servers then send the results to you.

8 When the transactions are complete, the buyer and seller are tasked with the all-important duty of rating the transaction experience. These ratings are crucial to eBay because they help to assure its users that they are not dealing with swindlers or deadbeats.

HDTV PLASMA DISPLAYS

3 When you type in a term to search for an auction, your search is sent off to separate search servers running a search application written using J2EE (Java), which is run on Sun Microsystems hardware.

4 The search servers send the search request to a cluster of 50 database servers running an Oracle database on a Sun SPARC computer. This database is in essence what eBay really is—it contains all the details of every single auction on eBay.

6 You browse through the results. When you find an auction in which you're interested, you make a bid. The web server sends the bid to an application server, which in turn sends the bid to the database servers that incorporate the bid into the database. The bid is now live and whomever visits that auction page will see it.

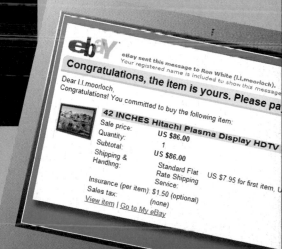

7 Flags in the database signal when the auction ends. At this time, the database sends all the information about the winning bid to the application server. The application server sends the information to the web server so it can be posted, and it automatically creates emails to be sent via email servers to the winning bidder and the seller.

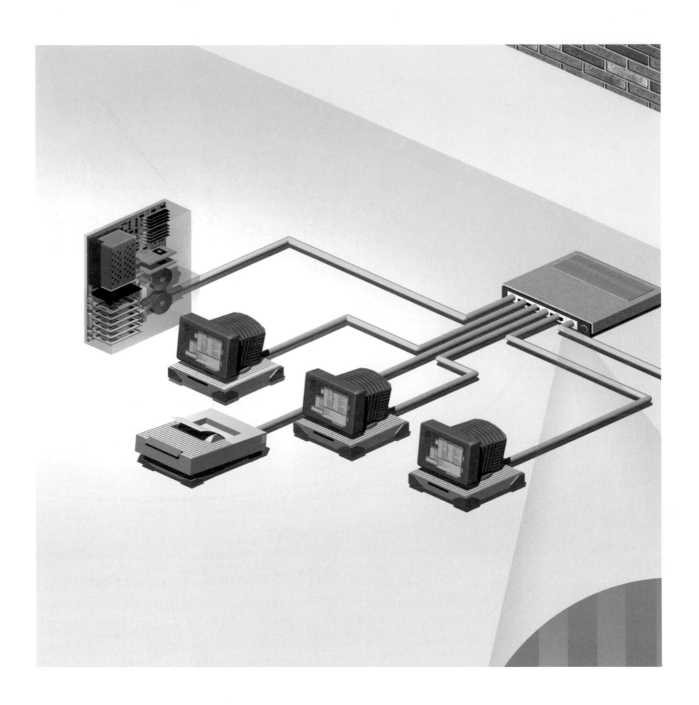

THE very nature of the Internet makes it vulnerable to attack. It was designed to allow for the freest possible exchange of information, data, and files—and it has succeeded admirably, far beyond its designers' wildest expectations. However, that freedom carries a price: Hackers and virus writers try to attack the Internet and computers connected to the Internet; those who want to invade others' privacy attempt to crack databases of sensitive information or snoop on information as it travels across Internet routes; and distasteful and pornographic sites have sprung up on the Web and on Usenet newsgroups.

This section of the book looks at a variety of security-related issues. You'll see how hackers target websites, invade your PC, and create vast armies of "zombie" networks that can be used to attack computers and sites whenever the hacker tells them to. You'll find out details about the dangers inherent in using wireless technologies, and see how viruses work. You'll also examine how websites can invade your privacy every time you visit.

There's a lot more in this section as well. Various tools have been developed to make transactions on the Net more secure and to help companies protect their sensitive data. You'll examine the thorny issue of pornography versus free speech and see how software can block children from visiting obscene sites or getting obscene materials. You'll also learn about some of the more controversial technologies on the Internet, such as cookies, which enable web servers to track your movements through their sites. This section also takes an inside look at an even more controversial technology, the National Security Agency's Echelon program, which allows it to wiretap, read email, and find out about people's Web surfing habits all over the world. You'll also look at how viruses work and how hackers attack Internet service providers (ISPs).

Chapter 44, "How Firewalls Work," looks at firewalls. Many companies whose networks are connected to the Internet have a great deal of sensitive information on their networks and want to ensure that their data and computers are safe from attack. The answer is to use firewalls— systems that allow people from inside a company to use the Internet but also stop people on the Internet from getting at the company's computers. This chapter also discusses personal firewalls— software people can use at home to ensure that hackers can't invade their own computers.

Chapter 45, "How Hackers Can Cripple the Internet and Attack Your PC," looks at attacks launched by hackers that can cripple ISPs and attack your computer as well. In a Denial of Service (DOS) attack, also called a *smurf attack*, or *smurfing*, a hacker targets an ISP and floods it with so much "garbage" traffic that none of the ISP's customers can use the service. Smurfing is one of the most common types of hacking attacks on the Internet. This chapter also examines the various ways hackers can attack your PC.

The chapter also gives you the rundown on zombie networks, which can be used by hackers to attack sites and computers at will. It also shows how viruses can invade your PC via email, and how hackers exploit browsers to invade your PC.

Chapter 46, "The Dangers of Wireless Networking," delves into the newest dangers to hit the Internet. Millions of people connect to the Internet wirelessly every day, using home wireless networks, wireless networks at work, public hot spots in cafes and similar locations, and via their cell phones. Every time they connect, they court danger, as this chapter shows you. The chapter details how hackers go "war driving" to find wireless networks to invade, and shows how they use a nefarious technique called an "Evil Twin" hack to fool you into giving up your personal information. The chapter also shows how you can protect yourself against wireless hacks and how B-list celebrity Paris Hilton had her cell phone hacked.

Chapter 47, "How Viruses Work," looks at viruses and how they are detected. Any program you download from the Internet has the potential for being infected with a virus and could infect your computer. You'll see just how these nasty data-killers work and look at antivirus tools that can detect and kill them. This chapter also examines how a special type of virus called a worm works. Worms are becoming increasingly common on the Internet, so you'll look at one of the most infamous worms—Melissa—and how it affected the Internet.

Chapter 48, "How Internet Sites Can Invade Your Privacy," explores controversial technologies that enable websites to track what you do when you're online. It covers cookies, web tracking, and web bugs, as well as a technology that can help preserve people's privacy—Internet passports. Some people worry that cookies and web tracking can invade their privacy. Others disagree, saying that cookies and web tracking can help customize the Web to users' interests. Cookies are bits of data put on a hard disk when someone visits certain websites. That data can be used for many purposes. One common use is to make it easier for people to use websites that require a username and password by storing that information and then automatically sending the information whenever it's requested. Passports enable people to decide what type of information about them can be tracked by websites. Web tracking enables those who run websites to see how people use their sites. Web bugs are another technique for tracking people's Internet use.

Chapter 49, "The Dangers of Spyware and Phishing," looks at two extremely common online dangers. Spyware gets onto your PC in a variety of ways, including piggybacking a ride on free programs, being installed without your knowledge from a website, pop-up ad, or via what are called drive-by downloads. There's a lot of different kinds of spyware that does a wide variety of damage, such as reporting on your surfing habits, stealing your passwords, and reporting every keystroke you make to a hacker.

The chapter also covers *phishing attacks*, which fool you into giving personal information such as your passwords to banking or financial sites. Both spyware and phishing attacks are done for financial reasons rather than malicious ones, and so the chapter follows the money trail to show you who's making money from the attacks.

Chapter 50, "Cryptography, Privacy, and Digital Certificates," examines cryptosystems and digital certificates. An enormous amount of information is sent across the Internet every day—everything from personal email to corporate data to credit card information and other highly sensitive material. All that information is vulnerable to hackers and snoopers. Because the information is sent in packets along public routers, the possibility exists that someone could intercept and decipher it. As a way to ensure that the sensitive material can't be looked at, sophisticated cryptosystems have been developed so that only the sender and receiver know what's in the packets.

The chapter also looks at digital certificates. On the Internet, no face-to-face communication takes place, so knowing whether people really are who they say they are can be difficult. Digital certificates are used to absolutely identify someone. If someone sends you an email, for example, a digital certificate will let you know that the person is who he says he is.

Chapter 51, "How Government and Workplace Surveillance Work," details an extremely controversial program that enables the federal government to read people's email and follow their Internet activity without people knowing about it. It also explains how your place of business can track all your Internet use.

Finally, Chapter 52, "Parental Controls on the Internet," takes a detailed look at the issues of pornography and free speech on the Internet. Explicit sexual material is posted on the Internet, and some people would like to fine and jail people and organizations that allow such material to be posted. Passing those types of laws raises a host of constitutional issues about free speech. As a way to solve the problem, companies create and sell software for parents that enables them to block their children from seeing obscene and violent material on the Internet. In this chapter, you'll see how one of the most popular pieces of parental control software works.

CHAPTER
44

How Firewalls Work

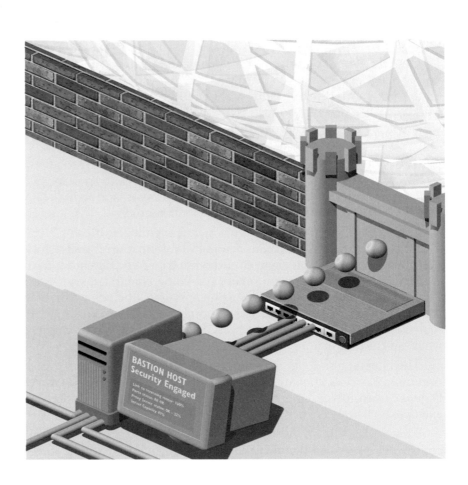

EVERY time a computer is connected to the Internet, it faces potential danger. Corporate local area networks (LANs) connected to the Internet, as well as PCs at home—especially those connected to a high-speed cable modem or DSL modem—are likely targets for hackers.

Due to the Internet's openness, every corporate network connected to it is vulnerable to attack. Crackers on the Internet could theoretically break into the corporate network and do harm in a number of ways: They could steal or damage important data; damage individual computers or the entire network; use the corporate computer's resources; or use the corporate network and resources as a way of posing as a corporate employee. The solution isn't to cut off the network from the Internet. Instead, the company can build firewalls to protect its network. These firewalls enable anyone on the corporate network to access the Internet, but they stop crackers, hackers, and others on the Internet from gaining access to the corporate network and causing damage.

Corporate firewalls are hardware and software combinations that are built using routers, servers, and a variety of software. They sit at the most vulnerable point between a corporate network and the Internet and can be as simple or complex as system administrators want to build them.

One of the simplest kinds of firewalls utilizes packet filtering. In *packet filtering*, a screening router examines the header of every packet of data traveling between the Internet and the corporate network. Packet headers have information in them such as the IP address of the sender and receiver, the protocol being used to send the packet, and other similar information. Based on that information, the router knows what kind of Internet service—such as FTP or rlogin—is being used to send the data, as well as the identity of the sender and receiver of the data. (The command, rlogin, is similar to Telnet, which enables someone to log into a computer. It can be dangerous because it enables users to bypass having to type in a password.) After this information is determined, the router can bar certain packets from being sent between the Internet and the corporate network. For example, the router could block any traffic except for email. Additionally, it could block traffic to and from suspicious destinations or from certain users.

Proxy servers are also commonly used in firewalls. A *proxy server* is server software that runs on a host in a firewall, such as a bastion host. Because only the single proxy server (instead of the many individual computers on the network) interacts with the Internet, security can be maintained. That single server can be kept more secure than can hundreds of individual computers on a network.

Home PCs connected to the Internet via high-speed cable modems or DSL modems are targets as well because if hackers can break into them, they can use them as launching pads for their attacks, while covering their tracks. *Personal firewalls* have become popular—software and hardware that sits on a home computer and protects the home computer in similar ways to how corporate firewalls protect corporate LANs.

How Corporate Firewalls Work

Internet Router (Choke Router)

Finance

To Manufacturing

1 The *firewall* shields the internal corporate network from the Internet. The internal network works as networks normally do—servers provide internal services such as email, access to corporate databases, and the capability to run programs from servers.

2 When someone on the corporate network inside the firewall wants to access the Internet, the request and data must go through an internal screening router (sometimes called a *choke router*). This router examines all the packets of data traveling in both directions between the corporate network and the Internet. Information in the packets' headers gives the router important information, such as the source and destination of the packet, the kind of protocol being used to send the packet, and other identifying data.

3 Based on the information in the headers, the screening router allows certain packets to be sent or received, but blocks other packets. For example, it might not allow some services, such as rlogin, to be run. The router also might not allow packets to be sent to and from specific Internet locations because those locations have been found to be suspicious. Conceivably, a router could be set up to block every packet traveling between the Internet and the internal network except for email. System administrators set the rules for determining which packets to allow in and which ones to block.

ping packet

ftp request

to: boogie@m-troller.com

to: noel@m-troller.com

ping packet

ftp request m-troller.com

to: mt@m-troller.com

Internet

Firewall

6 An *exterior screening router* (also called an *access router*) screens packets between the Internet and the perimeter network. The exterior screening router adds an extra level of protection by screening packets based on the same rules as the internal screening router. This protects the network even if the internal router fails. However, it might also add more rules for screening packets specifically designed to protect the bastion host.

Screened
Subnet
Firewall

Internal Network

BASTION HOST
Security Engaged

Bastion
Host

Exterior Router
(Access Router)

5 The bastion host is placed in a perimeter network in the firewall, so it is not on the corporate network itself. This further shields the corporate network from the Internet. If the bastion host were on the normal corporate network, an intruder could conceivably gain access to every computer on the network and to all network services. Isolating the bastion server from the corporate network by putting it in a perimeter network prevents an intruder from gaining access to the internal corporate network—even if there is a server break-in.

4 A *bastion host* in the firewall is the primary point of contact for connections coming in from the Internet for services such as receiving email and allowing access to the corporation's FTP site. The bastion host is a heavily protected server with many security provisions built in and is the only contact point for incoming Internet requests. In this way, none of the computers or hosts on the corporate network can be contacted directly for requests from the Internet, which provides a level of security. Bastion hosts can also be set up as *proxy servers*—servers that process any requests from the internal corporate network to the Internet, such as browsing the Web or downloading files via FTP. See the illustration later in this chapter for an explanation of how proxy servers work.

To Marketing

To HR

How Personal Firewalls Work

1 People who use high-speed connections, such as cable modems at home, might be prone to hackers' attacks because computers connected to the Internet in this way are more vulnerable and more enticing to the hackers. To protect home computers, many people have turned to *personal firewalls*—software that runs on the computer and protects the computer against Internet attacks. To understand how personal firewalls work, you first need to understand the concept of Internet ports. An *Internet port* isn't a physical device—rather it's a virtual entrance-way between your computer and the Internet. When you make an Internet connection, many of these virtual connections are opened up, and each has its own number and purpose. For example, email software usually uses port 110 on a mail server to get mail and uses port 25 on a mail server to send mail. FTP software usually connects to FTP servers using port 21.

137.42.1.1

PORT 31338   PORT 142   PORT 117

Personal Firewall

2 Personal firewalls work by examining data packets your computer receives. These data packets have a great deal of information in them, such as the sending computer's IP address, your computer's IP address, the port over which the packet will be transmitted, and other pieces of information. Firewalls can filter out packets being sent to certain ports. For example, a firewall can block all packets being transmitted to port 21 so that an FTP program can't be used to attack your PC. Firewalls can block every single port to your PC, or they can block them selectively—for example, only blocking ports that are commonly used in hacker attacks, such as blocking port 31338, which is one of the ports often used by the infamous Back Orifice Trojan horse.

3 One way that hackers can attack your computer is to plant a Trojan horse in it. That Trojan horse can then connect to a hacker on its own, which would give him complete control of your computer. Personal firewalls can tell you when programs from your PC attempt to connect to the Internet, and then only allow programs you know are safe to access the Internet—for example, your email software.

Back Orifice Trojan

146.45.78.122

112.98.12.34

4 Firewalls can also block specific IP addresses from contacting your computer. For example, if you know the IP of a hacker who has attacked you before, you can have your firewall block it from getting through to your computer.

FORBIDDEN IPs

123.54.12.0
137.23.122.8
247.07.19.1
175.125.3
244.6.07.89
44.32.1.189
27.123.

125.11.21.0

112.98.12.34

Personal Firewall

PORT 32   PORT 1338   PORT 21

**NAT
(Network
Address
Translation)**

6 Many personal firewalls keep a running log of every attempt made to attack or probe your PC. These logs can be sent to your ISP, which can use them to try to track down the hackers and shut them down.

102.147.12.32

LOG

131.244.34.12

5 Many home network routers include a hardware-based personal firewall that protects you from the Internet using a technique called *Network Address Translation* (NAT). With NAT, your true IP address is shielded from the Internet—it can't be seen by anyone or any application outside your home network. In essence, it's invisible and can't be reached by hackers.

ISP

How Proxy Servers Work

1 System administrators can set up proxy servers to be used for many services, such as FTP, the Web, and Telnet. System administrators decide which Internet services must go through a proxy server. Specific proxy server software is required for each kind of Internet service.

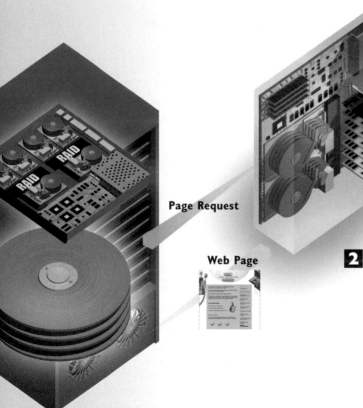

Internet Server

Page Request

Web Page

Proxy Web Server

Page Request

Web Page

2 When a computer from the corporate network makes a request to the Internet—such as to get a web page from a web server—it looks to that computer as if it were to connect directly to the web server on the Internet. In fact, however, the internal computer contacts the proxy server with its request, which in turn contacts the Internet server. The Internet server sends the web page to the proxy server, which then forwards the page to the corporate computer.

3 Proxy servers can be used as a way to log the Internet traffic between an internal corporate network and the Internet. For example, a Telnet proxy server could track every single keystroke in every Telnet session—and could also track how the external server on the Internet reacts to those keystrokes. Proxy servers can log every IP address, date and time of access, URL, number of bytes downloaded, and so on. This information can be used to analyze any attacks launched against the network.

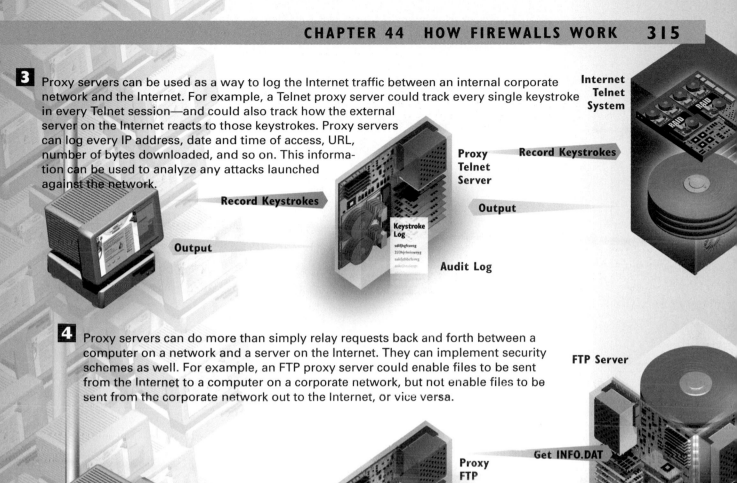

Internet Telnet System

Proxy Telnet Server

Record Keystrokes

Record Keystrokes

Output

Output

Keystroke Log

sdlfhgfcueg
333hjrhnioweyg
sakljchbcluveg
aokejhrxieygs

Audit Log

4 Proxy servers can do more than simply relay requests back and forth between a computer on a network and a server on the Internet. They can implement security schemes as well. For example, an FTP proxy server could enable files to be sent from the Internet to a computer on a corporate network, but not enable files to be sent from the corporate network out to the Internet, or vice versa.

FTP Server

Proxy FTP Server

Get INFO.DAT

Get INFO.DAT

INFO.DAT

INFO.DAT

External Network

Get File XYZ.ZIP

Request Denied

5 Proxy servers can also be used to speed up performance of some Internet services by *caching data*—keeping copies of the requested data. For example, a web proxy server could cache many web pages. Then, whenever someone from the internal corporate network wanted to get one of those web pages, that person could get it directly from the server at a high speed instead of having to go out across the Internet and get the page at a lower speed.

Proxy Web Server

Page Request

Cached Page

Cached Web Pages

Web Page

Web Server

CHAPTER

45

How Hackers Can Cripple the Internet and Attack Your PC

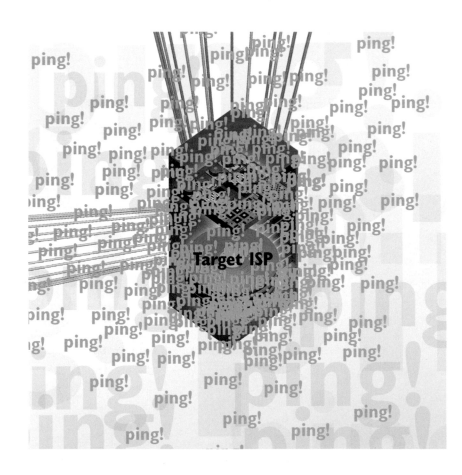

HACKERS are equal opportunity attackers—they attack individuals as well as websites by using a variety of software and malicious programs. Among hackers' many targets are Internet service providers (ISPs)—companies that sell access to the Internet. A hacker might target an ISP for several reasons: He might be angry at the ISP or at someone using the ISP, or he might attack the ISP for the mere thrill of it. Hackers also often attack big websites as well.

One of the most common attacks against an ISP or websites is a *denial of service (DOS)* or *distributed denial of service (DDOS)* in which a hacker incapacitates a network by flooding it with extraneous traffic. There are several ways that a hacker can launch a DOS or DDOS attack. One of the most popular ways is called a *smurf attack*, or *smurfing*. In a smurf attack, a hacker floods the ISP with so many garbage packets that all the ISP's available bandwidth is used up. The ISP's customers can't send or receive data and can't use email, browse the Web, or use any other Internet service.

In a smurf attack, hackers exploit a commonly used Internet service—ping (Pocket Internet Groper). People normally use *ping* to see whether a particular computer or server is currently attached to the Internet and working. When a computer or server is sent a ping packet, it sends a return packet to the person who sent the ping, which in essence says, "Yes, I'm alive and attached to the Internet." In a smurf attack, hackers forge the return addresses on ping requests so that, instead of going back to them, the return packets go to the hackers' target ISP. The hackers can use networks attached to the Internet as a way of relaying their ping requests and magnifying each ping request many times. In this way, a hacker can use networks attached to the Internet to flood the ISP with so many return ping packets that the ISP's customers can't use the ISP's services. Hackers can use multiple networks attached to the Internet in a single smurf attack. Smurf attacks are hard to ward off because the ping answering packets come from legitimate networks and not from the hacker.

Hackers don't just target ISPs, of course. They attack individuals as well. As you'll see in the illustration later in this chapter, hackers can take over people's computers to delete and steal files, steal personal information and passwords, and even use the person's computer as a launch pad for attacks on ISPs and websites.

One of the most insidious dangers on the Internet is zombies, computers that have been taken over by hackers, and will do their bidding. The reason for the name is obvious—in non-computer terms, a zombie is someone who has been dead, and then resurrected to do the bidding of a zombie master. The zombie has to follow the commands of his master, and has no will of his own. Hackers take over ordinary PCs and turn them into zombies.

How do hackers get into your PC to turn it into a zombie or to attack it in other ways? Often, right from the Web via your web browser, or else via email—and you'll see both means of attacks illustrated in the following pages.

How Smurf Attacks and DOS Attacks Work

1 In a smurf attack, or *smurfing*, and a denial of service, or DOS attack, a hacker targets an Internet service provider (ISP) and floods it with so much garbage traffic that none of the ISP's customers can use the service. Smurf attacks have become one of the most popular kinds of hacker attacks on the Internet. The attack starts when a hacker sends a series of *ping* (Packet Internet Groper) packets to a network attached to the Internet. Ping uses the *Internet Control Message Protocol*—a widely used protocol for, among other things, determining whether a particular computer is attached to the Internet and working properly. The network being pinged is not the target of the attack. Instead, it will be used as a way to attack the ISP.

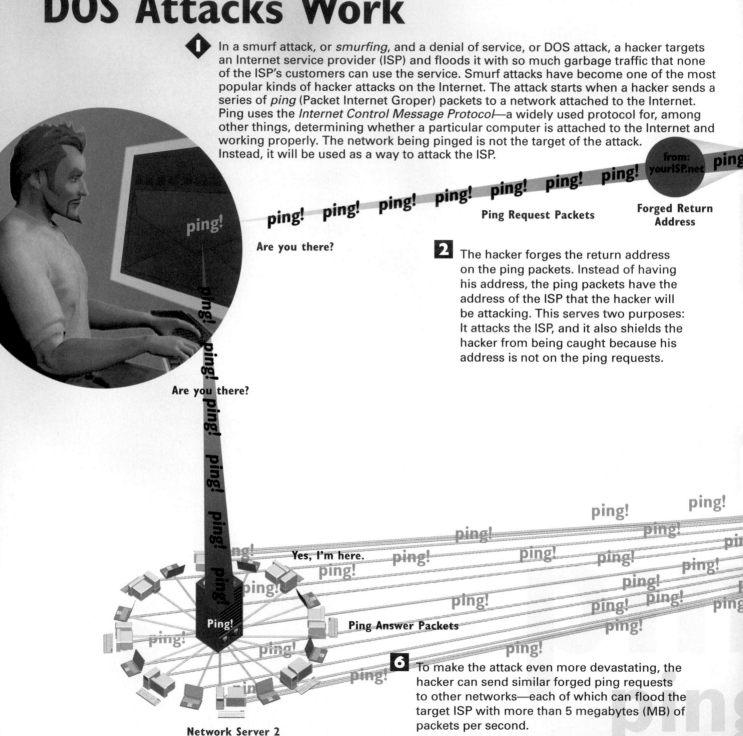

ping! ping! ping! ping! ping! ping! ping! ping

Ping Request Packets

from: yourISP.net

Forged Return Address

ping!

Are you there?

2 The hacker forges the return address on the ping packets. Instead of having his address, the ping packets have the address of the ISP that the hacker will be attacking. This serves two purposes: It attacks the ISP, and it also shields the hacker from being caught because his address is not on the ping requests.

Are you there?

Yes, I'm here.

ping! pi

Ping!

Ping Answer Packets

6 To make the attack even more devastating, the hacker can send similar forged ping requests to other networks—each of which can flood the target ISP with more than 5 megabytes (MB) of packets per second.

Network Server 2

3 The ping requests are sent in a constant stream to the network's *directed broadcast* address. This address, in turn, sends the ping requests to every computer attached to the network—which can be several hundred or more computers.

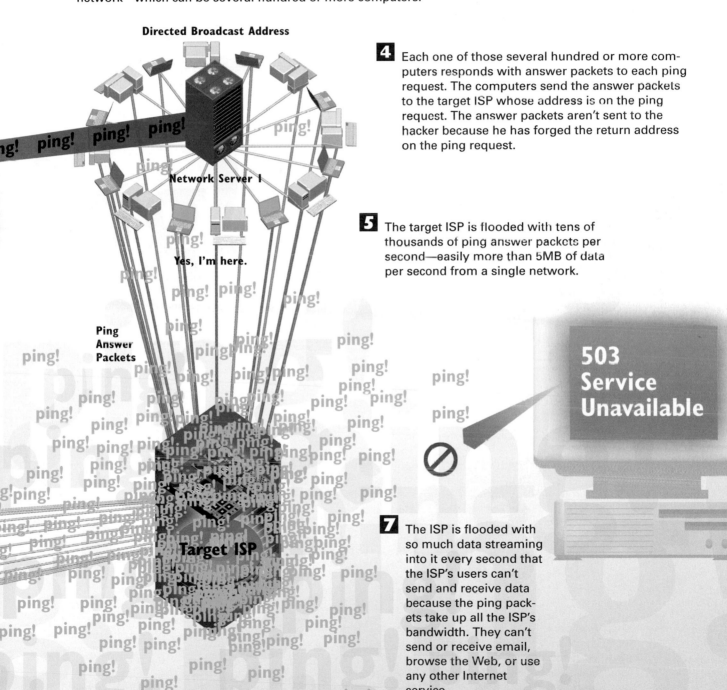

Directed Broadcast Address

ing! ping! ping! ping!

ping!

Network Server 1

Yes, I'm here.

Ping Answer Packets

Target ISP

4 Each one of those several hundred or more computers responds with answer packets to each ping request. The computers send the answer packets to the target ISP whose address is on the ping request. The answer packets aren't sent to the hacker because he has forged the return address on the ping request.

5 The target ISP is flooded with tens of thousands of ping answer packets per second—easily more than 5MB of data per second from a single network.

503 Service Unavailable

7 The ISP is flooded with so much data streaming into it every second that the ISP's users can't send and receive data because the ping packets take up all the ISP's bandwidth. They can't send or receive email, browse the Web, or use any other Internet service.

How Hackers Can Attack Your Computer

1 Hackers not only attack big websites and corporations, but also individual computers in homes or businesses. Hackers can do damage and use your computer in many ways. As a start to many of hacker's nefarious deeds, they need access to your computer. One common way they gain it is through the use of a program called SubSeven. Before the hackers can use the program, they have to get it on your computer. You can unwittingly get a copy of SubSeven on your computer in many different ways—for example, you can open a file in an email message and it can be installed to your computer without you realizing it, or you can be sent the program when you use Internet's IRC chat protocol.

Virus   Virus   27374 open?   Yes, come in!   Hacker

2 Hackers have automated tools that scan thousands of different computers to see which ones have SubSeven running on them. These tools send out *port probes*—packets that look at a specific virtual ports that all computers have when connected to the Internet. SubSeven uses port 27374, among other ports, and if it's running on a computer, it will open that port. A port probe alerts the hacker that port 27374 is open so that he knows he can take control of your PC.

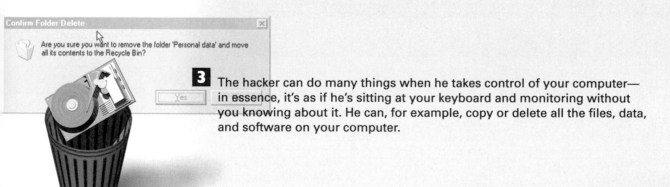

3 The hacker can do many things when he takes control of your computer—in essence, it's as if he's sitting at your keyboard and monitoring without you knowing about it. He can, for example, copy or delete all the files, data, and software on your computer.

4 He can find out personal information about you by looking through your files. For example, he might be able to gain access to your credit card number, bank account, and social security number, and then use that information illegally.

123-456-789-012

Amex, 101-11-33
$15,000 please.

Hacker

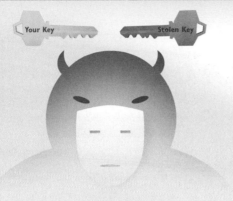

Hacker

5 He can gain access to all your passwords, which would enable him to pose as you on websites and break into data on your computer that you've tried to protect with passwords.

6 He can upload any files to, or download any files from, your computer. For example, he could use your computer to store copies of illegally copied software and could even enable other hackers to then download those illegal copies.

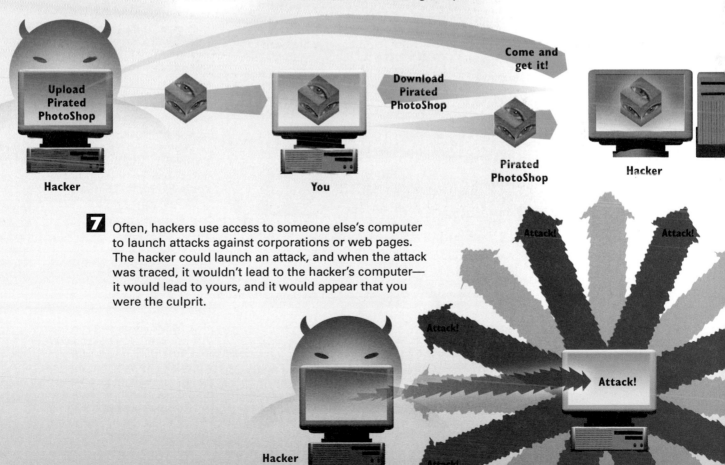

7 Often, hackers use access to someone else's computer to launch attacks against corporations or web pages. The hacker could launch an attack, and when the attack was traced, it wouldn't lead to the hacker's computer—it would lead to yours, and it would appear that you were the culprit.

How Email Viruses Travel in Your Email

From: L.L. Moorloch [DaddyMoorloch@apres.com]
Subject: Wait till you see the picture!|
Attachments: 🖼 Her sister.jpg.vbs (1 MB)

1 An unsuspecting victim receives an email that appears to have been sent by someone the victim knows, and the subject of the message is worded to entice the patsy to open the email, such as "Wild party pictures!!!"

2 Hidden within the email is one of three types of viruses.

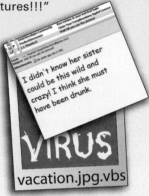

An **attachment virus** is a program attached to an email message. It pretends to be a photo or movie the victim can view on his computer. The name of the attachment is disguised to hide its true nature. For example, the attachment could be vacation.jpg.vbs. Many users notice the "jpg" and assume it's a vacation photo without realizing the "vbs" identifies the attachment as a Visual Basic script, a type of program. Attachments are the most common type of virus. Examples: Melissa, LoveLetter, and AnnaKournikova.

An **HTML virus** is **active content** code, essentially a small program written in **JavaScript** or **ActiveX** software languages. Active content is used on the Web whenever you buy something, fill in forms, vote in a poll, or take part in any other interactive pages on the Web. The HTML virus is not displayed when you open a message formatted in HTML. Examples: Kak worm, BubbleBoy, and HapTime.

A **MIME (Multi-Purpose Internet Mail Extensions) virus** takes advantage of a security hole in Outlook Express and Internet Explorer. The perpetrator fills in forms in the email's header with more information than the header can hold in its buffer—memory reserved for the form entries. When the buffer runs out of room to hold the entry, the overflow—the virus—spills into stack memory being used by the microprocessor to run programs, and the virus is executed instead of legitimate code. Example: Nimba.

3 What makes the virus launch its attack depends on what type of virus it is.

The **attachment virus** runs only when the victim double-clicks the attachment's filename.

The **HTML virus** jumps into action when the victim opens the message to read it. Merely displaying the message in the preview window also launches the virus.

The **MIME virus** can run even if it's not seen. Part of the code hidden in the header tells Outlook Express that the message is a .wav file—a Windows audio file. Outlook Express automatically executes the virus without the victim doing anything.

4 Viruses hidden in email do different kinds of mischief, but the first thing any of them does is propagate itself. It searches the victim's address book, old email, even documents created with Word or Excel. From these, it extracts names and email addresses.

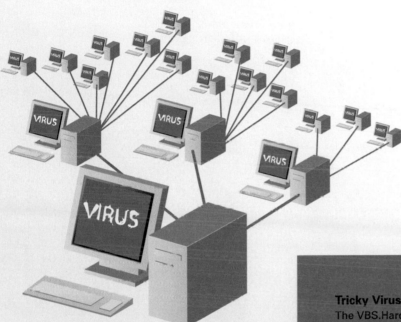

5 The virus uses the addresses to send duplicates of itself to the victim's friends and business acquaintances, hidden in the same email it rode into the computer. To make itself harder to trace, the virus might pick a name at random from the address book and put that in the From: field. In minutes, the virus spreads itself to hundreds of other computers, sometimes accompanied by haphazard attachments of letters and spreadsheets the virus has found among the victim's files.

6 Eventually, thousands of copies of the original virus deliver their payloads, which are anything from taunting messages to erasing hard drives. They might dump their payloads right after they've finished replicating themselves, after so much time has passed, or they might all go off at the same time on the same day.

Tricky Viruses

The VBS.Hard.A@mm virus is an attachment that comes on an email message warning against a nonexistent worm called VBS.AmericanHistoryX_II@mm. The subject of the message is "FW: Symantec Anti-Virus Warning"; the message promises more information in the attached memo.

When the attached file, www.symantec.com.vbs, is opened, it makes the Internet Explorer home page a phony website that warns about a fictitious worm. It also makes Outlook send copies of the bogus virus warning to everyone in the address book.

Each November 24, infected computers display the same message: "Don't look surprised! It is only a warning about your stupidity. Take care!"

How Zombies and Bot Networks Work

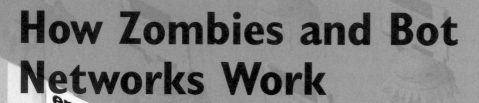

1 A *zombie*, also called a *Bot*, is a computer that can be taken over and controlled by someone remotely. Typically, a single person controls a zombie network of many thousands of infected computers. In one instance, a single zombie network was made up of more than 1.5 million PCs. An unsuspecting PC can become infected in many different ways, including via email, file-sharing networks, or directly over a network if network-file sharing has been turned on, with no security precautions.

The zombie software is installed on the PC. It turns off the PC's anti-virus software, and blocks access to security sites, so that the owner of the PC will not know his computer is infected.

2 The zombie connects to an IRC (Internet Relay Chat) channel, and lets it be known that it is available to carry out the commands of the owner of the zombie network.

3 The owner of the zombie network sends out a command over the IRC channel to tell all the PCs to perform a certain command—for example, to send out spam or phishing attacks.

4 The zombies obey the command, and each zombie sends out thousands of spams or phishing attacks. A single zombie network may send out many hundreds of thousands of spams and phishing attacks.

5 Because the spam and phishing attacks are carried out by the zombies, not the owner of the zombie network, he can't be traced to the attacks.

6 After the spam and phishing attacks have been sent out, the owner of the zombie network tells the zombies to go back to sleep. At any point, he can re-awaken them to do his bidding.

Note
Those who run zombie networks look to infect computers that have broadband cable and DSL connections, because they can send out many more messages per minute than computers connected to the Internet via dial-up. Broadband-connected PCs are also online all the time, while dial-up PCs are only available sporadically, when they have dialed into their ISPs.

How Hackers Exploit Browsers

1 Browser attacks target specific browsers, such as Internet Explorer or Firefox. Internet Explorer is the target of most attacks, because it is the most common browser, and also because it tends to have more security holes than other browsers.

2 One of the most common kinds of attacks is called a *buffer overflow attack*. A buffer is an area of memory allocated for a certain function. In a buffer overflow attack, the hacker writes code that downloads from a website, and floods a specific area of memory with so much data that it overflows into a nearby area of memory.

3 The data that flows into a nearby area of memory contains malicious code, and that code can bypass normal security functions because of a flaw in the browser.

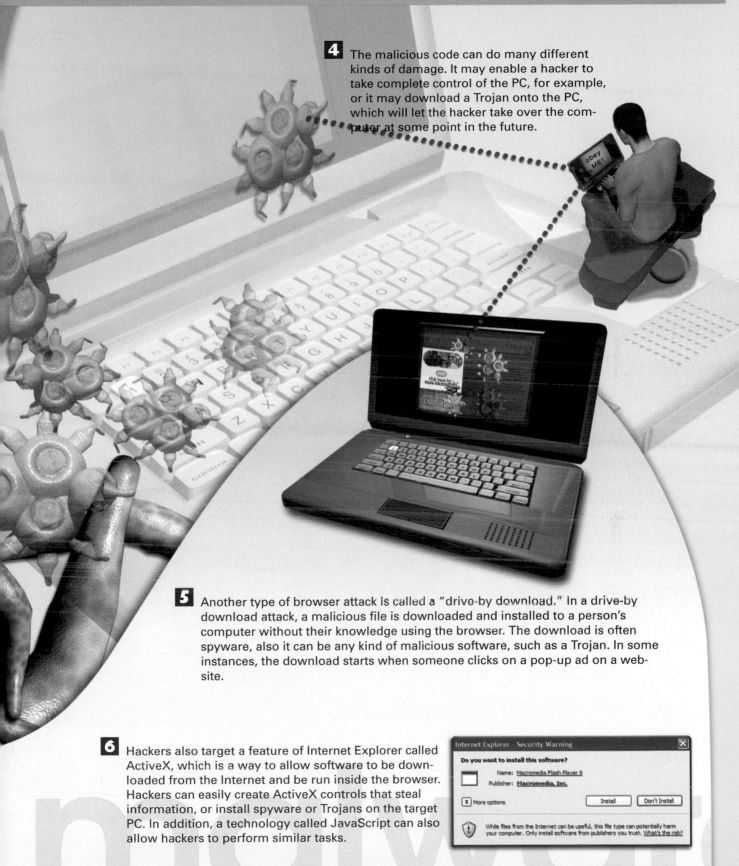

4 The malicious code can do many different kinds of damage. It may enable a hacker to take complete control of the PC, for example, or it may download a Trojan onto the PC, which will let the hacker take over the computer at some point in the future.

5 Another type of browser attack is called a "drive-by download." In a drive-by download attack, a malicious file is downloaded and installed to a person's computer without their knowledge using the browser. The download is often spyware, also it can be any kind of malicious software, such as a Trojan. In some instances, the download starts when someone clicks on a pop-up ad on a website.

6 Hackers also target a feature of Internet Explorer called ActiveX, which is a way to allow software to be downloaded from the Internet and be run inside the browser. Hackers can easily create ActiveX controls that steal information, or install spyware or Trojans on the target PC. In addition, a technology called JavaScript can also allow hackers to perform similar tasks.

CHAPTER

46

The Dangers of Wireless Networking

CONNECTING to the Internet wirelessly has become ubiquitous. (For details, see Chapter 9, "How Wireless Connections and WiFi Work.") Many people have wireless networks in their home, and in addition, many corporations are setting up wireless networks as well. They do it because it's much less expensive to set up a wireless network than a wired one, and more convenient for users as well—they can connect to the Internet and corporate network anywhere in the building, not just when they're next to an Ethernet port.

People also connect to the Internet when they travel, by using hot spots at cafes, airports, and other locations.

This wireless technology is called WiFi. But with all of WiFi's convenience, comes danger. The same technology that lets you browse the Web from your back porch can let invaders hop onto your network from outside your house or apartment.

By its very nature, WiFi is an open technology. A wireless router broadcasts its presence to any device with a WiFi adapter within its range, and if the router is unprotected, anyone who wants to can connect to it and use the network. That makes it easy for intruders to get in.

A common kind of intruder is called a "war driver." These people drive through areas of cities and suburbs known for having WiFi networks, and they search for unprotected networks they can break into. They use software that makes it easy to find unprotected networks. Some use high-powered antennas so they can find as many networks as possible. But, in fact, they don't even need this kind of equipment to get into networks. Software built directly into Windows XP, for example, makes it easy for anyone to find and connect to an unprotected network.

When war drivers target a business network, they may be looking for proprietary business information, or they may be looking to do malicious damage. When they target a home network, they may look for personal information, such as credit card numbers or they may also be looking to damage computers, as well.

But WiFi intruders can cause other problems—and these may even be more serious than stealing information or damaging computers. They can use the network for illegal activities, and if those activities are uncovered, it will look as if the owner of the network is guilty, because the war driver will be long gone.

Computers aren't the only devices that connect to the Internet wirelessly; cell phones do as well. Most cell phones are at heart computers—computers that are surprisingly powerful, and pack more power and memory than large computers of a dozen years ago.

And where there are computers, there are hackers. As cell phones get increasingly complex and powerful, they become more vulnerable to viruses and hackers. And as they get more powerful, cell phones have more data that hackers want to use. For example, B-list celebrity Paris Hilton had her cell phone hacked, and her personal address book and intimate photos that were on the phone were made available to the world when they were posted on the Internet.

How War Drivers Invade Your Network

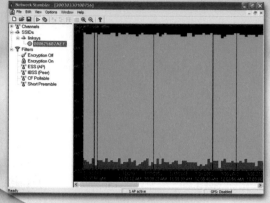

1 To go war driving, you need special software that can detect and report on any nearby WiFi networks within range of the computer. A particularly popular one, pictured here, is the free program NetStumbler, available from www.netstumbler.com. The software may work with only certain brands and models of WiFi cards.

2 Someone takes a WiFi-equipped laptop with NetStumbler and drives around with it in a car, looking for WiFi networks to tap in to. To increase the distance from which the networks can be detected, an antenna can be attached to the laptop's WiFi card. Often, a homemade "cantenna" is used—an antenna built using a tin can and copper wire.

3 One person drives, while the other watches NetStumbler for signs of any nearby networks. When NetStumbler detects a wireless network, it reports the network ID, the channel over which the network is broadcasting, whether encryption is being used, and similar information.

4 Based on the information that NetStumbler provides, the war driver can connect to the WiFi network, using software built in to the computer's operating system or that was provided along with the WiFi card, if the network isn't protected by encryption and security. (Many WiFi networks are left unprotected, in businesses as well as home.)

5 Once the war driver connects to the network, he has the same access rights as any other user, and so can use all the network's resources and data. If he is a hacker, he can also try to take control of the network or damage it.

6 NetStumbler can save the information about all the networks it finds during a day of war driving. That information can be shared with others, and also uploaded to a website, where it can be collated and published as a public map on the Internet, so that anyone can see where WiFi networks are located. Many people use these maps not for nefarious purposes, but so they can connect to the Internet using these networks when they are away from home.

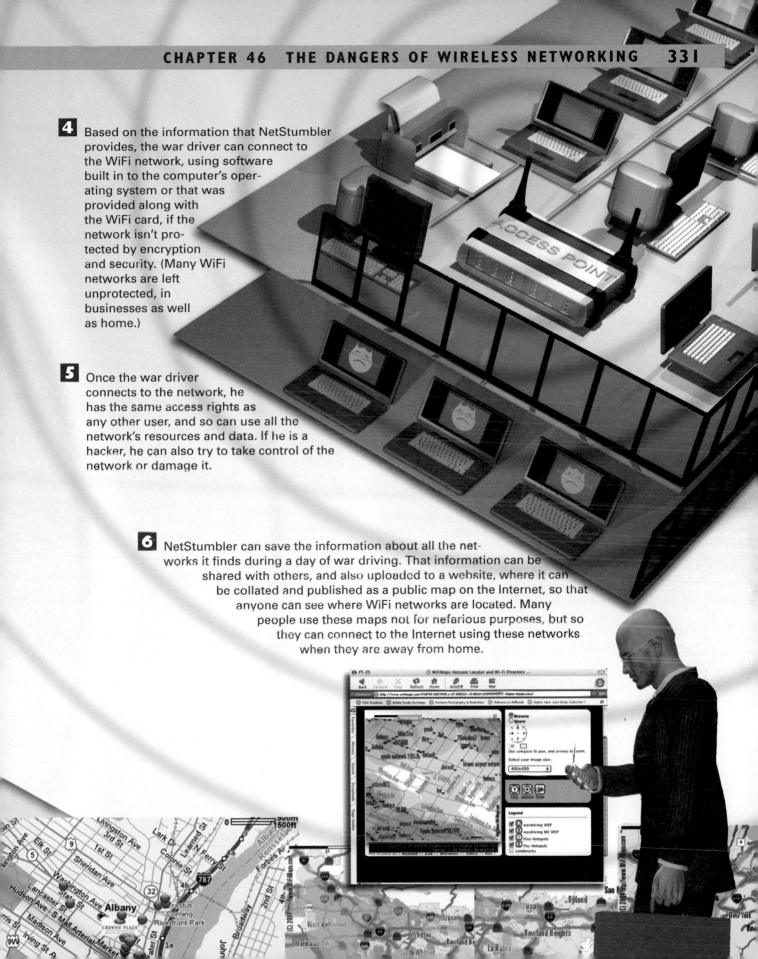

How "Evil Twin" Hacks Work

1 In an Evil Twin hack, a hacker creates a twin of an existing hot spot, to lure people into logging into his hot spot rather than the real thing. First a hacker finds a popular hot spot and finds its SSID—its network name. Next, he sets up a duplicate hot spot that has the same SSID as the real thing. He may use a small, hidden portable travel router to do this.

2 He may also use special software, such as one called hotspotter, that can turn an ordinary PC into a hot spot.

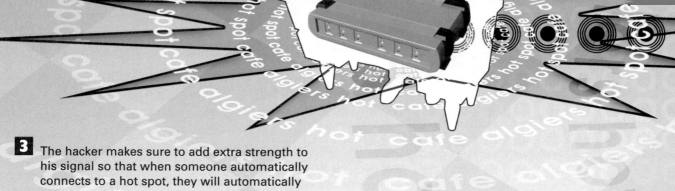

3 The hacker makes sure to add extra strength to his signal so that when someone automatically connects to a hot spot, they will automatically connect to his, because it has the strongest signal. The hacker may also jam the signals of the real hot spot, ensuring that someone will connect to his hot spot, not the real thing.

4 The hacker may set up a phony login screen that asks for credit card information, or if it is a for-pay hot spot, he will mimic the login screen of the real hot spot. That way, he can steal credit card information.

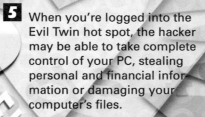

5 When you're logged into the Evil Twin hot spot, the hacker may be able to take complete control of your PC, stealing personal and financial information or damaging your computer's files.

How Paris Hilton's Cell Phone Was Hacked

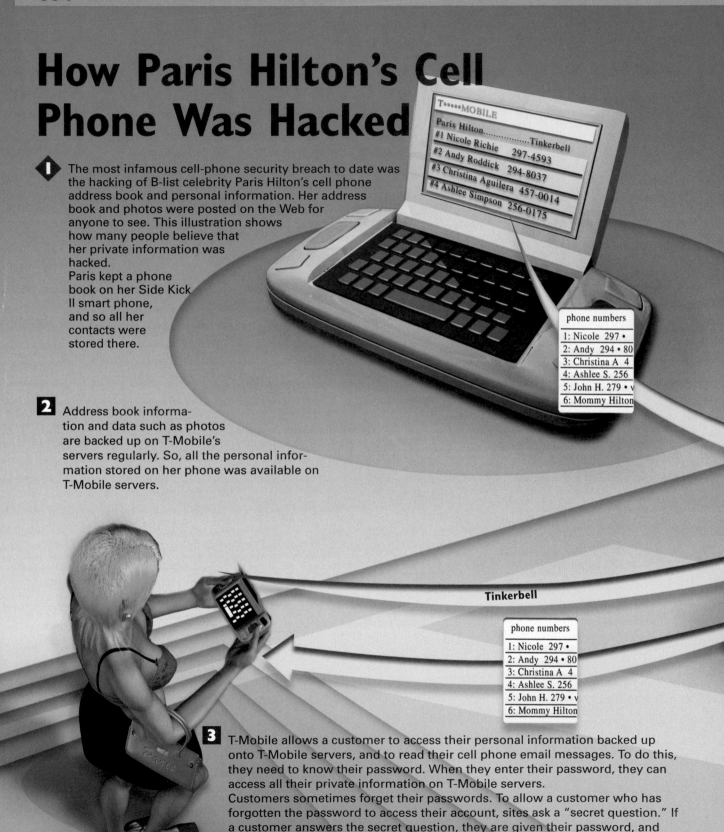

T••••MOBILE

Paris Hilton................Tinkerbell
#1 Nicole Richie   297-4593
#2 Andy Roddick   294-8037
#3 Christina Aguilera   457-0014
#4 Ashlee Simpson   256-0175

1 The most infamous cell-phone security breach to date was the hacking of B-list celebrity Paris Hilton's cell phone address book and personal information. Her address book and photos were posted on the Web for anyone to see. This illustration shows how many people believe that her private information was hacked.
Paris kept a phone book on her Side Kick II smart phone, and so all her contacts were stored there.

phone numbers

1: Nicole 297 •
2: Andy 294 • 80
3: Christina A 4
4: Ashlee S. 256
5: John H. 279 • v
6: Mommy Hilton

2 Address book information and data such as photos are backed up on T-Mobile's servers regularly. So, all the personal information stored on her phone was available on T-Mobile servers.

Tinkerbell

phone numbers

1: Nicole 297 •
2: Andy 294 • 80
3: Christina A 4
4: Ashlee S. 256
5: John H. 279 • v
6: Mommy Hilton

3 T-Mobile allows a customer to access their personal information backed up onto T-Mobile servers, and to read their cell phone email messages. To do this, they need to know their password. When they enter their password, they can access all their private information on T-Mobile servers.
Customers sometimes forget their passwords. To allow a customer who has forgotten the password to access their account, sites ask a "secret question." If a customer answers the secret question, they are given their password, and can access their account.

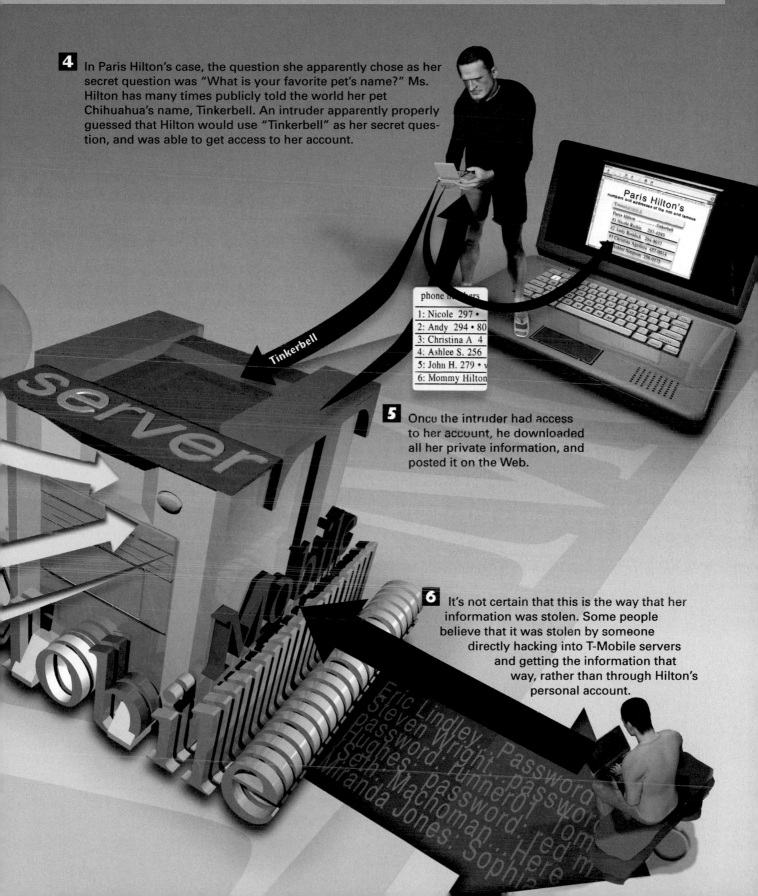

4 In Paris Hilton's case, the question she apparently chose as her secret question was "What is your favorite pet's name?" Ms. Hilton has many times publicly told the world her pet Chihuahua's name, Tinkerbell. An intruder apparently properly guessed that Hilton would use "Tinkerbell" as her secret question, and was able to get access to her account.

5 Once the intruder had access to her account, he downloaded all her private information, and posted it on the Web.

6 It's not certain that this is the way that her information was stolen. Some people believe that it was stolen by someone directly hacking into T-Mobile servers and getting the information that way, rather than through Hilton's personal account.

How Wireless Network Protection Works

1 No single method can protect home or corporate WiFi networks, and so a variety of measures have to be employed. The most basic protection is to use encryption, so that all communication is scrambled, and only those with the proper encryption keys can use the network or read its packets.

2 Networks can also allow only computers whose network adapters have specific *MAC addresses* to get on to the network. A MAC address is a unique number that identifies a network device. By allowing only certain MAC addresses on to the network, hackers can be blocked.

3 Wireless networks also use traditional network protection tools, such as firewalls and proxy servers. For more information about how firewalls work, see Chapter 44, "How Firewalls Work."

4 A new type of network protection is called a *honeypot*. There are several different types, but for wireless network, the most useful one is a honeypot that creates multiple false SSIDs (network identifiers). There is only one true SSID among the many false ones, and hackers cannot find the real SSID to hack into the network.

5 Network staff can position network antennas so that the signal does not reach outside the building. Much wireless hacking occurs in parking lots or other locations outside locations, and if the wireless signal does not reach outside, the network can't be hacked into.

6 One security risk comes from employees, who set up rogue access points. There are unauthorized access points that people set up without the knowledge of network administrators. They are not set up maliciously, but for people on the same floor or department to more easily get onto the network. But because they are set up without the network administrator's knowledge, they are often insecure, and a place where hackers can get in. So, network administrators use hardware devices to scan the building for these rogue access points, and dismantle them when they find them.

CHAPTER

47

How Viruses Work

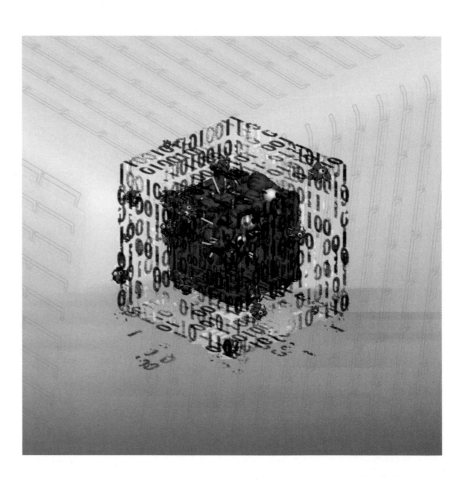

THE Internet, just like the rest of the world, is not a perfectly safe place to visit. If you download files from the Internet, there is a chance—a very small chance, but nonetheless a chance—that your computer could become infected with a virus.

Viruses are malicious programs that invade your computer. They can cause many different kinds of damage, such as deleting data files, erasing programs, or destroying everything they find on your hard disk. Not every virus causes damage; some simply flash annoying messages.

Although you can get a virus from the Internet by downloading files to your computer, the Internet is not the only place where viruses can be picked up. If you've sent files via email or on your company's internal network, you can get viruses that way as well. Instances have occurred when commercially bought, shrink-wrapped software has contained viruses.

The term *virus* is a somewhat generic term applied to a wide variety of programs. Viruses are written for specific kinds of computers, such as PCs or Macintoshes, because the files they infect run only on one kind of computer.

Traditional viruses attach themselves to programs or data files, infect your computer, replicate themselves on your hard disk, and then damage your data, hard disk, or files. Viruses usually attack four parts of your computer: its executable program files; its file-directory system that tracks the location of all your computer's files (and without which your computer won't work); its boot and system areas that are needed to start your computer; and its data files. At one time it was believed that data files could not be infected by viruses, but that is not the case—viruses have been written that infect data files too. For example, some viruses attach themselves to Microsoft Word macros and are launched whenever a particular macro is run.

Trojan horses are files or programs that disguise themselves as normal, helpful programs or files, but in fact are viruses. For example, if a program purported to be a financial calculator, but really deleted every file on your hard disk, that program would be called a Trojan horse.

Worms are programs designed to infect networks such as the Internet. They travel from networked computer to networked computer and replicate themselves along the way. The most infamous worm of all was released on November 2, 1988, the Robert Morris Internet Worm. The worm copied itself to many Internet host computers and eventually brought the Internet to its knees. A more recent worm, Melissa, was disguised as a Word document sent via email—and it wreaked enough havoc that it crashed many Internet and corporate mail servers by making use of the Outlook and Outlook Express email programs.

The best way to protect your computer against viruses is to use antiviral software. There are several kinds of antiviral software. A scanner checks to see whether your computer has any files that have been infected; whereas an eradication program will wipe the virus from your hard disk. Sometimes eradication programs can kill the virus without having to delete the infected program or data file, while other times those infected files must be deleted. Still other programs, sometimes called *inoculators*, do not allow a program to be run if it contains a virus and stop your computer from being infected. Malicious email programs can sometimes be stopped by disabling a built-in capability to run scripts in email software. Many antiviral programs build in all these capabilities, as a way of offering you the fullest protection.

How Viruses Infect Computers

1 A virus hides inside a legitimate program where it remains dormant until you run the infected program. The virus springs into action when you actually run the infected program. Sometimes the first thing the virus will do is infect other programs on your hard disk by copying itself into them.

Infected Application

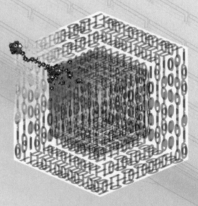

Newly Infected File

2 Some viruses place messages called *v-markers* or *virus markers* inside programs that they infect, and these messages help manage the viruses' activities. Each virus has a specific v-marker associated with it. If a virus encounters one of these markers in another program, it knows that the program is already infected so it doesn't replicate itself there. When a virus cannot find more unmarked files on a computer, that signals to the virus that there are no more files to be infected. At this point, the virus might begin to damage the computer and its data.

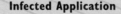

V-MARKER

Virus Marker

3 Viruses can corrupt program or data files so that they work oddly, not at all, or cause damage when they do run. They can destroy all the files on your computer, change the system files that your computer needs when it is turned on, and cause other types of damage.

Damaged File or Application

4 Software programs called *scanners* check for viruses and alert you to the viruses' presence. They work in many different ways. One method of detection is to check your program files for telltale virus markers that indicate the presence of a virus. Other methods include checking to see whether a program's file size has changed. Some types of antiviral programs run continuously on your computer and check any program for the presence of a virus before the program is run or downloaded.

SCANNING FOR VIRUSES

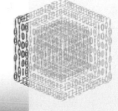

5 *Eradication programs* disinfect, or remove, viruses from software. Sometimes they can eradicate the virus without damaging the program that the virus has infected. In other instances, they have to destroy the program as well as the virus.

How Worms Work

1 Worms are programs that spread to computers and servers on a network, and disguise themselves as normal, helpful programs or files. One of the most well known worms of all time, called Melissa, used email to spread itself, and damaged many Internet and corporate mail servers. Here's how it did its work.

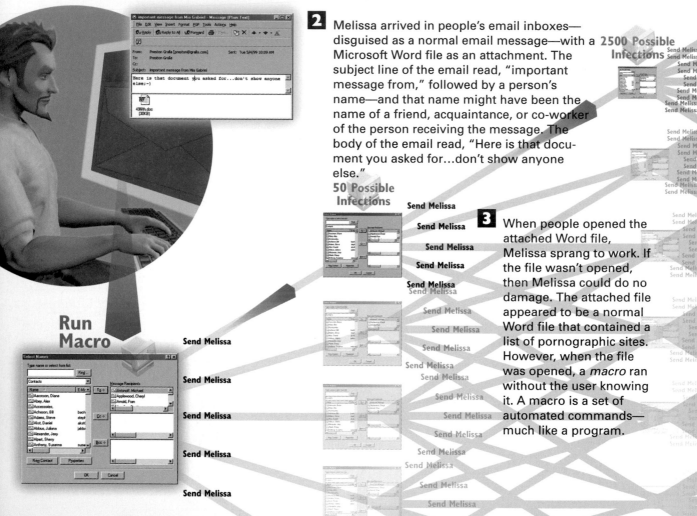

2 Melissa arrived in people's email inboxes—disguised as a normal email message—with a Microsoft Word file as an attachment. The subject line of the email read, "important message from," followed by a person's name—and that name might have been the name of a friend, acquaintance, or co-worker of the person receiving the message. The body of the email read, "Here is that document you asked for…don't show anyone else."

2500 Possible Infections

50 Possible Infections

Run Macro

Send Melissa

3 When people opened the attached Word file, Melissa sprang to work. If the file wasn't opened, then Melissa could do no damage. The attached file appeared to be a normal Word file that contained a list of pornographic sites. However, when the file was opened, a *macro* ran without the user knowing it. A macro is a set of automated commands—much like a program.

4 The macro checked to see whether the person had Outlook on his computer. Outlook is a Microsoft email program. If Outlook wasn't present, the macro wasn't able to do any damage. If Outlook was present, Melissa looked at the first 50 names in Outlook's address book, then made a copy of itself and mailed itself to all those 50 names without the person knowing this was happening. The email sent to each of those people looked exactly like the email the person received: The subject line of the email read, "important message from," followed by the name of the person who had been infected by Melissa. It appeared that the infected person was sending out a personal message.

**125,000 Possible
Infections**

5 Each of these 50 people, in
turn, received the infected
email and attached Word
document. When they
opened the attached file,
Melissa did the same thing
to them—automatically sent
itself to 50 more people.

6 The volume of email being sent
quickly became so great that
Internet and corporate email
servers were unable to keep up
with the demand for sending and
receiving messages—and many of
them crashed. Many Internet and
corporate mail servers were overwhelmed by the huge demand for
sending and receiving email, and
so normal mail—not just Melissa-
related mail—couldn't be sent or
received. The problem was finally
resolved when anti-virus software
was updated to include features
that could detect and kill Melissa.

Mail Server

IN
EMAIL
OUT

48

How Internet Sites Can Invade Your Privacy

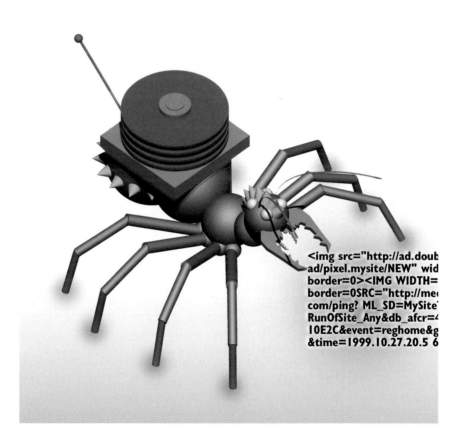

```
<img src="http://ad.doub
ad/pixel.mysite/NEW" wid
border=0><IMG WIDTH=
border=0SRC="http://me
com/ping? ML_SD=MySite
RunOfSite_Any&db_afcr=4
10E2C&event=reghome&g
&time=1999.10.27.20.5 6
```

PRIVACY issues are a big concern on the Net. Much information can be gathered about people when they use the Net, and it's not always clear who will use that information or how it will be used. In particular, three technologies that concern people are cookies, web tracking, and web bugs. Cookies and web tracking both serve useful purposes, but many people worry that there is a "Big Brother" aspect to them. Web bugs, on the other hand, can be used for nefarious purposes. One technology, Internet passports, might enable people to ensure that their privacy isn't invaded while still enabling websites to gather information that can be used to deliver specialized services to web surfers.

Cookies are bits of data put on a hard disk when someone visits certain websites. The most common use of this data is to make it easier for people to use websites that require a username and password. The cookie on the hard disk has the username and password in it, so people don't have to log in to every page that requires that information. Instead, the cookie sends the information to the server, and the person can visit the page freely.

Cookies can contain virtually any kind of information, such as the last time a person visited the site, the person's favorite sites, and similar, customizable information. They can be used to track people as they go through a website and to help gain statistics about what types of pages people like to visit. Although some people view them as invaders of privacy, they can also make the Web a much better place to visit by doing things such as making it easier to conduct electronic commerce.

Although cookies can be used to track how people use a website, many other methods can be used, as well. In one method, web server logs are examined in detail. This would make it possible, for example, to identify the most popular pages on the site, the sites people have just visited, how many pages people read in a typical visit, and similar information. Other methods include using software *sniffers* that examine every packet coming into or going out of a website. Webmasters can use this tracking information to help create better sites—but they can also use it to assemble demographic information to sell to advertisers. The second illustration in this chapter shows the functionality of web tracking software from a company called Accrue.

Web bugs can also trace people's paths through a website. Web bugs get their name not in reference to an error in a program, but instead from the term *to bug* as in "to wiretap." More dangerously, web bugs can be included in email, and they can actually enable people to view some of your email, as you'll see in the illustration later in this chapter.

To allay people's privacy concerns, a variety of technologies and standards are being developed. They include the Platform for Privacy Preferences (P3P), the Internet Content and Exchange standard (ICE), and the Open Profiling Standard (OPS). Generically, we'll call these Internet *passports*. These Internet passports let people control which information about themselves they'll allow to be released to websites—and how that information can be used. And passports let people control what type of information can be gathered about their surfing and how that information can be used, as well. In general, the more information that people allow to be gathered about themselves, the more specialized services they'll gain on the Web, such as customized news feeds.

Another privacy concern is posed by *spyware*, software that watches your surfing activities without you knowing about it, reports on them, and then delivers targeted ads to you, based on your activity. Spyware typically is installed on your computer when you install a piece of free software, such as the file-sharing software.

How Cookies Work

1 *Cookies* are pieces of data placed on a computer's hard drive by a web server; they can be used for a variety of purposes. They can store usernames and passwords, for example, so that people don't have to continually log on to a site that requires registration; or they can enable people to fill electronic shopping carts with goods they want to buy. Cookies also store the name of the site that placed the cookie. Only that site can read the cookie information, so information from one site can't be shared with information from another site. Cookie information is put into a special file on a hard disk. The location and files vary according to the type of computer and the browser. On PCs using Netscape, for example, the information is put into a file called COOKIES.TXT. That single text file holds all the cookies, and each cookie is one line of data in the file.

Web Server

CGI Script

Password: pg
Username: who

www.buyshop.com

Buyshop.com cookie?

```
# Netscape HTTP Cookie File
# http://www.netscape.com/newsref/std/cookie_spec.html
# This is a generated file! Do not edit.
.ad-up.com          TRUE    /barryl/public_html   FALSE   946079999   Ad-OpUser      125101
www.lego.com        TRUE    /cgi-bin/pirat  FALSE   883699199       &r      &n=unknown&pf=&b=26t=16f=8
.gowest.com         TRUE    /       FALSE   946684799   IHTERSE 155.40.99.171138680490BA657
.hotbot.com         TRUE    /       FALSE   937396800   ink     180DH12pE48N364m0540m400053959C1536
.focalink.com       TRUE    /       FALSE   946641600   SB_ID   ads80.21677B490F1091100935
.boston.com         TRUE    /       FALSE   946684799   IHTERSE hia.tiac.net277D3054056212370
.netscape.com       TRUE    /       FALSE   1609372800  MOZILLA HB2_ID=0FGHKEIIRJSSPTS[-]HB2_VERS=
.netscape.com       TRUE    /       FALSE   1609372800  HS_IBD  IBD_SUBSCRIPTIOHS=IHE005[IHC010[I9
.realaudio.com      TRUE    /       FALSE   946845740   uid     1992792405034722865
.nytimes.com        TRUE    /       FALSE   946684799   PV      27.7278
.nytimes.com        TRUE    /       FALSE   946684799   ID      .7.-22=6
.nytimes.com        TRUE    /       FALSE   942109160   libuser .7.-22=6
.nytimes.com        TRUE    /       FALSE   942109160   libq    =6-.9*-.9cW.-22=cBZP9*c6/+0529+0
.netscape.com       TRUE    /       FALSE   946684799   NETSCAPE_ID     100Ac010,13bf8f76
ad.doubleclick.net  FALSE   /       FALSE   942191940   IAF     tcecb50
.infoseek.com       TRUE    /       FALSE   982131378   InfoseekUserId  8480FC0465B09557036A0EAA357
.software.net       TRUE    /       FALSE   946684799   ADUBL   http://www.software.net/FKSH020051
.yahoo.com          TRUE    /       FALSE   883699200   10400   domain=gpath=39312F312F7765770733f4
.usj.com            TRUE    /       FALSE   946635010   user_type       subscribed
www.maricle.com     FALSE   /       FALSE   1293753600  EGSOFT_ID       -185.40.99.171=1575746728.1
www.download.com    FALSE   /       FALSE   946590400   csr     -9193.3056A416.790
.family.com         TRUE    /       FALSE   946681200   ch_stateID      49193.3056A416.790
Buyshop.com                 TRUE            123702  132
```

buyshop.com   True   123702   132

3 If no cookie is associated with the URL, the server places a cookie inside the cookie file. Some sites might first ask a series of questions, such as name and password, and then place a cookie on the hard disk with that information in it. This is typical of sites that require registration. Commonly, a CGI script on the server takes the information the user has entered and then writes the cookie onto the hard disk.

2 When you visit a site, your browser examines the URL you're visiting and looks into your cookie file. If it finds a cookie associated with that URL, it sends that cookie information to the server. The server can now use that cookie information.

Buyshop.com cookie

4 As you travel through a website, more information might need to be put into your cookie. On a site where you can purchase goods online, for example, you might put goods into an electronic shopping cart. Every time you did this, new cookie information would be added, detailing the goods you wanted to buy. When new cookie information is put in, a CGI script deletes the old cookie information and puts in a new cookie. When you leave a site, your cookie information remains on your hard disk so the site can recognize you the next time you decide to visit—unless the cookie has specifically been written to expire when you leave the site.

Delete old cookies; put on new cookies

5 The server takes actions based on your cookies—for example, displaying your electronic shopping cart. If the site enables you to buy online, it might have asked for your credit card number. For security reasons, that number is not stored in your cookie. Instead, it is stored on a secure server. When you decide to buy something, you enter a secure area with your browser. Your cookie then sends an ID to the server that identifies your shopping session, and the server then displays your credit card information, enabling you to buy online.

BUYSHOP.COM

Delete old cookies; put on new cookies

6 After you order something from your electronic shopping cart—or after you decide to delete something out of the shopping cart—a new cookie is put on your hard disk; this one does not include the goods you bought or decided to take out of your shopping cart.

Web Server

The server www.amazon.com wishes to set a cookie that will be sent to any server in the domain .amazon.com The name and value of the cookie are: session-id-time=867052800

This cookie will persist until Mon Jun 23 03:55:00 1999

Do you wish to allow the cookie to be set?

OK   Cancel

7 Because some people don't like cookies to be placed on their hard disks, browsers give people control over whether to accept cookies, to not accept cookies, or to ask each time a cookie is being placed on the hard disk. Pictured is the message you get if you've asked to be told each time a cookie is placed on your hard disk.

How Websites Track Your Activities

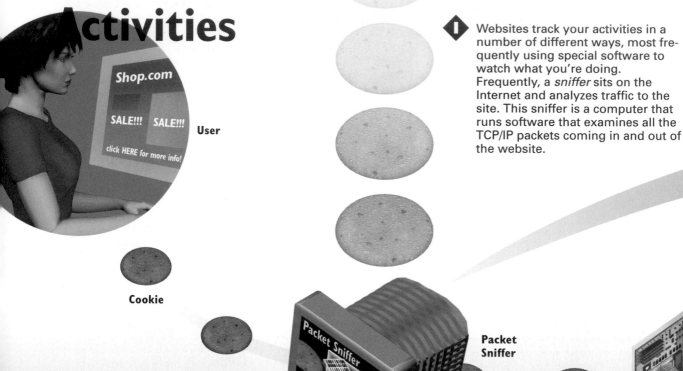

User

Cookie

IP Packet

User

Shop.com

SALE!!!   SALE!!!

click HERE for more info!

Games.com

REVIEWS   JOIN

Packet Sniffer

Packet Sniffer

137.42.6.72

Web Server

1 Websites track your activities in a number of different ways, most frequently using special software to watch what you're doing. Frequently, a *sniffer* sits on the Internet and analyzes traffic to the site. This sniffer is a computer that runs software that examines all the TCP/IP packets coming in and out of the website.

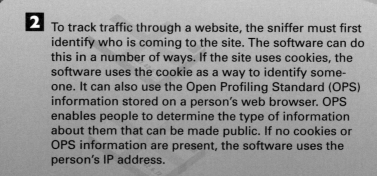

2 To track traffic through a website, the sniffer must first identify who is coming to the site. The software can do this in a number of ways. If the site uses cookies, the software uses the cookie as a way to identify someone. It can also use the Open Profiling Standard (OPS) information stored on a person's web browser. OPS enables people to determine the type of information about them that can be made public. If no cookies or OPS information are present, the software uses the person's IP address.

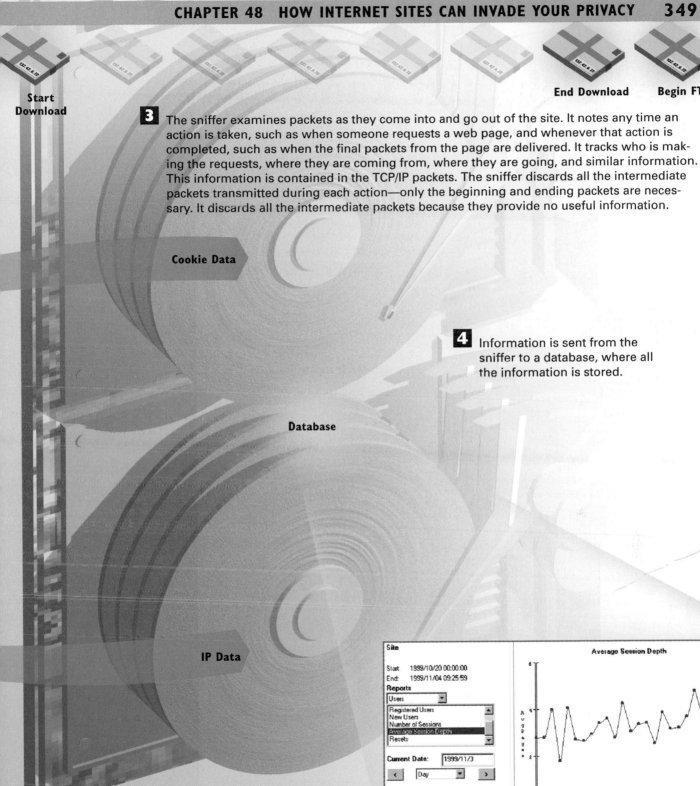

Start Download

End Download

Begin FTP

3 The sniffer examines packets as they come into and go out of the site. It notes any time an action is taken, such as when someone requests a web page, and whenever that action is completed, such as when the final packets from the page are delivered. It tracks who is making the requests, where they are coming from, where they are going, and similar information. This information is contained in the TCP/IP packets. The sniffer discards all the intermediate packets transmitted during each action—only the beginning and ending packets are necessary. It discards all the intermediate packets because they provide no useful information.

Cookie Data

4 Information is sent from the sniffer to a database, where all the information is stored.

Database

IP Data

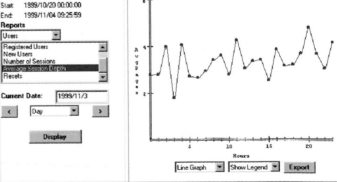

Server Traffic Analysis

5 Many types of reports can be created out of the database, such as the average amount of time people spend on a site, the average number of pages they read per visit, the most popular pages on a site, sites people have just visited, sites they're going to visit, and other information.

How Web Bugs Can Invade Your Privacy

WebMailApp

Add to email:
contents=
document.body.
in HTML;

1 A *web bug* is a piece of HTML code placed on web pages or in email messages that can be used to silently gather information about people, track their Internet travels, and even allow the creator of the bug to secretly read a person's email. In this illustration we'll look at web bugs used in email. Email web bugs can be placed only in HTML email, so the person creating the bug must create an HTML-based email message.

2 In the HTML code for the message, the person puts in a small piece of JavaScript code that has the capability to read the entire contents of an email message.

Email

```
<img src="http://ad.doubleclick.net/
ad/pixel.mysite/NEW" width=1 height=1
border=0><IMG WIDTH=1HEIGHT=1
border=0SRC="http://media.preferences.
com/ping? ML_SD=MySiteTE_MySite_1x1_
RunOfSite_Any&db_afcr=4B31-C2FB-
10E2C&event=reghome&group=register
&time=1999.10.27.20.5 6.37">
```

4 The person sends the email message. The recipient opens the message in an HTML-enabled email reader, such as Outlook. (Note: If the recipient doesn't have an email reader, the web bug won't work.)

3 The person also puts a web bug into the email message. The web bug is an HTML reference to a tiny graphic—the smallest possible on a computer screen is one pixel by one pixel—that is transparent so that it can't be seen. This tiny graphic is also called a *clear gif* because *gif* refers to a common web graphics format. When someone reads her HTML message, her computer gets the graphic from a server—and that server then can get information about the person's computer.

Web Server

5 The JavaScript runs and reads the entire email message. The person's email software contacts the remote server to get the clear gif. It does more than get the gif, though—it also sends identifying information about the computer, such as its IP address and the time the message is being read. It also sends the contents of the email message, as taken by the JavaScript. At this point, that doesn't really matter because the sender of the message knows the contents of the message because she created it. But the sender now knows identifying information about the recipient of the mail.

Get Graphic

IP 47.32.21.2 read 5:10 09/12/02

Get Graphic

IP 132.21.23.4 read 6:20 10/13/02

Cookie

• clear.gif

6 The server sends the gif, but can also send a cookie along with it. It can match this cookie with the identifying information sent via the web bug, and with those pieces of information track a person's use of the Internet. For example, if the piece of mail that set all this in motion was a piece of junk mail, the sender would be able to know who responded to the offer, and track what he did in response—visiting a particular web page or buying specific products, for example. That information could then be kept in a database.

7 If the recipient of the message sends the message along to someone else, and sends a message along with it, the whole process starts all over. Now, however, when the web bug sends the contents of the email message, it contains the person's comments—so the mail has effectively been wiretapped. This continues so that every time a new person gets the message, the wiretap continues.

Forwarded Email

How Internet Passports Work

2 When the user visits a website, the information in the profile the person has put into his passport is sent to the site's web server.

Username: JonJohnson
Password: JIF

Welcome Jon Johnson

INTERNET PASSPORT
OK - News Sharing
NO - Buying Information

3 The server examines the information in the passport. In this instance, the profile includes a username and password—so the username and password are sent to the website, automatically logging in the person to a special portion of the site that allows only those who have already registered at the site. The server might then send a welcome message to the person logging in.

Web Server

Utah: 107
Chicago: 103

No Buying Information

INTERNET PASSPORT

OK - News Sharing

NO - Buying Information

Name: Jon Johnson
Username: Jordan
Password: JIF

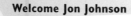
Reads Sports Scores

Passport

1 Internet *passports* are designed to let people decide what personal information they will allow to be released to websites. A variety of technologies are involved with Internet passports, including the Platform for Privacy Preferences (P3P), the Internet Content and Exchange standard (ICE), and the Open Profiling Standard (OPS). The passport lives inside a web browser. A user fills out a profile in the browser, determining what information can be made available to websites, such as name, address, occupation, username and password, and age. The user also decides which type of information about his surfing habits can be shared among websites—and which can't. In this instance, the person has decided that information about what news stories he reads can be shared, but not information about what products he buys.

4 While on the site, the person reads news about the latest sports scores, then buys an electric razor and a book about sailing. The website puts into the person's profile that he has read sports scores, but not that he has bought a razor and a book—because the person's profile said it would allow information about what news stories he reads to be shared, but not information about what he buys.

5 The person visits another website. The information in the profile the person has put into his passport is sent to the site's web server. The server sees that the person has recently read a story about sports scores, so it sends to him a daily digest of the latest sports news. Because the profile doesn't have any information about what the person has bought, it doesn't send any information about special sales on the site.

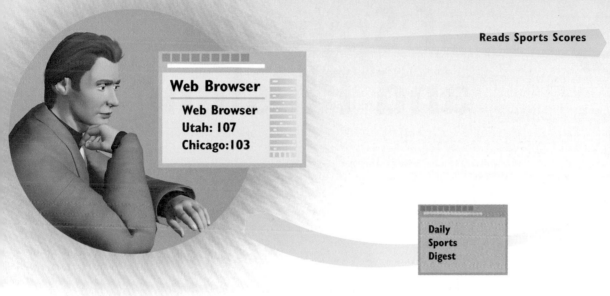

Reads Sports Scores

Web Browser

Web Browser
Utah: 107
Chicago:103

Daily
Sports
Digest

News Site

6 The person now surfs to a different website. This site allows in only people who have agreed, in their profiles, to allow their online buying habits to be shared among sites. Because the person has said he doesn't want that information to be shared, the person is not allowed onto the site.

Buying Site

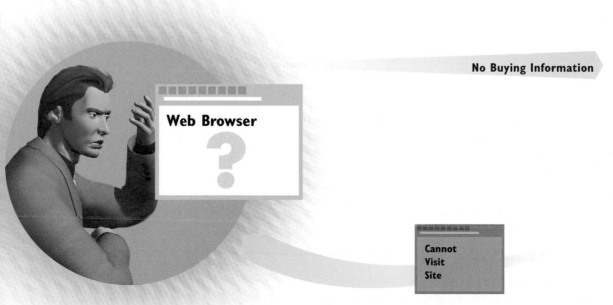

No Buying Information

Web Browser

?

Cannot
Visit
Site

CHAPTER
49

The Dangers of Spyware and Phishing

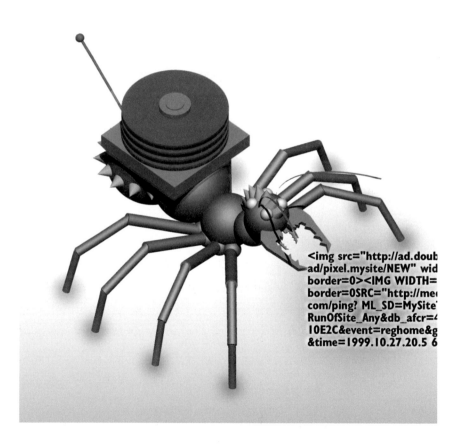

<img src="http://ad.doub
ad/pixel.mysite/NEW" wid
border=0><IMG WIDTH=
border=0SRC="http://mec
com/ping? ML_SD=MySite
RunOfSite_Any&db_afcr=4
10E2C&event=reghome&g
&time=1999.10.27.20.5 6

THESE days, possibly the biggest danger you face when you go onto the Internet is spyware—a type of malicious software that can invade your privacy and wreak havoc on your PC. Spyware is a relatively new phenomenon; it does not have a long history as do viruses, Trojans, and worms.

Spyware is an umbrella name for many different types of malicious programs. But these kinds of programs have several things in common. First, all of them, one way or another, spy on your behavior. They may watch what web pages you visit, and report that information to a server or person, or may track your web searches. They may allow people to record every keystroke you make. They may open up a "back door" into your computer so that hackers can later take control of your PC when they want.

The second thing they have in common is that they install without your knowledge, or by tricking you. One common way they get on your PC is when you install a piece of software, such as file-sharing software. When you install that software, spyware often comes along for a ride, and installs itself without your knowledge, or misleads you about what the program actually does.

Unlike many viruses, spyware is not created for malicious reasons—it is there to generate cash. One kind of spyware swarms your PC with dozens of pop-up ads, and you most likely click some of them to close them. But every time you click, the spyware purveyor makes money, because he has a business arrangement with a merchant or website to drive traffic to it.

Another kind of lucrative Internet attacks is so-called "phishing"—attacks in which you're sent an email from what appears to be a bank, financial institution, or commerce site such as PayPal, Amazon, or eBay, but in fact are forged sites.

The emails warn that you must log on to your account, perhaps to verify information, or perhaps to be sure your account does not expire. You're told to click a link to get to the site. When you get to the site, it looks like the real thing, but it's a spoof. Log on, and all your information is stolen.

Why has phishing become so widespread? Because it pays off—big-time. Fraudsters can make massive amounts of revenue by draining bank accounts and participating in identity theft.

While phishing fraud is widespread, it's actually not that difficult to protect against. Spam filters catch most phishing attempts, and some email programs, such as Outlook, now include built-in anti-phishing tools. Additionally, browsers include anti-phishing tools that warn you when you're about to go to a website that is most likely a spoof. Additionally, there are browser add-ins that you can install that fight spoofs and phishing as well.

But the best protection is the simplest: Never click a link in an email that claims to be from a financial institution, no matter how legitimate the email seems.

Because there is money to be made from surfing, phishing attacks and spyware aren't going away any time soon. But as you'll see in this chapter, anti-spyware can combat them, so there are ways to keep yourself safe, and protect your privacy.

How Spyware Works

1 Spyware sits in the background of your computer, watches what websites you visit, then reports on your activities. Based on those activities, targeted ads are delivered to you. But first, the spyware has to get onto your computer. Often, you get spyware by downloading a free program, or clicking a pop-up ad. Spyware comes along for the ride without you knowing it. When you install the program you've chosen, spyware gets installed as well, without telling you.

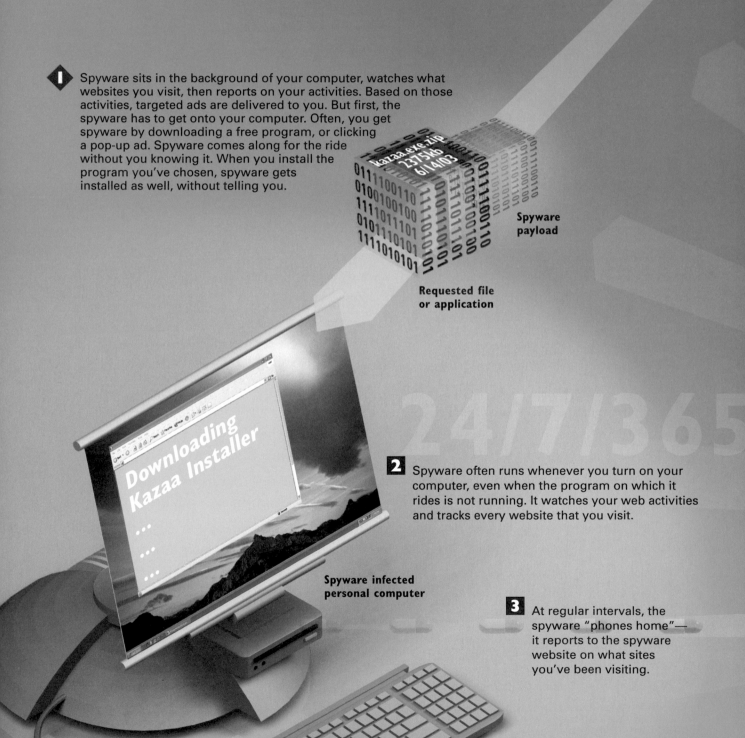

Spyware payload

Requested file or application

kazaa.exe.zip
2375kb
6/14/03

Downloading Kazaa Installer

Spyware infected personal computer

2 Spyware often runs whenever you turn on your computer, even when the program on which it rides is not running. It watches your web activities and tracks every website that you visit.

3 At regular intervals, the spyware "phones home"— it reports to the spyware website on what sites you've been visiting.

5 Based on that profile, the website delivers targeted ads to you. The ads appear whenever you run the program on which the spyware piggybacked onto your system. When you delete the program on which the spyware piggybacked onto your system, the spyware typically does not get deleted. It keeps watching your surfing activities and reporting on them, although it can't deliver ads based on that information, because the program on which it was piggybacked has been deleted. To delete the spyware, you need a special spyware detector and killer, such as Ad-Aware from www.lavasoft.com.

Pop up, pop under, self launching Web ads

REPORT
8253417 profile:
likes sports,
cares about money

sites visited:
sportsillustrated.com
money.com

4 Based on the sites you've been visiting, the spyware website creates a profile about your surfing activities.

Automated report

SPYWARE HQ

Following the Spyware Money Trail

1 There are many different types of spyware that make money for spyware creators or users in many different ways. This illustration shows how much spyware includes a money trail that includes reputable, well-known websites and merchants.

MERCHANT SITE

ID:spyguy ID:spyguy ID:spyguy ID:spyguy ID:spyguy

2 Much spyware is intended to make money from *affiliate programs*, in which any user can sign up to make money by delivering ads for the site or merchant. First, someone who wants to make money from spyware signs up for an affiliate program with a website or merchant. The person gets a code that identifies him, so he can be paid for every link or click to the merchant.

3 Some merchants monitor those who sign up for their affiliate programs, but many do not. Those looking to make money from spyware look for merchants who do not do a good job of policing their affiliate programs.

4 Those looking to make money from spyware are often not spyware authors. Instead, they make a deal with a spyware author, in which spyware includes links to the person's affiliate program ID. The spyware author shares the money from the program with the person looking to make money from spyware.

Electronics.com

GREAT DEALS

Download now

Last Chance

50% OFF
order now

click here

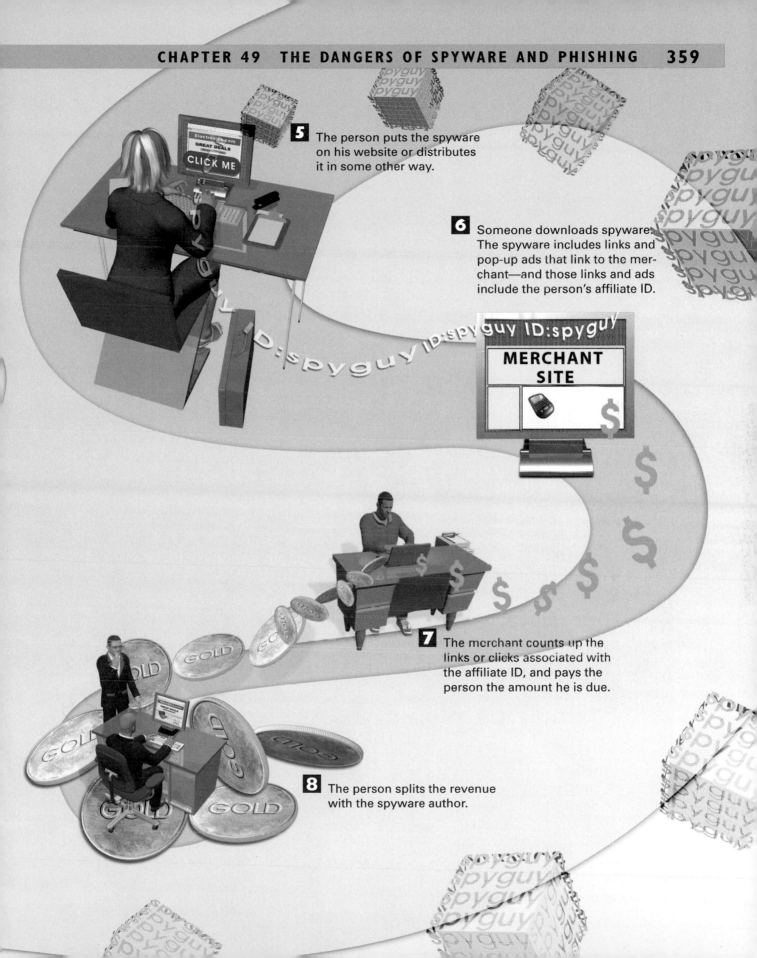

5 The person puts the spyware on his website or distributes it in some other way.

6 Someone downloads spyware. The spyware includes links and pop-up ads that link to the merchant—and those links and ads include the person's affiliate ID.

MERCHANT SITE

7 The merchant counts up the links or clicks associated with the affiliate ID, and pays the person the amount he is due.

8 The person splits the revenue with the spyware author.

How Phishing Works

1 To hide the identity of the phisher, phishing attacks are not sent from the phisher's computer. Instead, a phisher uses or hires a person who controls an army of thousands of zombie PCs whose owners don't know they have been turned into zombies. The person controlling the zombie army tells them to send out the email composed by the phisher.

2 The email is sent to tens of thousands or more people; specific individuals are not targeted. The email list may be provided by the person who controls the zombie army, may be bought from spammers, or may have been accumulated by the phisher.

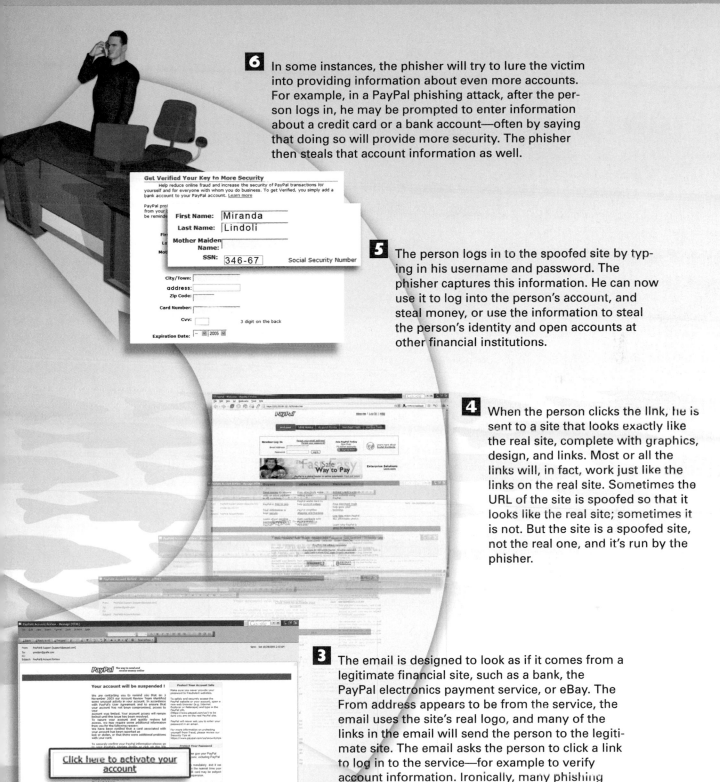

6 In some instances, the phisher will try to lure the victim into providing information about even more accounts. For example, in a PayPal phishing attack, after the person logs in, he may be prompted to enter information about a credit card or a bank account—often by saying that doing so will provide more security. The phisher then steals that account information as well.

Get Verified Your Key to More Security

Help reduce online fraud and increase the security of PayPal transactions for yourself and for everyone with whom you do business. To get Verified, you simply add a bank account to your PayPal account. Learn more

First Name:	Miranda
Last Name:	Lindoli
Mother Maiden Name:	
SSN:	346-67	Social Security Number

City/Town:
address:
Zip Code:
Card Number:
Cvv: 3 digit on the back
Expiration Date: __ 2005

5 The person logs in to the spoofed site by typing in his username and password. The phisher captures this information. He can now use it to log into the person's account, and steal money, or use the information to steal the person's identity and open accounts at other financial institutions.

4 When the person clicks the link, he is sent to a site that looks exactly like the real site, complete with graphics, design, and links. Most or all the links will, in fact, work just like the links on the real site. Sometimes the URL of the site is spoofed so that it looks like the real site; sometimes it is not. But the site is a spoofed site, not the real one, and it's run by the phisher.

3 The email is designed to look as if it comes from a legitimate financial site, such as a bank, the PayPal electronics payment service, or eBay. The From address appears to be from the service, the email uses the site's real logo, and many of the links in the email will send the person to the legitimate site. The email asks the person to click a link to log in to the service—for example to verify account information. Ironically, many phishing attacks warn people their account has been compromised and asks them to log in to help protect their account.

Following the Phishing Money Trail

1 Phishers rarely work by themselves. They are usually part of a larger crime organization. The Russian mafia has been especially active in phishing, and is responsible for a significant number of phishing attacks.

Zombie PC

Zombie PC

2 The phisher pays someone who controls a fleet of zombies to send out the phishing attack from the zombie PCs.

sending passwords and account information

Zombie PC

3 The phisher compiles a large list of bank accounts, credit card information, PayPal logins, and similar information from the phishing attack.

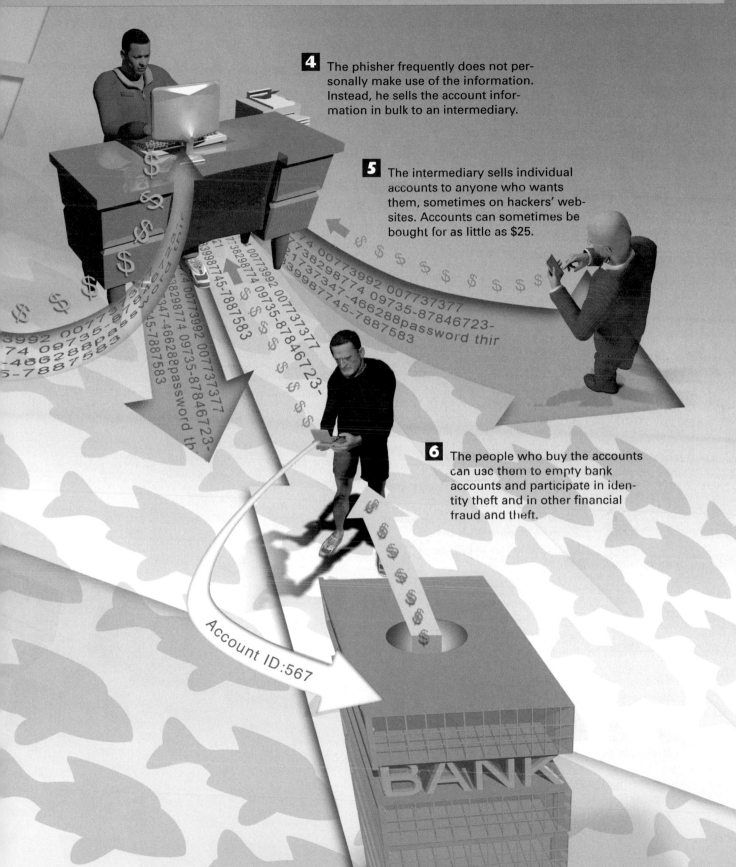

4 The phisher frequently does not personally make use of the information. Instead, he sells the account information in bulk to an intermediary.

5 The intermediary sells individual accounts to anyone who wants them, sometimes on hackers' websites. Accounts can sometimes be bought for as little as $25.

6 The people who buy the accounts can use them to empty bank accounts and participate in identity theft and in other financial fraud and theft.

Account ID:567

BANK

How to Protect Against Spyware

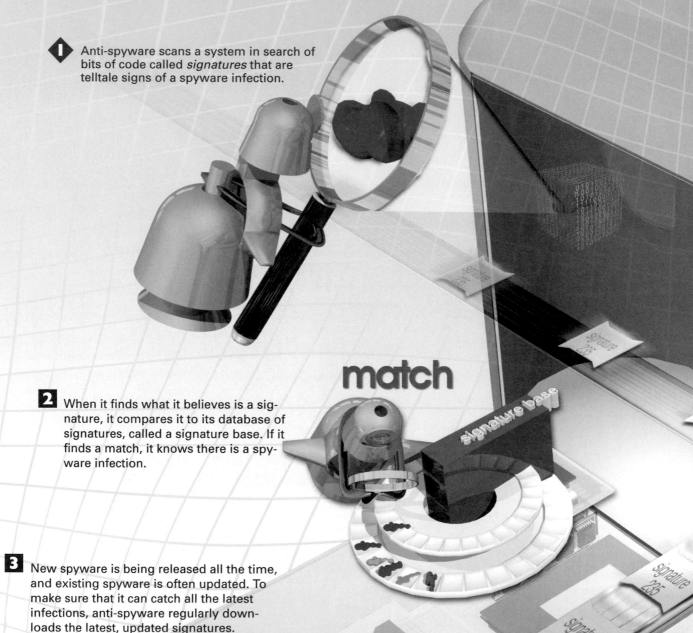

1 Anti-spyware scans a system in search of bits of code called *signatures* that are telltale signs of a spyware infection.

2 When it finds what it believes is a signature, it compares it to its database of signatures, called a signature base. If it finds a match, it knows there is a spyware infection.

3 New spyware is being released all the time, and existing spyware is often updated. To make sure that it can catch all the latest infections, anti-spyware regularly downloads the latest, updated signatures. In some instances, particular pieces of spyware don't leave telltale signatures. In other instances, spyware constantly morphs, making detection difficult. So some anti-spyware doesn't only search for signatures, but looks for telltale suspicious behavior as well.

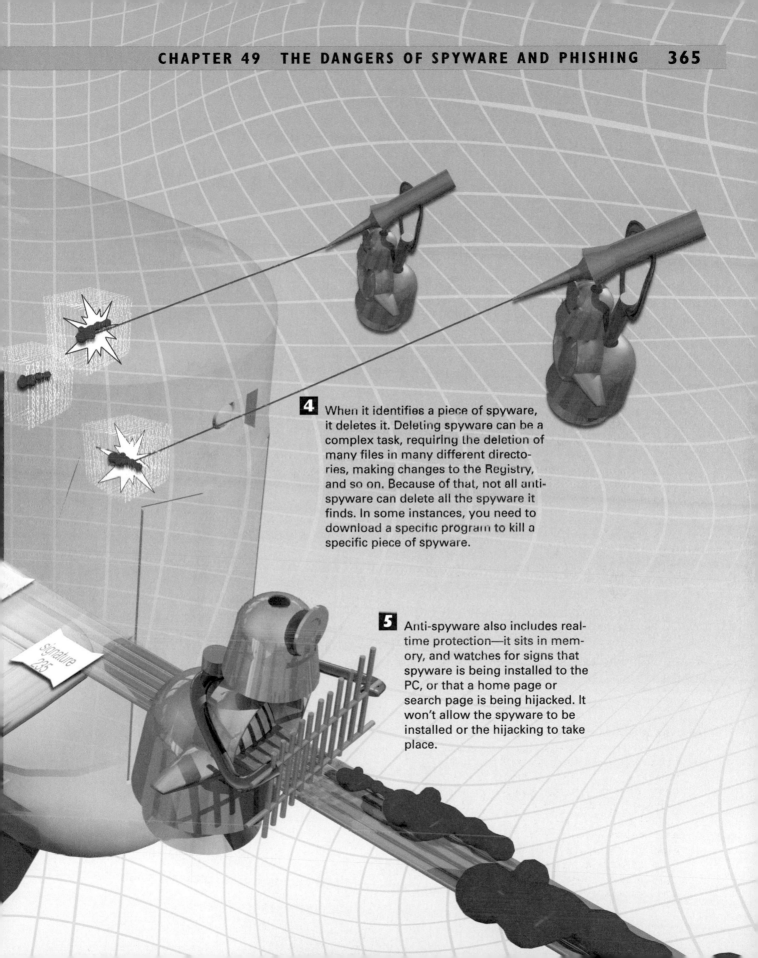

4 When it identifies a piece of spyware, it deletes it. Deleting spyware can be a complex task, requiring the deletion of many files in many different directories, making changes to the Registry, and so on. Because of that, not all anti-spyware can delete all the spyware it finds. In some instances, you need to download a specific program to kill a specific piece of spyware.

5 Anti-spyware also includes real-time protection—it sits in memory, and watches for signs that spyware is being installed to the PC, or that a home page or search page is being hijacked. It won't allow the spyware to be installed or the hijacking to take place.

CHAPTER

50

Cryptography, Privacy, and Digital Certificates

THE Internet is a notoriously insecure network. Anything you send across it can be easily snooped upon. This is of particular concern when highly confidential information, such as corporate data and credit card numbers, is transmitted across the Internet. Unless there is some way to protect that type of information, the Internet will never be a secure place to do business or send private, personal correspondence.

Another related concern is that it can be difficult to know whether the person sending the information across the Internet, such as credit card information, is really who he says he is. There are ways for people to forge identities and steal credit card numbers, and financial institutions and other businesses require ways to verify the identity of the person sending the information.

Several ways have been developed to solve these problems. At the heart of them is *encryption*—a way of altering information so to anyone other than the intended recipient it will look like meaningless garble. When the recipient gets the information, it needs to be *decrypted*—that is, turned back into the original message by the recipient, and *only* by the recipient. Many complex cryptosystems have been created to enable this type of encryption and decryption.

Cryptosystems use what are called *keys*—secret values computers use in concert with complex mathematical formulas called *algorithms* to encrypt and decrypt messages. If someone encrypts a message with a key, only someone else with a matching key can decrypt the message.

There are two kinds of common encryption systems: secret-key cryptography and public-key cryptography, also called asymmetric cryptography. Public key cryptography is what is commonly used on the Internet.

In *public-key cryptography*, two keys are involved: a public key and a private key. Each person must have both a public key and a private key. The public key is made freely available, whereas the private key is kept secret on the person's computer. The public key can encrypt messages, but only the private key can decrypt messages the public key has encrypted. If someone wants to send a message to you, for example, she would encrypt it with your public key. But only you, with your private key, would be able to decrypt the message and read it. Your public key could not decrypt it.

Digital certificates use encryption to verify that the person sending information—such as a credit card number, a message, or anything else over the Internet—really is who she says she is. The certificates place information on a person's hard disk and use encryption technology to create a unique digital certificate for each person. When someone with a digital certificate goes to a site or sends email, that certificate is presented to the site or attached to the email, and it verifies that the user is who she claims to be.

Digital certificates are issued by certificate authorities. These certificate authorities are private companies that charge either users or companies for the issuance of the certificates. You might be familiar with one such certificate authority, called VeriSign. Digital certificates contain information such as your name, the name of the certificate authority, the certificate's serial number, and similar information. The information has been encrypted in a way that makes it unique to you.

How Cryptosystems Work

1 Gabriel wants to send a confidential message over the Internet to Mia. Mia needs some way to decrypt the message, as well as a way to guarantee that Gabriel—and not an imposter—has actually sent the message. First, Gabriel runs his message through an algorithm called a *hash function*. This produces a number known as the *message digest*. The message digest acts as a sort of "digital fingerprint" that Mia uses to ensure that no one has altered the message.

2 Gabriel now uses his private key to encrypt the message digest. This produces a unique digital signature that only he, with his private key, could have created.

3 Gabriel generates a new random key. He uses this key to encrypt his original message and his digital signature. Mia needs a copy of this random key to decrypt Gabriel's message. This random key is the only key in the world that can decrypt the message—and at this point, only Gabriel has the key.

4 Gabriel encrypts this new random key with Mia's public key. This encrypted random key is referred to as the *digital envelope*. Only Mia can decrypt the random key because it was encrypted with her public key, so only her private key can decrypt it.

5 Gabriel sends a message to Mia over the Internet composed of several parts: the encrypted confidential message, the encrypted digital signature, and the encrypted digital envelope.

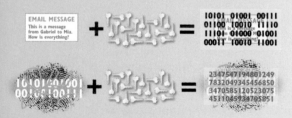

Original Message

Hash function

Message digest

PUBLIC
Gabriel's public key

PRIVATE
Gabriel's private key

PUBLIC
Mia's public key

+ PRIVATE =

6 Mia gets the message. She decrypts the digital envelope with her private key and out of it gets the random key Gabriel used to encrypt the message.

EMAIL MESSAGE
This is a message from Gabriel to Mia. How is everything?

7 Mia uses the random key to decrypt Gabriel's message. She can now read the confidential message he sent to her. However, she can't yet be sure that the message hasn't been altered en route to her or that Gabriel was definitely the sender.

◀ PUBLIC +
23475471948B1249
7832049345456850
3470585120523075
45110459347058S1
= 10101001001
00100100111

8 Mia now uses the random key and Gabriel's public key to decrypt his encrypted digital signature. When she does this, she gets his message digest, the message's "digital fingerprint."

EMAIL MESSAGE
This is a message from Gabriel to Mia. How is everything?
+ $[a, b^3 \sim q_4]$
$C^4 \sim cosineb-1^1$
= 10101001001
00100100111

9 Mia uses this message digest to see whether Gabriel indeed sent the message and that it was not altered in any way. She takes the message she decrypted and runs it through the same algorithm—the *hash function*—that Gabriel ran the message through. This produces a new message digest.

EMAIL MESSAGE
This is a message from Gabriel to Mia. How is everything?
+ $[a_2 b^3 \sim q_4]$
$C^4 \sim cosineb-1^4$
= 10101001001
00100100111

identical

PUBLIC +
23475471948B1249
7832049345456850
3470585120523075
45110459347058S1
= 10101001001
00100100111

10 Mia compares the message digest she calculated to the one she got out of Gabriel's digital signature. If the two match precisely, she can be sure that Gabriel signed the message and that it was not altered after he composed it. If they don't match, she knows that either he didn't compose the message or that someone altered the message after he wrote it.

PRIVATE

Mia's private key

Digital signature

Random key

10101 01001 00111
01100 10010 11110
11101 01000 01001
00011 10010 11001

Encrypted message

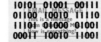
23475471948B1249
7832049345456850
3470585120523075
45110459347058S1

Encrypted digital signature

00100 00011 00101
11100 00001 01011

Encrypted random key (digital envelope)

How Digital Certificates Ensure Internet Security

1 A digital certificate is used to guarantee that the person who sends information or email over the Internet or who makes a financial transaction really is who he says he is. Digital certificates are issued by certificate authorities (CAs). To get a digital certificate, you typically visit a CA site and request a certificate. You then provide information about yourself, such as your name and other identifying information.

2 You are issued a digital certificate, which has been digitally signed to guarantee its authenticity. The certificate is data unique to you and is put on your hard disk, along with a private key.

3 The digital certificate is composed of information such as your name, the name of the CA, the unique serial number of the certificate, the version number of the certificate, the expiration date of the certificate, your public key, and the digital signature of the CA. The exact format of the certificate is defined by a standard known as X.509.

Name:	**Gabe Gralla**
Authority:	**VeriPure**
Serial Number:	**000518**
Version Number:	**3**
Expires:	**11/9/01**
Key:	**87162552**
Digital Signature:	**00101001110**

4 When you want to send email to someone and have her know for certain that it is you and no one else who has sent the mail, you attach the digital certificate to your email message. One of the things the certificate does is sign the message with a private key that you were given as part of the digital certificate.

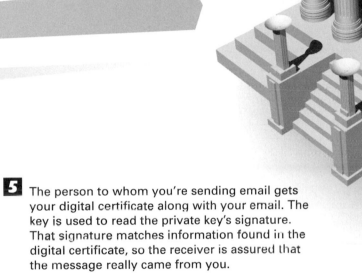

5 The person to whom you're sending email gets your digital certificate along with your email. The key is used to read the private key's signature. That signature matches information found in the digital certificate, so the receiver is assured that the message really came from you.

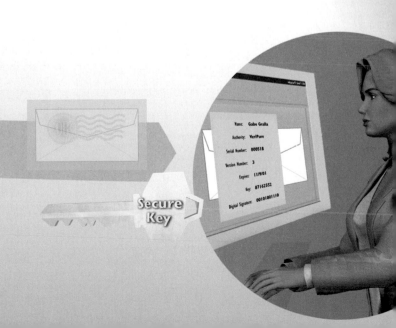

Secure Key

Name: Gabe Gralla
Authority: VeriPure
Serial Number: 000518
Version Number: 3
Expires: 11/9/01
Key: 87162552
Digital Signature: 00101001110

CHAPTER 51

How Government and Workplace Surveillance Work

HACKERS aren't the only ones who at times invade people's Internet privacy. So does the federal government and many corporations. The FBI and National Security Agency (NSA) invade some people's privacy by wiretapping their Internet connections, and corporations may snoop on their employees' Internet use to make sure they don't do anything illegal or harassing to others.

Particularly controversial has been President George W. Bush's decision to let the super-secret National Security Agency (NSA) tap phone calls and Internet use of American citizens without first getting a warrant. There is a well-defined legal procedure for such taps, with secret courts that allow them, and presidents for years have used them. But President Bush's decision to bypass the courts has been extremely controversial, and as this book goes to press, Congress had planned to hold hearings on the matter.

Two other controversial programs for gathering personal communications have been the Carnivore program run by the FBI, and the Echelon program run by the NSA. The Carnivore program was used to wiretap people's Internet connections. It has been discontinued, but the FBI continues to use similar technology.

Carnivore was the Internet equivalent of a wiretap—it allowed FBI agents to examine everything that a suspect does on the Internet, from sending and reading email, to browsing the Web, sending and receiving files via FTP, and, in fact, anything else someone does. It literally allows agents to examine and keep copies of every bit of information sent to and from an individual.

Just as a special warrant is required for a law enforcement agency to obtain a wiretap, a special warrant was required for the FBI to obtain a Carnivore tap.

With Carnivore, the FBI placed a computer at the Internet service provider (ISP) of the target of the investigation. It then tapped in to the line of the ISP and examined all the ISP's Internet traffic, using filters and software to get copies of the target's traffic and discarding the rest. Depending on the warrant, the FBI might target only portions of the target's Internet usage— for example, email but not FTP.

Civil libertarians and those concerned with privacy issues criticized Carnivore. They worried that it could easily be abused, and they argued that the simple fact of tapping into someone's Internet usage is an invasion of privacy.

The existence of Carnivore was acknowledged by the FBI, but the NSA doesn't acknowledge the existence of its Echelon data-gathering operation, which is the largest data gathering operation in the world. It literally listens in on the world's communications and stores information it believes is relevant. We don't know exactly how the program operates, because that is classified, but based on public records, we illustrate its basic outlines.

In the workplace, a variety of snooping tools can be used, ranging from those that log every packet that comes into and out of the network, to those that watch people's actual keystrokes. In addition, most emails are traceable, even if companies are not monitoring their emails. Microsoft Exchange servers, for example, have message-tracking abilities and retention settings that can track email even if it's been deleted. One reason for corporate snooping is to make sure people aren't making unauthorized use of the Internet. Another is to ensure the Internet is not being used in a harassing manner. For example, courts have ruled if an employee displays a pornographic website on his computer, it could be considered sexual harassment. No matter the reasons, however, many employees are made uncomfortable by such snooping and should realize that everything they do at work may be tracked by their employer.

How the National Security Agency's Echelon Spy System Works

1 The National Security Agency's (NSA) Echelon system is a top-secret way to intercept and interpret telephone, email, Internet, fax, and other electronic communications all over the world. Because the precise nature of the way it works is classified, we don't have an exact picture of it, but based on public resources, this illustration shows the general outline of how it works.

2 Listening stations throughout the world point satellite dishes at the international telecommunications satellites (Intelsats) that most countries of the world use. A ring of Intelsats hovers stationary above the equator, each of which handles tens of thousands of simultaneous phone calls, email messages, faxes, and other communications. The stations are pointed at different satellites and intercept every communication in their targeted satellites.

3 Intelsats carry much of the world's telecommunications traffic, but not all of it. There are also undersea cables, land-based systems, land-based microwave networks, and regional telecommunications satellites. Echelon taps into each of those in different ways. For example, Echelon may tap directly into the undersea cables at the points they emerge from the sea. And Echelon may tap into microwave networks by placing listening stations somewhere along the microwave route.

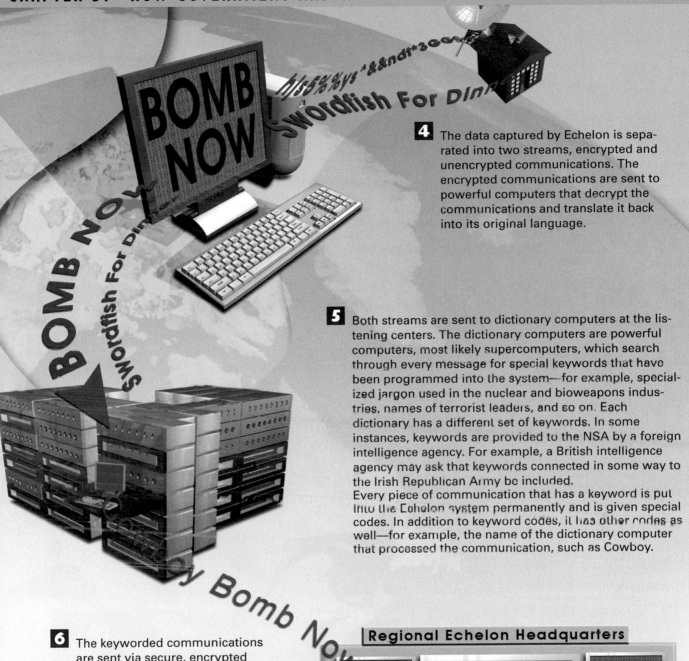

4 The data captured by Echelon is separated into two streams, encrypted and unencrypted communications. The encrypted communications are sent to powerful computers that decrypt the communications and translate it back into its original language.

5 Both streams are sent to dictionary computers at the listening centers. The dictionary computers are powerful computers, most likely supercomputers, which search through every message for special keywords that have been programmed into the system—for example, specialized jargon used in the nuclear and bioweapons industries, names of terrorist leaders, and so on. Each dictionary has a different set of keywords. In some instances, keywords are provided to the NSA by a foreign intelligence agency. For example, a British intelligence agency may ask that keywords connected in some way to the Irish Republican Army be included.
Every piece of communication that has a keyword is put into the Echelon system permanently and is given special codes. In addition to keyword codes, it has other codes as well—for example, the name of the dictionary computer that processed the communication, such as Cowboy.

6 The keyworded communications are sent via secure, encrypted communications links to regional Echelon headquarters, where communications experts sift through the communications using powerful computers in search of useful intelligence. They then pass along that intelligence to agencies that might find it useful, both inside and outside the United States.

Regional Echelon Headquarters

How the FBI's Carnivore System Invaded Your Privacy

1 Before it was disbanded, the FBI's system for tracking people's Internet use, including reading their emails and seeing what websites they visited, was called Carnivore. The data-gathering portion of Carnivore was a Pentium-based system, on which the Carnivore packet sniffing software ran. No keyboard or monitor was attached to the computer, so no one at the ISP could make use of it.

Dedicated Phone Line

FBI

2 The computer was attached via a dedicated phone line and a 56K modem to the FBI offices. The FBI ran an off-the-shelf program called PcAnywhere to enable it to control the Carnivore software and computer remotely. The dedicated connection was not connected to the Internet and all data was encrypted, using both PcAnywhere's encryption and other encryption programs.

CARNIVORE

3 FBI agents have the right to monitor only someone against whom they've obtained a wiretap warrant. The warrant also might require they gather only certain types of information about that person—for example, only his email messages. Agents used the Carnivore software to set filters, which filtered out all the data they didn't want and focused only on the data they wanted. So, for example, they set a filter that said only to track packets to and from a particular person, or only to examine his email, or email and web usage.

Save all packets to and from IP 168.2.9.100

Discard all other packets

```
1 00001    1101001
10010 0    10 10 11
11  100    011  100
   1010 1   1 00001
1101001    10010 0
10 10 11   11  100
011  100    1010 1
   1010 1   1101001
```

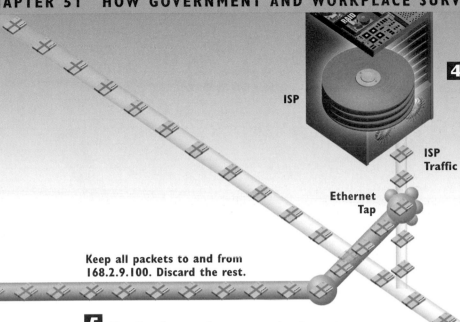

ISP

ISP Traffic

Ethernet Tap

4 An Ethernet tap was placed at the Internet service provider (ISP) of the target. This tap allowed traffic to flow through the ISP as it would ordinarily flow. But it also took a copy of every packet flowing through the ISP and sent it to the Carnivore computer.

Keep all packets to and from 168.2.9.100. Discard the rest.

5 The Carnivore software examined every packet and discarded those that were supposed to be filtered out. The remaining packets, the ones targeted by Carnivore, were stored on a removable 2 gigabyte Jaz drive.

6 The removable drive was delivered to the FBI offices, and data from it was examined using two pieces of software: Packeteer and CoolMiner. Packeteer reassembled all the packets and put them into a form that CoolMiner used. CoolMiner was used to examine the information—for example, it can be told to look only at email messages or only packets sent using the HTTP protocol. With CoolMiner, the FBI reconstructed all the target's activities, including sent and received email.

2GB Jaz Disk

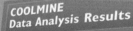

FBI

COOLMINE
Data Analysis Results

Application Protocols		Internet Chat	
AOL	0	AOL IM	
FTP	0	ICQ	0
Gopher	1	ICQ Msgs	0
Web Traffic	1	Chat	1
Lotus	0	NetMeeting	0
Internet News	0	Yahoo Pager	0
Printer	1		
Telnet	0		
		Email	
		IMAP	1
Network Protocols		POP3	0
Net Bios	0	Sent Mail	1
TCP	0	Exchange	1
UDP	1	MS Mail	1
Unknown	0	CC Mail	0

How Internet Workplace Surveillance Works

www request

1 One of the most common ways that companies track employee Internet behavior is through the use of packet sniffers. Packet sniffers are software that examines or "sniffs" every packet of data traveling across the network and stores it to a log file. An unfiltered sniffer captures every packet to the log, while a filtered sniffer only captures specified packets—for example, only packets that have passed into the network from the Web from specified websites.

www request

Local Network

Log File

www log for user #8369519302417
sex.com — ALERT!
stuff.com
kinky.com — ALERT!
bicycles.org
cnn.com
singles.com — ALERT!

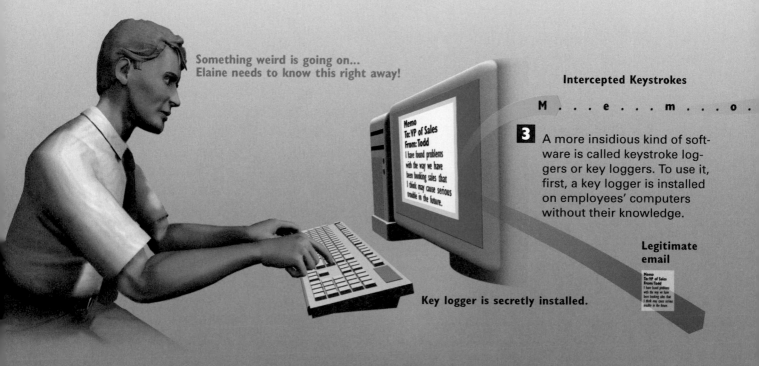

Something weird is going on...
Elaine needs to know this right away!

Intercepted Keystrokes

M . . . e . . . m . . . o .

3 A more insidious kind of software is called keystroke loggers or key loggers. To use it, first, a key logger is installed on employees' computers without their knowledge.

Legitimate email

Key logger is secretly installed.

Gross

Yuk!   Not again!

We are paying him to work...

Not again!   Does he ever listen?

Yuk!   What the heck is he thinking?

He was warned 6 times!

The Internet

2 Once the packet sniffer saves the packets to a log file, technical support staff can use log software to examine the file and reconstruct employee Internet behavior.

www log for user
#8369519302417
sex.com
stuff.com
kinky.com
bicycles.org
cnn.com
singles.com

Administrator

Log File

Local Network

PINK SLIP

#@$%*&!   The jig is up!

t . . . o . . . v . . .   **Keystrokes**

4 After the software is installed, it sends a record of every key pressed on the computer back to a person, or saves the record to a log. Every single keystroke is recorded, and so all computing activity is recorded, not just Internet activity. For example, a key logger can record every word of every document created on the computer.

Memo
To: VP of Sales
From: Todd
I have found problems with the way we have been booking sales that I think may cause serious trouble in the future.

Crooked Financial Executive

CHAPTER

52

Parental Controls on the Internet

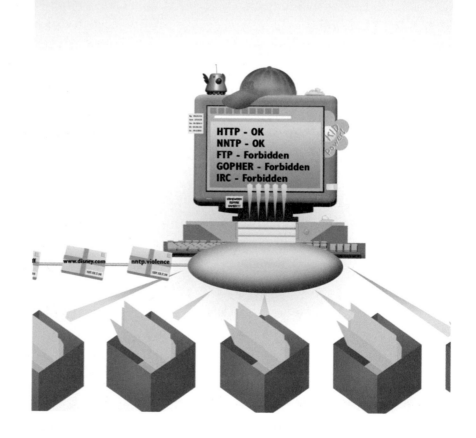

THE very nature of the Internet—the way it allows free, unfettered flow of information among people—has gotten it a lot of bad publicity. Much has been made of the fact that erotic and pornographic information is available on the Internet—everything from pictures to discussions about subjects many people find objectionable. The truth is that that kind of content makes up a very small part of what's available on the Internet, and the objectionable content is not exactly in public view—you have to do a bit of digging to find it.

However, just the fact that this type of information is available to anyone who wants to see it, including children, has made people uncomfortable. In fact, the U.S. Congress and other legislative bodies have tried to take steps to ban certain types of content from being available on the Internet, or to ban libraries and other public facilities from allowing access to certain material. As a result of these efforts, controversial laws have been passed against online pornography. The laws have then been overturned by the courts. For example, a law called the Communications Decency Act was ruled unconstitutional by the Supreme Court.

The real answer to the problem, though, doesn't lie with legislation. The answer lies with technology—software that enables parents to ensure that their children are not seeing objectionable material. A number of companies make and sell software that will do this, such as SurfWatch, Net Nanny, and CyberPatrol. These companies check sites for content and then bar children from getting to those sites containing content that is unsuitable for them. Some routers used for home networks also include filtering capabilities built in to them.

Online services such as America Online have a variety of ways to block access to objectionable material on the Internet. Some allow parents to block children from using services such as the World Wide Web, chat, or newsgroups completely. Others license technology from software makers, such as those that manufacture SurfWatch, to enable anyone on their service to block Internet sites they don't want their children to visit.

One group working on the issue is Platform for Internet Content Selection (PICS), which is trying to give parents control over the type of material to which their children have access. The group is trying to develop industry standards for technology that would allow the content of all sites and documents on the Internet to be rated according to its suitability for children. Additionally, the group would create standards to enable software to be developed for blocking sites based on those suitability ratings.

Businesses are also concerned with the type of Internet material their workers are accessing over corporate networks. Getting at and displaying sexual material can be interpreted as sexual harassment and can lead to serious legal ramifications. Additionally, most companies simply don't want their workers accessing that material on company time. Some companies now lease the same software parents are buying. Instead of installing the software on individual computers, though, the software is installed on a server, and it checks all incoming Internet traffic to every computer in the company.

How Parental Controls Work

1 The SurfWatch module examines the URL of every address coming toward the TCP/IP stack. It looks specifically for five types of URLs: http, nntp, ftp, gopher, and IRC. It takes each of those five types of URLs and puts it in its own separate "box." It allows the rest of the Internet information coming in to go through. SurfWatch checks for these types of URLs because they are the ones most likely to contain objectionable material.

2 SurfWatch software is installed on a computer that a parent wants to monitor to ensure that children can't get to objectionable material on the Internet. When a child launches software to get onto the Internet, SurfWatch latches onto Winsock or MacTCP, depending on whether a PC or Macintosh is being used. A SurfWatch software module sits "in front" of Winsock or MacTCP (which we'll generically call a TCP/IP stack) and monitors the TCP/IP data stream coming to the TCP/IP stack from the Internet.

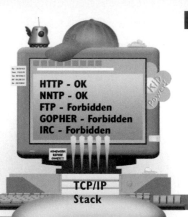

HTTP - OK
NNTP - OK
FTP - Forbidden
GOPHER - Forbidden
IRC - Forbidden

TCP/IP
Stack

SurfWatch

irc.adultstuff   ftp.nastystuff   www.disney.com   nntp.violence

www.disney.com   nntp.sex   ftp.nastystuff   gopher.sex   irc.dogs

HTTP (Web)   **NNTP (News)**   **FTP (FTP)**   **GOPHER (Gopher)**   **IRC (Internet Chat)**

Objectionable URLs:
meanstuff.com,
naughtystuff.com,
sexystuff.com,
violentstuff.com

3 Every URL in each of the boxes is checked against a database of the URLs of objectionable sites. If SurfWatch finds that any of the URLs are from objectionable sites, it doesn't allow that information to be passed on to the TCP/IP stack, blocking the site and preventing information from being viewed. It alerts the child that the site has been blocked. SurfWatch checks thousands of sites and lists in its database the ones that are found to be objectionable.

Objectionable words: sex, violence, pornography, guns

4 If the URL is not in the database, SurfWatch does another check of the URL. This is called *pattern matching*. It looks at the words in the URL and checks them against a database of words to see whether any of them indicates a request for objectionable material. Often, people creating objectionable material put representative words in the URL to draw attention to the site. If SurfWatch finds a matching pattern, it doesn't allow that information to be passed on to the TCP/IP stack, blocking the site and preventing information from being viewed. It also alerts the child that the site has been blocked.

PICS

5 There is another way that SurfWatch eventually might check for objectionable sites. A rating system called PICS (Platform for Internet Content Selection) embeds information about the content in its documents—saying, for example, whether objectionable material can be found there. If SurfWatch uses this system and finds that the URL is of a site containing objectionable material, it won't allow that information to be passed on to the TCP/IP stack, blocking the site and information from being viewed. It also will alert the child that the site has been blocked.

6 If the URL is not found to be of an objectionable site after the checks have been completed, the URL is passed to the TCP/IP stack and then to the Internet software, where the child can view it and interact with it. SurfWatch does all the checking practically instantly, so there is no apparent delay in getting material from the Internet.

7 Because the Internet is growing so quickly, and so many new sites are being created every month, the SurfWatch database of objectionable sites could become outdated. To solve the problem, SurfWatch automatically updates the database of sites every month. That way, the list of sites is always kept current.

KID SITES 101
KIDSEARCH
TEENSTREETS
DISNEY.FUN

TCP/IP
Stack

SurfWatch

SurfWatch
Update

www.disney.com

New SurfWatch Data

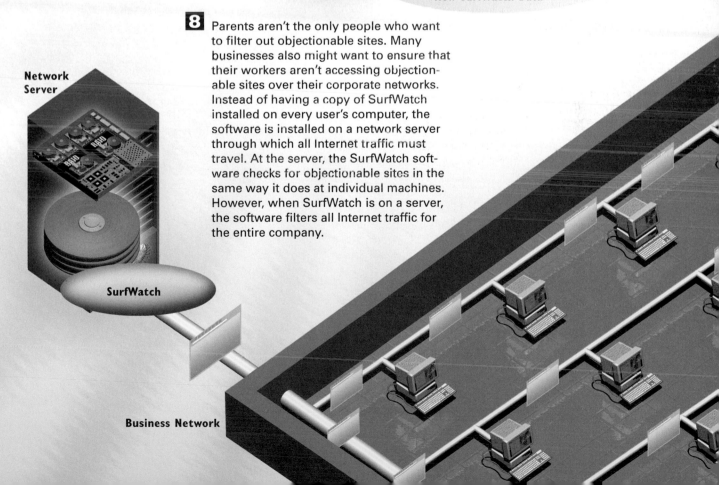

8 Parents aren't the only people who want to filter out objectionable sites. Many businesses also might want to ensure that their workers aren't accessing objectionable sites over their corporate networks. Instead of having a copy of SurfWatch installed on every user's computer, the software is installed on a network server through which all Internet traffic must travel. At the server, the SurfWatch software checks for objectionable sites in the same way it does at individual machines. However, when SurfWatch is on a server, the software filters all Internet traffic for the entire company.

Network
Server

SurfWatch

Business Network

Glossary

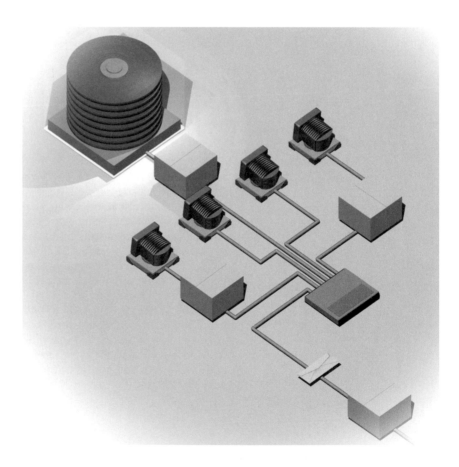

802.11   See *WiFi*.

ActiveX   A technology for Microsoft Internet Explorer that enables programs to be downloaded and run in your browser.

Address   An Internet location, such as a URL, an IP address, or an email address.

Agent   A piece of software that goes out across the Internet and does a job for you—for example, finding the best prices on a product you want to buy.

AJAX (Asynchronous JavaScript and XML)   A technique that allows developers to create interactive websites that function more like desktop programs than slow, static websites.

ASCII characters   Plain-text characters that you get by pressing keys on your keyboard.

Attachment   See *File attachment*.

Audio file   A file you can download or play from the Internet that has music or sounds in it.

Avatar   A picture that represents you in picture-oriented chat rooms.

Bandwidth   A measure of the amount of data that can be sent across an Internet connection over a unit of time.

BitTorrent   A peer-to-peer file sharing program used to share music and video files. It is designed to distribute very large files to many people without using up a significant amount of server resources and bandwidth.

Blog   A web-based publication, often in diary or column format, often updated on a daily basis, or many times a day. Also called a weblog.

Bluetooth   A wireless networking standard that allows devices of many different kinds to communicate in a peer-to-peer fashion; that is, without having to use a server or other hardware to connect them.

Bot   Short for robot. A computer that has been taken over by a hacker and can be used to attack websites, send spam, launch phishing attacks, or for other purposes.

Bridge   A device that connects local area networks with each other.

Broadband connection   A very fast Internet connection, such as via a cable modem or DSL.

Browser   See *Web browser*.

Buddy list   In instant messaging software, a list of friends you create so that you are alerted whenever one of your "buddies" comes online.

Cable modem   A device used to connect a computer to the Internet at very high speeds over cable TV lines. The device isn't a true modem, though, and uses a network card inside the computer to connect to the cable line.

Cache   A place on a computer or server that temporarily stores items such as web pages and graphics so they can be more quickly retrieved.

Carnivore   An FBI hardware and software system that can be used to read people's email and track everything they do when they are on the Internet.

Chat   A way that two or more people can communicate in real-time by typing messages on their keyboards.

Chat room   A location in cyberspace where people go to chat.

Client   A piece of software running on a local computer or device that communicates with a central server.

Client pull animation   A web animation technique in which the web browser requests a series of images that, when displayed one after another, appears to be animated.

Client/server architecture   A model of computing in which clients on local computers cooperate with distant servers to complete tasks. The Internet is largely based on client/server architecture.

Coaxial cable   The type of cable used for cable TV connections. It can also be used to provide high-speed access to the Internet, via cable modems.

Common Gateway Interface (CGI)   A communications protocol that enables web servers to communicate with applications such as databases.

Cookies   A bit of data put on your computer by a web server that can be used to track what you do when you are on the Web.

Cryptosystems   Systems used to encrypt data and then decrypt data so that only the intended recipient can read it.

Decryption   A method of unscrambling encrypted data so that it can be understood.

Denial of Service (DOS) attack   A method hackers use to attack Internet service providers or websites that involves inundating the server(s) with bogus traffic.

Digital certificate   A key used to encrypt and decrypt information; it can be used to guarantee that you're the sender of a message or to verify the authenticity of a person sending you a message.

Digital signature   An encrypted electronic "signature" that identifies you as the sender of a message—and that can't be forged.

Digital subscriber line (DSL)   A way of giving a computer high-speed access to the Internet using existing phone lines. A DSL modem is required.

Domain   An area of the Internet owned by a company or person, such as zdnet.com.

Domain name server   A server that translates Internet addresses, such as www.zdnet.com, into their IP addresses, such as 128.42.23.68, and vice versa.

Domain Name System (DNS)   The system that translates Internet addresses, such as www.zdnet.com, into their IP addresses, such as 128.42.23.68, and vice versa.

Download   To transfer information or files from the Internet to your computer.

Dynamic Host Configuration Protocol (DHCP)   A protocol used to renew an IP address or provide a new IP address to a computer when it connects to a server. When you connect to the Internet using an Internet service provider, you usually are given a different IP address every time you connect.

Dynamic HTML (DHTML)   A group of HTML-related technologies that allows for greater interactivity and animation on web pages.

Dynamic IP address   An IP address delivered via DHCP; with a dynamic IP address, the IP address of a computer will be different each time it goes onto the Internet.

Echelon   A program run by the spy agency the National Security Agency, that snoops on web use, email use, Internet use, and phone calls around the world.

Email filter   A way of automatically sorting incoming email so that some are automatically routed to certain folders or deleted, based on the sender and the content of the message. Email filters can be used to cut down on spam sent to you.

Email reader   A piece of software used to send and receive email.

Encryption   A method of scrambling data so that it can be read only by its intended recipient.

Ethernet   The most common local area networking standard.

Evil Twin attack   An attack in which a hacker creates a hot spot virtually identical to a real hot spot, fooling people into using it. The hacker can then steal information from the computers connected to the Evil Twin.

Ewallet   An electronic wallet that contains your credit card information or electronic money so you can use it to easily shop at many online shopping sites.

Extensible Markup Language (XML)   An extension of HTML that separates the content of a web page from its display. It can be used to allow designers to easily create web pages to be displayed on many different devices, such as computers, cell phones, and PDAs.

File attachment   A file attached to an email message or a newsgroup posting. Any type of file can be attached to email or newsgroup postings.

File compression   Shrinking the size of a file so that it can be transferred more quickly over the Internet and/or consumes less space when saved to storage media.

File extension   The letters on the end of a filename that are used to identify the type of file it is. For example, files with .doc extensions are Microsoft Word files.

Firewall   A hardware or hardware/software combination that protects computers on a network from being attacked by hackers or snoopers.

Flash   An animated movie played over the Web, created using Macromedia Flash software.

FTP (File Transfer Protocol)   A way of downloading files on the Internet. See also *Download*.

Gateway   A device that connects local area networks with each other and can translate data from one network to another.

GIF (Graphics Interchange Format)   A common graphics format used on web pages. Files in this format end in .gif.

Grid Computing   A technology that allows the power of many computers to be combined into one large system.

Helper application   See *Plug-in*.

Hops   The number of times a packet of information needs to be sent to different routers before reaching its destination.

Host   See *Server*.

Hot spot   A public wireless access point that allows people to connect to the Internet using WiFi technology.

HTML (Hypertext Markup Language)   The computer language that forms the basis of the World Wide Web. Web browsers interpret HTML commands and display web pages based on the HTML commands.

HTTP (Hypertext Transfer Protocol)   An Internet protocol that defines the way web browsers and web servers communicate with each other.

Hub   A device that connects several computers to one another on a network.

Hub/Router   A combination of a hub and router that connects computers, routes data among them, and provides access to the Internet or other networks. Home networks commonly use a hub/router.

Hyperlink   A link on a web page that sends you to another web page or resource.

Hypertext   Text that, when clicked, sends you to another piece of text or location.

Image map   A static image that has been turned into a clickable image with different clickable parts.

Instant message   A chat-like message sent to another individual in a private, one-on-one conversation.

Instant messaging software   Software that enables people to know when their friends are online and lets them send person-to-person messages.

Internet-enhanced TV   The use of Internet technologies to add interactivity and web links to television broadcasts.

Internet service provider (ISP)   A company that provides dial-in or some other type of access to the Internet for a monthly fee.

Internet telephony   The use of the Internet to make telephone calls.

Intranet   A private network inside a corporation that uses Internet technology.

IP address   An Internet address that is a series of four numbers separated by dots, such as 155.40.112.23. Every time you go onto the Internet, you use an IP address; without it you can't do things such as surf the Web.

IPTV   A technique that uses the basic IP Internet protocol to deliver interactive TV into homes.

IPv6   The newest version of the basic IP Internet protocol. It allows for a far greater number of available IP addresses and adds other new features, including increased security.

IRC (Internet Relay Chat)   A standard that enables people to chat with each other over the Internet. You need special IRC software to chat via IRC.

ISDN (Integrated Services Digital Network)   A method of establishing a high-speed connection to the Internet using telephone lines. Special lines and modems are needed for ISDN.

Java   A programming language used to create programs that can be run inside web browsers or on a variety of computers. The strength of Java-written programs is that they can be written once and can then run as is in a variety of computers.

JavaScript   A technology that enables web designers to use a variety of interactive features on web pages.

JPEG (Joint Photographic Experts Group)   A common graphics format used for web pages. Files in this format end in .jpg.

Kazaa   A popular program used for sharing music files, movie files, and other kinds of files with others.

Key   A piece of data used to encrypt or decrypt information.

Key logger   A piece of software that records every keystroke someone makes on a computer and then sends the information to someone who wants to monitor that computer. Also called keystroke loggers or keystroke interceptors, this software can be used for workplace surveillance.

Lightweight Directory Access Protocol (LDAP)   A protocol that enables the creation of Internet white pages, which let people look up other people's email addresses.

Listserv   A type of software that manages sending and receiving email broadcasts and discussions. The term often is used generically to describe an email broadcast.

Local area network (LAN)   A network that connects computers together in a relatively small area using privately owned communication channels (not public satellites or telephone lines).

MacTCP   Software for Macintosh computers that interprets TCP/IP commands.

Mail header   The part of an email message that contains the subject line, the sender, the receiver, and similar information.

Mail server   A server that delivers or receives email.

Mailing list   See *Listserv*.

MBone (Multicast backbone)   A high-capacity Internet backbone used for transmitting broadcasts using the Multicast IP protocol.

Message board   A public area online where people can read and send messages.

Metasearch software   Software that can search through many search engines simultaneously and report back the results.

Microbrowser   A browser that a cell phone or similar device uses to browse the World Wide Web.

Microsoft Outlook   A popular email program.

Moderated newsgroup   A newsgroup in which all postings first have to go through a moderator before being posted.

MP3 file   A type of digital file used to store audio. This type of file uses data compression techniques that yield relatively small file sizes while preserving near-CD quality sound.

Multicast IP   A protocol that enables video and audio broadcasts to take place, while using a minimum of bandwidth.

Name server   A server that translates Internet addresses, such as www.zdnet.com, into their IP addresses, such as 145.45.23.45.

Napster   A once-popular program that was used for sharing music files in the MP3 format with others.

.NET   A technology from Microsoft that runs programs and services remotely across the Internet, and also delivers services automatically to people's desktops. It's similar to web services, but uses a different technology for creating the programs and services.

NetCam   A video camera that attaches to a computer and often is used for Internet video-conferencing or videochat.

Network address translation (NAT)   A technique in a local area network that provides an internal IP address to computers inside the network, while masking the IP address to the outside world. It also enables several computers on the local area network to share an external IP address.

Network card   An add-in card put into a computer so it can get onto a network.

Newsgroup   A discussion area on the Internet.

Newsgroup reader   A piece of software used to read newsgroups.

Node   A portion of a network through which many computers are connected.

Online auction   Just like a real-life auction, except that it's done online.

Opt out   A policy that lets you say you don't want to receive junk mail or similar information.

Packet   A piece of data broken down into pieces for transmitting over the Internet or another network.

Packet sniffer   A piece of software that can track, examine, and log every packet of information that travels across a network.

Packet switched network   A network in which there is no unbroken connection between sender and receiver; instead data is broken into packets, sent, and then reassembled when received. The Internet is a packet switched network.

Palm Query Application (PQA)   A small piece of software on a wireless Palm device that enables it to get information from the Internet using web clipping.

Palmtop computer   A small computer, such as the Palm, that fits in the palm of your hand and is often used for keeping track of schedules, to-do lists, and a calendar; it also can be used for wireless communications.

Parental controls/content filtering   A feature of America Online, some routers, and some add-in software that lets parents decide where kids can go on America Online and the Internet and how they can use America Online and the Internet.

Passport   A technique that enables people to determine what information to give to websites and what information to keep private.

Password   A set of private letters and numbers or words you type in to give you access to a service or site.

Peer-to-peer file sharing software   Software that allows people to share files with one another, most frequently music files and, increasingly, video files and movies.

Peer-to-peer network   A network that enables computers or other devices to connect directly with one another without having to use a server or other hardware to connect them.

Personal Digital Assistant (PDA)   A small handheld computer, such as a Palm device or Windows CE device.

Personal firewall   A hardware or hardware/software combination that protects an individual computer from being attacked by hackers or snoopers.

Phishing attack   An attack in which a person is lured to a website that looks like a legitimate financial site, but is in fact a scam. When a person types in his user name and password, the scammer steals it.

Piconet   A network formed by the connection of two or more Bluetooth devices with one another.

Plug-in   A piece of software that installs in a browser or works in concert with a browser, such as for displaying different types of video.

Podcast   A method of distributing media files, in particular sound files, allowing people to subscribe to radio-like broadcasts that are downloaded to their PCs or portable music player such as an iPod.

Point-to-Point Protocol (PPP)   A protocol for computers to connect to the Internet using dial-up modems.

POP 3 (Post Office 3)   A communications protocol used by email servers to deliver email.

Pretty Good Privacy (PGP)   A program used to encrypt and decrypt information. It's especially useful for sending out private email that only the sender and recipient can understand.

Private key   Someone's key in an encryption scheme that only one person can use. It's used in concert with that individual's public key to encrypt and decrypt information. See also *Key* and *Public key*.

Proxy server   A server located between a client, such as a web browser, and the server the client is trying to contact, and which tries to fulfill the request before sending it to the server. For example, a proxy server could be used to speed up the delivery of web pages.

Public key   Someone's key in an encryption scheme that anyone can use. It's used in concert with that individual's private key to encrypt and decrypt information. See also *Key* and *Private key*.

Really Simple Syndication (RSS)   A technology that allows notification when a web page or blog has changed or new information is available.

RealPlayer   A popular piece of software that plays video and audio files.

Registrars   Private companies that accept payment from companies and individuals who buy Internet domains.

Router   A piece of hardware that sends packets to their proper destinations along networks, including the Internet.

Routing table   A database in a router that details the various paths packets can take en route to their destinations.

Search engine   A website that lets you perform searches throughout the Internet.

Secure site   A site that encrypts your credit card information as it's sent across the Internet so the credit card number can't be stolen.

Serial Line Internet Protocol (SLIP)   A protocol for computers to connect to the Internet using dial-up modems. It's not as effective as a similar protocol, called PPP.

Server   A computer that performs some task for other computers, such as sending or receiving email or delivering web pages.

Server push animation   A web animation technique in which a server sends a series of images to a browser that, when displayed one after another, appear to be animated.

Service Registry   A repository of information about web services. Service Registries can be searched through as a way for individuals or companies to find web services to run.

SET (Secure Electronic Transactions)   The electronic encryption and payment standard that a group of companies, including Microsoft, Netscape, VISA, and MasterCard, is pushing to become the standard for doing electronic commerce on the Internet.

Shockwave   An animated movie played over the Web, created using Macromedia Director software.

Shopping cart   A list of items someone wants to buy when at an online store.

SMTP (Simple Mail Transfer Protocol)   A communications protocol used to send email.

Smurf attack   One type of Denial of Service attack in which a network is overwhelmed with replies to forged PING requests. See *Denial of Service attack*.

SOAP (Simple Object Access Protocol)   A communications protocol used by web services and .NET.

Socket   Software that understands and interprets TCP/IP commands.

Spam   Junk email sent to people who haven't requested it. Most spam is commercial offers and can also be fraudulent.

Spam filter   Software that can filter out spam before it is received.

Spamoflauge   The act of hiding a spammer's true email address so the true sender of the spam can't be traced.

Spider   Software that gathers information from the Web and puts it into a large database that can be searched by search engines.

Spyware   Software that spies on a person's Internet activities or keystrokes, and reports on them to a server or hacker.

SSL (Secure Sockets Layer)   A technology that scrambles information as it's sent across the Internet so hackers can't read it.

Static IP address   A fixed IP address that never changes. Unlike a dynamic IP address, it is permanent, so the IP address of the computer never changes whenever it goes onto the Internet.

Streaming audio   See *Streaming media*.

Streaming media   A technique that enables you to view and listen to audio and video files from the Internet while they're still downloading to your computer. With streaming media, you can view and listen to audio and video files only a few seconds after you click them.

Streaming video   See *Streaming media*.

T1 line   A high-speed line that can carry data at a rate of 1.544Mbps.

T3 line   A high-speed line that can carry data at a rate of 44.746Mbps.

TCP/IP (Transmission Control Protocol/Internet Protocol)   The communications protocols that underlie the Internet.

TCP/IP stack   See *Socket*.

Telnet   A way of accessing a host computer from your own computer over the Internet.

Trojan horse   A malicious program that appears to be benign, but in fact is doing damage to your computer. Some Trojan horses can give hackers complete access to the computers of people who run them.

TRUSTe   A company that sets voluntary standards for privacy on the Internet and that gives out "seals" that companies can post on their websites if the companies adhere to those privacy rules.

Uniform resource locator (URL)   An address on the Internet, such as http://www.zdnet.com, which enables computers and other devices to visit it.

Universal Description, Discovery and Integration (UDDI)   A group of specifications that lets companies publish information about themselves and their web services, and lets others search through that information in order to find a web service, bind to it, and run it.

Universal Serial Bus (USB)   A technology that enables many devices to connect to a computer, such as NetCams, scanners, and digital cameras. The devices can be attached to one another in daisy-chain fashion, allowing many to be connected at once.

Unmoderated newsgroup   A newsgroup in which postings don't have to go through a moderator before being posted.

Upload   To transfer a file from your computer to another computer or to a server.

Usenet   A system of more than 14,000 discussion areas called newsgroups.

Videoconference   A conference among several people in which they can talk to one another and see each other using video cameras over the Internet.

Virtual Private Network (VPN)   An encryption technique that enables people to connect to their corporation's network over the Internet, while protecting the data from being seen by anyone else.

Virtual reality (VR)   The simulation of reality on a computer screen or over the Internet.

Virtual Reality Modeling Language (VRML)   The language used to create virtual reality websites.

Virus   A malicious program that attacks a computer.

Voice over Internet Protocol (VoIP)   A technique for making telephone calls using the Internet's basic IP protocol.

WAP Transaction Protocol (WTP)   A communications protocol, part of the Wireless Access Protocol (WAP) that is the equivalent of the Internet's TCP/IP protocols and enables cell phones and similar devices to access the Internet.

War driving   A technique for finding WiFi networks and attempting to access them.

Web browser   A piece of software that enables people to browse the World Wide Web.

Web bug   A technique that enables websites or people to track people's activities when they visit the Web or use email.

WebCam   A video camera that sends live still or video images to a website.

Web clipping   A technique that enables Palm devices to get information from the Internet.

Weblog   See *Blog*.

Web page template A preformatted design for a web page that includes colors, fonts, layout, and other elements. Templates make creating web pages easy—you only have to put in your own words, pictures, and content.

Web Services A technology that allows programs and services to be run remotely across the Internet, and also allows services to be delivered automatically to people's desktops. It's similar to .NET from Microsoft, but uses a different technology for creating the programs and services.

Web tracking A technique used by websites that tracks what people do when they visit a website.

WebTV A product that lets you access the Web on your television set.

Web white pages Websites that contain information that can be searched through for identifying information, such as email addresses, phone numbers, and addresses.

Whiteboard In videoconferencing, an application that enables several people to work on the same screen simultaneously.

WiFi A family of wireless networking technologies, also known as 802.11, that allow computers and other devices to connect to each other and to the Internet without wires.

Wiki A website that lets groups of people work together to create and edit information.

Wikipedia A free, online encyclopedia created by thousands of volunteers working together using the world's largest wiki.

WiMax A technology that delivers high-speed, wireless Internet access to an entire metropolitan area.

Winsock Software for Windows that interprets TCP/IP commands.

Wireless access point A device that connects wireless devices, such as a computer equipped with a wireless network card, to a network.

Wireless access protocol (WAP) An Internet protocol that defines the way cell phones and similar devices can access the Internet.

Wireless Markup Language (WML) A markup language related to HTML that is used to create websites that cell phones and similar devices can visit.

WMLScript A scripting language that enables interaction between cell phones and the Internet.

Workgroup software Software that enables groups in a corporation to work more closely and effectively with each other and does things such as route documents among people and allow people to run whiteboard applications.

World Wide Web   The most popular portion of the Internet, it allows you to view pages that include text, pictures, video, sound, and various forms of interactivity.

World Wide Web Consortium (W3C)   The group that develops standards for the evolution of the World Wide Web.

WSDL (Web Services Description Language)   A language used in web services and .NET technology to create a description of the web service that will be run.

XML   See *Extensible Markup Language*.

Zombie   A computer taken over by a hacker and used to attack websites, send spam, launch phishing attacks, or for other purposes.

Index

T

X - Y - Z

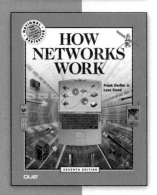
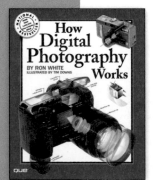